While the influence of French philosopher Henri Bergson on modernism has long been debated, this is the first thorough, current examination of the ways in which his ideas are manifest in British modernism. Mary Ann Gillies shows that he played a central role in the development of British literary modernism.

Focusing on the work of T.E. Hulme, the Men of 1914, the Bloomsbury Group, T.S. Eliot, and John Middleton Murry, Gillies convincingly demonstrates that Bergson's theories underlie the literary aesthetics of the period that forms the intellectual basis of modern literature. She then turns her critical eye to five major modernist writers – Eliot, Virginia Woolf, James Joyce, Dorothy Richardson, and Joseph Conrad – and provides insightful and detailed Bergsonian readings of their major works.

Drawing on material not previously available, Gillies persuasively argues that Bergson was a major intellectual force in British literature during the first thirty years of the twentieth century.

MARY ANN GILLIES is assistant professor of English, Simon Fraser University.

# Henri Bergson and British Modernism

MARY ANN GILLIES

McGill-Queen's University Press
Montreal & Kingston • London • Buffalo

© McGill-Queen's University Press 1996
ISBN 0-7735-1427-9

Legal deposit third quarter 1996
Bibliothèque nationale du Québec

Printed in the United States on acid-free paper

This book has been published with the help of a grant
from Simon Fraser University.

---

**Canadian Cataloguing in Publication Data**

Gillies, Mary Ann, 1959–
    Henri Bergson and British modernism
    Includes bibliographical references and index.
    ISBN 0-7735-1427-9
    1. Bergson, Henri, 1859–1941 – Influence.
    2. Modernism (Literature) – Great Britain. 3. English
    literature – 20th century – History and criticism.
    I. Title.
    PR830.B47G54 1996   820.9'1   C96-900332-3

---

This book was typeset by Typo Litho Composition
Inc. in 10/12 Palatino

*For my mother*

# Contents

# Acknowledgments

During my decade of work on Henri Bergson and British Modernism, I have incurred a number of significant debts.

As a doctoral student, I received grants from the Rhodes Trust (Rhodes Scholarship) and from the Social Sciences and Humanities Research Council of Canada (Doctoral Fellowship). This book is a substantially revised version of my dissertation, which was supervised by Lord Quinton. Simon Fraser University's University Publications Committee provided a grant toward the publication of this book.

During the lengthy revision process, I benefited from the assistance of many individuals. I thank Philip Cercone at McGill-Queen's University Press for his unwavering belief in this project and for his astute advice; Wendy Dayton, who skilfully edited the text, improving it in many ways; and Joan McGilvray, who saw it through the publication process. Carole Gerson's assistance at a critical time in the preparation of the manuscript was truly generous. I also would like to thank the following individuals for their advice and support: Kathy Mezei, Patricia Srebrnik, Betty A. Schellenberg, Leith Davis, John Kelly, June Sturrock, Joseph McAleer Jr., Norman Ingram, Sandra Djwa, Ila Burdette, Elona Malterre, Anthony Warrens, Judith Heaton, and Dr. Robin Fletcher and his wife, Ginny.

Some parts of chapter 4 originally appeared in my article "T.S. Eliot and Henri Bergson: An Uneasy Relationship" *Literary Half-yearly* 29, no. 2 (July 1988): 1–13. In addition, chapter 8 is a revised version of my article "Conrad's *The Secret Agent* and *Under Western Eyes* as Bergsonian Comedies," *Conradiana* 20, no. 3 (1988): 195–213.

Finally, my family encouraged me during my long journey toward this point and also kept me solidly grounded in the here and now. My brother Alan was particularly generous with his time. I gratefully acknowledge my debt to them.

# *Abbreviations*

Throughout the text I use parenthetical citations. In most cases, the short title of the work clearly indicates which text is being cited. However, for Bergson's texts and for four of Virginia Woolf's, I use abbreviations; the following is a list of these texts and abbreviations.

Works by Bergson:

TFW  *Time and Free Will*
M&M  *Matter and Memory*
CE  *Creative Evolution*

Works by Virginia Woolf:

JR  *Jacob's Room*
Dalloway  *Mrs Dalloway*
TTL  *To The Lighthouse*
TW  *The Waves*

*Henri Bergson and British Modernism*

# Introduction

Henri Bergson was a leading intellectual force in the early years of this century. His ideas were common currency, in the academic as well as the fashionable societies throughout Europe and North America. It is surprising, then, that his influence on Anglo-American writers has been studied at length only recently – by Paul Douglass, in *Bergson, Eliot & American Literature* (1986), and Tom Quirk, in *Bergson and American Culture* (1990). These two authors establish quite convincingly that Bergson had an important role to play in the development of writers such as Faulkner, Eliot, Cather, and Stevens. Bergson's place in American Modernism is thus charted, the conclusion being that "in technique and theme ... modern American Literature is profoundly entangled with Bergson" (Douglass, 177).

Given the interest in Bergson in American literature, I expected a similar re-examination of his role in the development of British Modernism to have occurred. But that is not the case. The only lengthy study of Bergson's influence on British writers is Shiv Kumar's *Bergson and the Stream-of-Consciousness Novel* (1963). And that, although it provides many valuable insights into Bergson's impact on Joyce, Woolf, and Richardson, is limited in significant ways. Not only does it not refer to material unearthed since 1963 – the omission of material from Virginia Woolf's diaries and letters is particularly upsetting – it is also hampered by its desire to "bring out the *parallelism* between the notion of the stream of consciousness as it appears in [Woolf, Joyce, and Richardson] and the Bergsonian concept of flux" (S. Kumar, viii). This latter focus, thanks to its exploration of only a narrow spectrum of Bergson's theories and their impact on British Modernism, unfortunately narrows the scope of the study, rendering its conclusions limited. More recent studies concerning British Modernism, however, have acknowledged Bergson's larger role in its genesis.

Sanford Schwartz, for example, devotes a chapter to Bergson in his *Matrix of Modernism: Pound, Eliot and Early Twentieth Century Thought* (1985), while Michael Levenson's *A Genealogy of Modernism* (1984) looks at Bergson as a figure in Modernism. As well, Frederick Burwick and Paul Douglass, in their collection of essays *The Crisis in Modernism: Bergson and the Vitalist Controversy* (1992), examine Bergson's place in the revival of Vitalism in Britain at the turn of the century. None of these works, however, provides the detailed, lengthy treatment given American Modernism by Douglass or Quirk. It was the absence of such a study that prompted this present project.

In this book, I chart Bergson's role in the development of British Modernism in a way that goes beyond the brief examinations provided in the more general studies. In part one – the first three chapters – I outline the areas of Bergson's philosophy to which the modernist writers responded. Chapter one presents those theories of Bergson that had the most appeal for modernists. Chapters two and three deal with Bergson's entrance into British discussions and his specific impact on the men and women involved in devising the terms of modernist literature. In part two – chapters 4 to 8 – I provide Bergsonian readings of five major modernists: T.S. Eliot, Virginia Woolf, James Joyce, Dorothy Richardson, and Joseph Conrad.

A study of this nature poses several problems at the outset. The first centred on the question of influence and how that term should be applied to the writers examined. I do not believe in the *Zeitgeist* theory: the notion that certain ideas are in the air, and that Bergson was one of many affected by them, rather than one who was developing distinctive ideas of his own in response to the issues of the day. Bergson was certainly concerned with the major issues of his time – it is impossible not to be so concerned – but I would suggest that those who argue thus have a limited notion of the way in which a society constructs its ideas. I choose, too, to work with a broader notion of influence than that presented, for example, by Harold Bloom in his *Anxiety of Influence*. Indeed, I am not so much concerned with establishing the various stages that writers go through in their relationship with mentors or predecessors. Rather, I am more interested in the social contextualization of the arts, as discussed by Janet Wolff in *The Social Production of Art*. And I particularly appreciate her argument:

Even when artistic production is a more "individual" activity, as in painting or writing a novel, the collective nature of this activity consists in the indirect involvement of numerous other people, both preceding the identified "act" of production (teachers, innovators in the style, patrons, and so on), and mediating between production and reception (critics, dealers, publishers). More generally, the individuality of the artist, and the conditions for his or her specific piece of work, are entirely dependent on the existence of the structures and institutions of artistic practice, which facilitate that work. (Wolff 118–19)

Many of her ideas have influenced contemporary approaches to the arts. What is important for this study, however, is the notion that artistic activity "consists in the indirect involvement of numerous other people."

I would broaden Wolff's list of figures who have an impact on artists, however, to include those individuals whose ideas are well known in society and whose works prompt widespread debate. Thus Bergson's ideas, which were very much at the centre of debate in Britain around the time that Modernism was beginning to take root (1909–1914), would become part of the indirect involvement of other people in the creation of an individual's artwork. I do not propose in this book to undertake a specific historical-materialist analysis of Modernism, as Wolff's theory would suggest; instead, I use her notion of the social nature of art to replace other notions of influence. I contend that because literature is inextricable from the social conditions and institutions in which it is produced, these things have a profound influence on, or role in, its production. In this sense, then, Bergson exerted an influence on modernists, because he was part of both the general social condition of the time – his theories were widely known and reflected the major social concerns of his day in ways that were unique to him – and the institutional establishment – he occupied a chair at a prestigious institution (Collège de France) and his personal appearances in Britain were sponsored by three universities (Oxford, Birmingham, and London), all of which were leaders in producing individuals to help run the different institutions that shaped and supported the social structures of the day.

The second problem lay in establishing the study's parameters. This involved two separate, but complementary, steps. First, I had to decide which of Bergson's works and ideas to include; second, I had to determine which modernist writers to discuss.

I decided that Bergson's writings published prior to World War 1 would be the primary focus of the study. Though 1922 has often been cited as the year that Modernism emerged – because of the publication of major modernist works such as Woolf's *Jacob's Room*, Eliot's *The Wasteland*, and Joyce's *Ulysses* – I believe that the working out of a modernist aesthetic actually occurred well before 1922, with 1909–1914 being a crucial period. Thus the Bergsonian works that might have influenced writers struggling to establish a separate identity from their predecessors would have been the major studies – *Time and*

*Free Will, Matter and Memory* and *Creative Evolution* – all of which were available in English translations by 1911. In addition, I include Bergson's essay on comedy – *Laughter* – in my study of Conrad.

As to which of the many Bergsonian ideas to focus on, I decided to examine three broad themes as representative of the central points of intersection between Bergsonian philosophy and modernist writings. The first focuses on the problem of origins in the rationalist, materialist world of the early twentieth century. Here the question revolves around knowing how to define the world in an empirical way, while at the same time accounting for the need for some sort of ordering myth or structure to deal with origins and the continued existence of this world. The second focuses on the need to deal with the problems of identity. Here the question is the nature of the self, particularly in light of the discoveries of contemporary psychology. The third focuses on the problems of representation in art. At issue here is the constant shifting of the basis and modes of representation. Bergsonian philosophy deals at length with each of these subjects, and the way in which modernist writers responded to Bergson's treatment of these topics is the common ground explored by this study.

The second task, choosing which writers to include, proved something of a challenge. Using Wolff's argument unmodified meant that all writers of this period could be considered open to Bergson's influence; hence a study of any one of them would reveal Bergsonian traces. But I wanted to be more selective than this, for two reasons. The first reason is that both Douglass and Quirk dealt with major modernist figures when demonstrating Bergson's central role in the formation of American Modernism. By choosing to deal primarily with major figures, I, too, could then demonstrate Bergson's central role, albeit in British Modernism. The second reason concerns the more practical aspects of space and focus: even if a single book has sufficient space to explore all the writers influenced by Bergson – a dubious proposition – such a study, cast too broadly, simply becomes too diffuse. I thus decided to choose those writers who make a major contribution to defining Modernism and who best show signs of Bergsonian influences.

The third major concern was with the reception of this book. I am not engaged in a major revision of modernist poetics. Nor is it new to say that Bergson influenced Modernism. But illustrating exactly how Bergson influenced Conrad, for example, or John Middleton Murry *is* new. Mind you, I am not redefining Modernism so much as fleshing out a part of it that others have noted and then left by the wayside. This process creates its own problems for me as a critic. I necessarily examine Modernism and Bergson from a late twentieth-century position. This limits me as a reader of modernist texts and as a commentator about them. Of course, my position grants me certain insights not available to many previous critics; the access to Woolf's non-fictional writings or to unpublished essays of Eliot, for instance, means that I have materials that earlier critics may not have had. But the very same position denies me the possibility of reconstructing Modernism as it was in the first two decades of this century. Further, I cannot present Modernism unmediated by subsequent works – whether creative (those moving beyond Modernism), or critical (those colouring my opinions about the period). Thus my construction of Modernism is necessarily a post-modern one. I nevertheless write my version of Modernism based on evidence that was pulled out of the period in a systematic way. For example, I examine the gaps of the period as much as the statements made openly by writers – such as Hulme's clear acknowledgement of Bergson' influence on him, and the silence maintained by Woolf. I also accept that literature emerges from a social context and that this means that many forces will influence the construction of a text. In this case, I argue that inasmuch as Bergson is an important player in the social concerns of the time, his ideas become an essential part of Modernism's social context. Thus I have participated in the ongoing rewriting of Modernism; despite my limitations as a critic removed from the period, I have attempted to be faithful to its sources and to capture the spirit and shape of the period under study.

### CHAPTER ONE

# Henri Bergson: Antecedents, Philosophy, and Context

This chapter deals with Bergson's philosophical antecedents, his philosophy, and his fall from popularity in the aftermath of World War I. The section on philosophical antecedents emphasizes Bergson's French heritage, to help explain why he articulated a metaphysical philosophy in an era dominated by Positivism. The section on Bergson's philosophy focuses on the three themes outlined in the introduction: Bergson's vision of the world, what constitutes the self, and the nature of art.

## BERGSON'S PHILOSOPHICAL ANTECEDENTS

Many of Bergson's critics underscore his enduring debt to the French spiritualist philosophers prominent in the academies of the mid-nineteenth century. Bergson is seen as heir to the school of thought that includes such eminent Frenchmen as Félix Ravaisson, Jules Lachelier, Maine de Biran, and Émile Boutroux. At the École Normale Superieure, Bergson first studied under the guidance of another well-known spiritualist, Leon Olle-Laprune, before coming under the dynamic tutelage of Boutroux. The spiritualist philosophy associated with men like Boutroux and Ravaisson

recognized the autonomies of body and soul and asserted that the faculties of the latter were clearly superior to the properties of the former, especially since they transcended death itself. To sustain such a new approach, which claimed to bring philosophy more closely in touch with reality, mechanism had to be attacked, its postulates had to be proved false, and it had to be relegated to its own sphere in the physical world, the only world it was truly capable of comprehending. (Grogin, 11)

There is no denying that spiritualist ideas – particularly the central concern about the place of free will in a determinist world – became important features of Bergson's philosophy. Indeed, it may be possible to ascribe much of Bergson's initial popularity to the fact that he was seen to have assumed the spiritualist mantle. But how much Bergson's initial engagement with the ideas of the spiritualists determined the subsequent course of his own philosophy is really a moot point, for although he does embrace their insistence that the inner life is important, he also asserts his independence from them in other aspects of his complex philosophy.

To argue that Bergson was simply the successor to these nineteenth-century thinkers and that he did little but frame the standard spiritualist ideas in terms that were appealing to a twentieth-century audience disillusioned with the rationalist, determinist society of the Third Republic is to present a corrupt account of both his work and his academic training. Bergson's initial training was in physics and mathematics; in fact, he won prizes in mathematics while still a student and his first publication was an answer to a mathematical problem (Bergson, "Solution"). Like most young intellectuals in the post-Darwinian era, he was forced to confront the radical discoveries of natural science; thus his most famous work, *Creative Evolution*[1], clearly demonstrates his wide knowledge of contemporary evolutionary theories and their scientific bases. Furthermore, throughout his life he maintained an interest in the sciences, being as well read in contemporary scientific literature as he was in philosophy. His work reflects this lifelong interest in both the spiritual and physical realms. Critics often dismiss Bergson's statements about the necessity of understanding both spiritual and physical worlds, citing them as proof of the contradictions inherent in his philosophy. Yet remarks such as those found in the introduction to *Matter and Memory* indicate a willingness to accept the findings of rational, physical science, coupled with the insistence that certain facets of life, although less amenable to these types of analyses, are nonetheless crucial for a full understanding of what it is to be a human being. For example, Bergson writes:

This book affirms the reality of spirit and the reality of matter, and tries to determine the relation of the one to the other by the study of a definite example, memory. It is, then, frankly dualistic. But, on the other hand, it deals with body and mind in such a way as, we hope, to lessen greatly, if not overcome, the theoretical difficulties which have always beset dualism, and which cause it, though suggested by the immediate verdict of consciousness and adopted common sense, to be held in small honour among philosophers. (*M&M*, xi)

Bergson's express aim in this book, as in all of his work, is not to exile rationalist thought or determinism in favour of an equally unidimensional and exclusive spiritualist tradition. Rather, he hoped to find a way of wedding the two and thereby allowing philosophy, and other intellectual endeavours, to mirror what the ordinary individual's common sense said: that the world consists of physical and spiritual aspects that necessarily work in consort to define human beings and their existence. It is this deceptively modest aim that forms the fundamental basis of Bergson's philosophy.

## BERGSON'S PHILOSOPHY

### World View

In the introduction to his first major work, *Time and Free Will*, Bergson explained what he wished to achieve:

The problem which I have chosen is one which is common to metaphysics and psychology, the problem of free will. What I attempt to prove is that all discussion between the determinists and their opponents implies a previous confusion of duration with extensity, of succession with simultaneity, of quality with quantity: this confusion once dispelled, we may perhaps witness the disappearance of the objections raised against free will, of the definitions given of it, and, in a certain sense, the problem of free will itself. (*TFW*, xix-xx)

While this accurately projects what he does in his study, the issue of free will is overshadowed by the concepts he uses to prove its existence and importance. In fact, *Time and Free Will* is remembered less for Bergson's assertions about free will than for its radical reorientation of the two dimensions of time and space. The statement above hints at what is to come in the study proper by asserting the confusion of those qualities that Bergson describes as temporal – duration, succession, and quality – and those that are spatial – extensity, simultaneity, and quantity. Nevertheless, this brief statement does not prepare the reader for the revolutionary reordering of the world that results from Bergson's insistence on privileging time over space. In effect, he defends the concept of free will by turning the prevailing view of the world on its ear, insisting that when time is accepted as the dimension in which actual life occurs there will no longer be a problem in accepting the fact that free will is an integral part of the make-up of individuals. In fact, in this study Bergson argues that, by accepting the spatial concept of the world as wrongheaded and the temporal concept as correct, the whole problematic issue of free will is eliminated. The central elements of Bergson's time theory provide the cornerstone of his entire philosophy; they also help to establish his vision of the world.

In *Time and Free Will* Bergson attacks traditional depictions of time. Time has become spatialized; according to Bergson, "By introducing space into our perception of duration, [we corrupt] at its very source our feeling of outer and inner change, of movement, and of freedom" (*TFW*, 74) Bergson discusses the Eleatic paradoxes and Zeno's paradox of the arrow in order to demonstrate that the only way that time may be a quantitative entity is to falsely ascribe spatial quantities to it. He claims that this sort of spatializing occurs in every aspect of life: the day is artificially divided into twenty-four, sixty-minute segments; the month into intervals of anywhere from twenty-eight to thirty-one days; and the year into 365 days; life is referred to in terms of spans of years; and civilization, in terms of centuries. All these divisions, and the many other ways that time is carved up, exist for the convenience of human beings and help circumscribe and control the natural environment. Bergson insists that when time is no longer spatialized, it may be possible to become aware of life's true nature. He argues:

There are … two possible conceptions of time, the one free from all alloy, the other surreptitiously bringing in the idea of space. Pure duration [*durée*] is the form which the succession of our conscious states assumes when our ego lets itself *live*, when it refrains from separating its present state from its former states … it need not be entirely absorbed in the passing sensation or idea; for then, on the contrary, it would no longer *endure*. Nor need it forget its former states: it is enough that, in recalling these states, it does not set them alongside another, but forms both the past and the present states into an organic whole, as happens when we recall the notes of a tune, melting, so to speak, into one another. (*TFW*, 100)

Although both the times discussed here are essential to Bergson's discussion, the one that occupies most of his attention is *durée*.

Bergson explains *durée* as internal time, the time of active living; as something inapplicable to the world outside the self, because the individual cannot perceive *durée* unless it is cut into segments and thus spatialized. Bergson defines *durée* throughout his first work, but the best description of it is found in chapter 2, where he writes that "duration properly so called has no moments which are identical or external to one another, being essentially heterogeneous, continuous, and with no analogy to number" (*TFW*, 120). In other words, inner time, or experienced time, resists attempts to spatialize it. Real time is simply when no moment is ever recoverable; when no moment is ever perceived as external to the living of it until after it has been experienced. For Bergson, then, time is a quality, not a quantity. This explains that common experience of having time collapse or expand when an individual is under some stress; or of having time seem to fly when we want to prolong some particular experience, yet crawl when we would prefer to see the experience finished. Measured by standard external units, however, time neither flies nor crawls but continues to move in its well-regulated manner. Bergson's view of time removes the external standard and replaces it with what the internal sense of time reveals: real time is that in which people live; it is qualitative, not quantitative, in nature.

It is easy to see why many people call Bergson's time theories relativistic. The privileging of *durée* seems to indicate that Bergson viewed all existence as a continual free-flowing flux in which no states ever remain permanent and no states ever recur. However, this is only half the story. It is true that Bergson raised *durée* over *l'étendu* (clock time), but he did not dispense with *l'étendu* entirely. According to Bergson, for human beings to have an existence outside their inner world, they need to construct an external reality. Hence they use the method of science – the spatialization of time – to reconstruct their lived experience of *durée*. In other words, though real living goes on in the indivisible realm of *durée*, this world is broken into segments so we can explain, analyse, and even understand the nature of experiences. Although the conscious reconstruction of our experiences distorts them, this distortion is inevitable, because of the impossibility of ever halting the flow of *durée* and because of the equally inevitable human need to violate this flow in order to assert our will over the natural environment.

The context within which Bergson first presented his ideas on time contributes to their continuing misapprehension. Bergson, attempting to defend the notion of free will by demonstrating how limited and incorrect definitions of time can result in denial of free will, devotes over half of *Time and Free Will* to the issue of free will. Thus his treatment of time is but a preliminary to the main discussion of the work's central issue. Given that he wishes to use *durée* as the foundation of his central thesis, it is not surprising that he stresses the importance of *durée* over *l'étendu*. It is nevertheless important to recognize that Bergson does not claim that *durée* alone accounts for how we live. While he establishes *durée* as the more important of the two times and also the realm to which is assigned the most fundamental aspects of our life, Bergson is aware that pure *durée* alone is insufficient for human existence. We live in an internal world, he says, as well as the external world that we construct by spatializing time. To remain always in *durée* would result in an isolated existence bordering on madness, for humans need the society of others. Yet to live always in external time is equally destructive, for this would prevent genuine growth and self-knowledge. Far from erecting a simple relativistic world, Bergson recognizes that some sort of combination of the spatialized, scientific time world and the relativistic world of *durée* accounts for the total experience of living. In his reconstruction of the relationship of time and space, Bergson offers an alternative world view that privileges the world of our experience – the source of life – at the expense of the external world – that realm outside us that we reconstruct according to our own internal sense of life.

In *Time and Free Will*, Bergson participates in the post-Renaissance shift in perspective from an externally validated world – one which locates meaning in institutions such as the church, the law, or the Academy – to an internally validated one – most clearly defined by Descartes's dictum "I think, therefore I am." But in his repeated insistence on the necessary relationship between time and space, he is walking a fine line between the internalization of the world and the imposition of the external world on the internal. This is the first example of what was to become a characteristic of Bergsonian philosophy: the attempt to mediate between the extremes of two opposing positions. In the process of this mediation, he establishes a middle ground in which the two theories can live in a somewhat hostile, uncomfortable truce. In the case of his world view, the truce is clearly weighted in favour of an internal, temporal view. But by firmly rejecting the solipsistic escape into the self that might result by excluding space, Bergson presents a vision that accounts for the primacy of individual experience, while also allowing for the presence of others' experiences and for other objects that exist externally to the individual self. Bergson escapes the extremes of positivism and determinism with his vision, thereby providing another choice for those seeking alternatives to the limited range of world views. He reinforces this vision in his most famous work, *Creative Evolution*.

*Creative Evolution*, published in 1907, was an immediate success. In this book Bergson was trying to reconcile what Darwinian evolutionary theory had made to seem irreconcilable: he wanted to bring together the scientific facts of evolution, which he accepted with some qualifications, and the notion that there is some central force that exists at the heart of things and that directs the flow of life. In other words, Bergson continued to insist on a world view that permits the coexistence of a materialist theory (scientific evolution) and a spiritualist theory (the central force in the world which can never really be known). Bergson identifies the force that incorporates both these theories as the *élan vital*.

For Bergson, the *élan vital* bridges the gap between the physical – matter – and the spiritual – life. Far from being some mysterious entity that is either at the command of organisms or outside their grasp, it is the *"original impetus* of life, passing from one generation of germs to the following generation of germs through the developed organisms which bridge the interval between generations. This impetus, sustained right along the lines of evolution among which it gets divided, is the fundamental cause of variations, at least those that are regularly passed on, that accumulate and create new species" (CE, 92). According to Bergson, this force tends toward the creation of new species, adapting old ones to their changing environment. It exists both in global terms – all living organisms are subject to the push of the *élan vital* – and on individual terms – each organism has its own *élan vital* that accounts for its evolution. The microcosm and the macrocosm are both fueled by the life force, argues Bergson, although their conflicting interests often engender either adaptations that are good for the general environment and not for individual, or change that is good for the individual and not for the general environment. Thus, though the life force tends to push all organisms in one direction, there is not always harmony in the universe – thanks to the variety of species and their diverse needs and interests, as well as their differing adaptive abilities. While Bergson feels that creative evolution is optimistic, because it does not espouse a mechanist theory in which adaptation is purely an organism's response to external stimuli, he notes that it is not teleological, because the adaptations do not occur so that the organism can reach some final state of evolutionary perfection. Although Bergson does not admit in this work to believing that a form of supreme being lurks behind the *élan vital*'s controlled direction, his whole theory of creative evolution implies such a presence, thus enabling him to marry the seemingly incompatible theory of evolution with the notion of a being from whom life springs. Here again, Bergson finds a middle ground between two dominant ideological camps and presents an alternative world view.

Both *durée* and the *élan vital* point toward a consistent world view: the presence of a "real" material world, as well as living beings that are subject to the natural forces (chief among them the *élan vital*) that direct the growth and changes occurring in the world. Bergson argues that human beings truly live in *durée* – this is where the growth and change occur – but make sense of the "real" world external to them by spatializing it and thereby rendering it immobile but comprehensible. Bergsonian philosophy distinguishes between living and reconstructing, by claiming that living occurs in a temporal plane and reconstruction in a spatial plane, but insists that the totality of human life is explained by the interaction of the two. This interaction that Bergson presents as a new vision of the world is an important contribution to twentieth-century thought.

## The Self

In *Matter and Memory*, his lengthy discussion on the nature and function of memory published in 1896, Bergson examines the notion of body-mind dualism. He openly asserts that this book "affirms the reality of spirit and the reality of matter, and tries to determine the relation of the one to the other by the study of a definite example, that of memory. It is, then, frankly dualistic" (*M&M*, xi). But Bergson's dualism does not reprise previous philosophical discussions of the relationship between body and mind, although he naturally places his work in its proper context. Instead, he centres his examination of memory on the idea that the body is "a centre of action, and only a centre of action" (*M&M*, 303) and develops his argument by discussing the consequences that result from this assertion. Of particular interest are his ideas of perception and memory, and the concept of self that results from his treatment of the duality of matter and spirit.

Bergson attacks both the realist and the idealist definitions of perception. He argues that the question is not whether objects exist in themselves (realists) or only exist in our minds (idealists) but whether perception is a cognitive act. Bergson maintains that perception is an action, and that pure perception is a recording of sensations provoked by contact with objects external to the mind. He says "In pure perception we are actually placed outside ourselves, we touch the reality of the object in an immediate intuition [of it]" (*M&M*, 84). Pure perception – which is very like *durée* – is only an ideal, he continues, because "perception is never a mere contact of the mind with the object present; it is impregnated with memory-images which complete it as they interpret it" (*M&M*, 170). One could say, then, that memory allows awareness of perceptions; it is memory that permits the existence of consciousness. As Bergson puts it:

Our perception presents us with a series of pictorial, but discontinuous, views of the universe; from our present perceptions we could not deduce subsequent perceptions, because there is nothing which foretells the new qualities into which they will change … The qualitative heterogeneity of our successive perceptions of the universe results from the fact that each, in itself, extends over a certain depth of duration, and that memory condenses in each an enormous multiplicity of vibrations which appear to us all at once, although they are successive. (M&M, 76–7)

In other words, memory is the bridge between the perceptions of an event or object and the recollection of it. Although we as individuals cannot simply reconstruct the perception, since each perception is completely infused with memories of other perceptions, we can make an approximate recollection of it that will help in the construction of external reality. Having dealt with the issue of perception, Bergson turns to the issue of memory itself.

He asserts, much like Descartes, that there are two types of memory: voluntary memory (cerebral memory) and involuntary memory (pure recollection). Unlike Descartes, Bergson maintains that every sensation is retained by one of the two memories. Bergson differentiates clearly between the two: "The past appears to be stored up ... under two extreme forms: on the one hand, motor mechanisms which make use of it; on the other hand, personal memory-images which picture all past events with their outline, their colour and their place in time" (M&M, 102). He differentiates them clearly by describing the way they function: "The first, conquered by effort remains dependent on our will; the second, entirely spontaneous, is as capricious in reproducing as it is faithful in preserving" (M&M, 102). Cerebral memory, as the repository of habitual actions, is therefore tied to the body. Motor functions, learned by dint of long practice and stored in habit memory, are thus liable to recall when the will is deliberately exerted to bring them forward to consciousness' attention and for use. It is important to note that Bergson does not give the brain a privileged position: it is just another organ," an instrument of analysis in regard to the movement received, and an instrument of selection in regard to the movement executed. But in the one case as in the other, its office is limited to the transmission and division of movement"(M&M, 20). Also, the brain is not the mind; that exists elsewhere, as a product of Bergson's mémoire par excellence (pure recollection). Moreover, although involuntary memory records all the perceptions of past experience, these perceptions, unlike those in habit memory, cannot always be called forward. For Bergson, then, the brain acts as a processor of sorts, permitting limited access to involuntary memory; although the criteria for access are unknown, they seem to include the utility of the perception to the present moment. Indeed, the more useful the perception stored in involuntary memory is to the present moment, the more likely it will be spontaneously recalled. It is clear that Bergson's two memories are not equal in stature; involuntary memory is privileged over voluntary memory, although both are necessary for a proper functioning memory system. Having established the nature of memory, Bergson next turns to the central issue of the book – the mind-body relationship.

Although the body and mind exist in a union, Bergson believes that the mind can exist after the body's physical demise. To him, the body is the recipient of physical sensations, while the mind is a separate, non-physical entity that is capable of existence after the body's decay because it does not depend on physical sensations, and the movement they provoke, for its own existence. Further, the mind's life is revealed through the agency of pure memory, for if pure memory "is not attached to, produced by, or preserved in, brain tissue, its continuity beyond the decomposition of our organism is a very plausible hypothesis" (Kolakowski, 48). For Bergson, the immortality of the mind is both central and ultimately unprovable. Bergson puts this idea in terms of the body-mind issue when he discusses pure memory:

My actual sensations occupy definite portions of the surface of my body; pure memory, on the other hand, interests no part of my body. No doubt it will beget sensations as it materializes; but at that very moment it will cease to be a memory and pass into the state of a present thing, something actually lived; and I shall only restore to its character of memory by carrying myself back to the process by which I called it up, as it was virtual, from the depths of my past. It is just because I made it active that it has become actual, that is to say, a sensation capable of provoking movements. (M&M, 179)

Pure memory, like *durée*, just is. Bergson then employs this idea to arrive at the sense of a self that illustrates the separateness of mind from body.

The self, says Bergson, is a real entity that experiences continuous growth by reabsorbing and reinscribing the whole of its experiences and perceptions at any single moment; each moment it presents a new "whole" self to the world, but paradoxically this "new" self is a compilation of "old" selves. The self cannot exist without memory, for the self is in fact memory. Leszek Kolakowski makes this difficult point clearer when he says:

There can be no distinction between the form of memory and its actual content, between the ego and the perceptions and recollections that are put "into" or superimposed "on" it. I am what I remember, consciously or otherwise ... I am new at every moment but, by including the whole of my past in my present, I remain the same person. And, if we make an effort to free ourselves from our space-related mental habits, we see that there is no contradiction

between our never being identical at any two points or segments in time ...
and being a continuous personal existence. (Kolakowski, 47)

Self, which is memory, depends on both the body and the mind for its
existence. As Bergson says, "Spirit borrows from matter the perceptions on which it feeds, and restores them to matter in the form of
movements which it has stamped with its own freedom" (*M&M*, 332).
Just as Bergson's ideas about time permitted a redefinition and new
understanding of the general physical phenomenon of existence, his
ideas about memory allow a reassessment of how it works, while permitting a new understanding of individual existence. For if memory is
self, then self is dual; but not in the restrictive traditional sense that
saw self as dual by virtue of consisting of the equal, but separate, qualities of a real physical thing and an abstract concept. Self is both of
these things and neither of these. Its "thingness" comes to the fore
when a spatialized series of perceptions is presented to the world and
is called "ourself"; its "abstractness" assumes centre stage when it becomes clear that the flow of perceptions and memories that produce a
self can never be halted. Practically speaking, Bergson acknowledged
that the only way anyone can function in society is to use an external,
spatialized self; however, this does not mean that it is the real self. As
Bergson argued throughout *Matter and Memory*, a person may know
matter by access to its physical qualities that act on the body, and the
spirit by realizing that the way the body reacts to perceptions is gov-
erned by memory, since no perception is free from memory and memory is spirit. But because no one can know pure spirit or pure matter,
the self that is presented to the world and that a person knows becomes like the body, in that it is "an object destined to move other objects [and it] is, then, a centre of action" (*M&M*, 5). Although it is not
the self, it assumes the external representation of the self, even though
Bergson insists that it must not be mistaken for the real thing.

Bergson best addresses the issue of what the self is in *An Introduction to Metaphysics*. Here he says:

There is, beneath these sharply cut crystals and this frozen surface [self], a
continuous flux which is not comparable to any flux I have ever seen. There is
a succession of states, each of which announces that which follows and contains that which precedes it. They can, properly speaking, only be said to
form multiple states when I have already passed them and turn back to observe their track. Whilst I was experiencing them they were so solidly organized, so profoundly animated with a common life, that I could not have said
where another commenced. In reality no one of them begins or ends, but all
extend into each other. (*INTRO*, 9–10)

The self, according to Bergson, consists of a solidified upper layer, a crust, which is the apparently stable, whole person that is projected to the external world. It is this projection that allows one to function in the world. But this self can also be considered atrophied and effectively dead, because it ceases to be mobile. Thus the real living being consists of the many interpenetrating and constantly mobile selves that exist below the surface of the solidified crust. And the link between the two layers of self is primarily memory. In their own ways, each of the two layers of self are important for an individual's wholeness. Here again, Bergson's usual philosophical method of mediating between two apparently contradictory views is evident. On the one hand, he agrees with contemporary psychologists such as Freud, who maintain that the tumultuous inner world provides the true essence of the self; yet he also upholds previous theorists' contentions that it is the surface layer that deserves the title of self, because that is the layer that presents a stable and coherent personality to the world. By embracing both points of view, Bergson creates a third view.

## Art

Immediately prior to the outbreak of World War I, Bergson told T.E. Hulme that his next book would be about aesthetics and ethics.[2] Unfortunately, this book was never written, although Bergson did deal with comedy in *Laughter*. However, clues to his aesthetics are scattered throughout his earlier works: music, language, dance, and the visual arts are all discussed in a manner that is clearly an extension of his philosophical system. Gathering these comments together reveals how Bergson viewed art and the creative activity that produces it.

Before examining Bergson's loosely formulated aesthetics, it is necessary to look at one crucial concept: intuition. Although Bergsonian intuition has come under fire for its vague and often difficult to grasp meaning, Bergson addresses the issue squarely in *Creative Evolution*: intuition allows one to penetrate to the heart of *durée* in any object or living thing. By intuition, Bergson meant "instinct that has become disinterested, self-conscious, capable of reflecting upon its object and of enlarging it indefinitely" (*CE*, 186). Intuition, "by the sympathetic communication which it establishes between us and the rest of the living, by the expansion of our consciousness which it brings about, … introduces us into life's domain, which is reciprocal interpenetration, endlessly continued creation" (*CE*, 187). But intelligence cannot be dispensed with, for it is "from intelligence that has come the push that has made [intuition] rise to the point it has reached" (*CE*, 187). Together, these two statements permit a fuller understanding not only of objects external to the individual, but also of the inner world. It seems that, for Bergson, when we turn our gaze inward, we intuitively enter into an understanding with ourself and then employ our intelligence to explain what intuition has revealed. Again, there are parallels here that link this concept to the rest of Bergson's philosophy: intuition is like *durée*, a quality that is experienced but that needs a spatialization, provided here by intelligence, to interpret or reconstruct it. Like *durée*, intuition cannot be defined in precise, scientific terms. Hence intuition, like its counterpart, has often been dismissed as some sort of mysticism. Intuition, however, like *durée*, does describe the events and experiences summoned by interactions with self, others, or objects that escape more precise descriptions. Therefore it cannot be dismissed as easily as Bergson's critics might have wished. Because it provides a good account of the workings of the spirit, it also works well as an account of our unmeasurable life experiences.

Arthur Szathmary, one of Bergson's first and most perceptive aesthetic commentators, notes: "Bergson conceives of art, not as an expression superimposed upon the more vital aspects of experience, but as the finest rendition of experience itself" (Szathmary, 50). For Bergson, all aspects of life are aesthetic because art is not found simply in static objects. Art is an experience of life that may be reconstructed in an object, but whose meaning is released when the object's perceiver penetrates to its living elements. Szathmary comments on the continuity between Bergson's general philosophic concepts and his aesthetic notions in a telling manner: "By the expansion of the term 'aesthetic', Bergson suggests a criticism of all esoteric and mythological interpretations of art; he points to the immediate approach through sensory discrimination. More than this, he suggests that the lesser experiences – our everyday contact with natural objects – may be 'aesthesized' and 'heightened'" (Szathmary, 54). Art becomes much more than a finished poem, painting, or symphonic score; for Bergson, art is the experience of these things. The real art lies behind the object (or deep within it); in aesthetic experience and through aesthetic experience both artist and audience are joined in a common activity – the rediscovery of the emotions, perceptions, and impressions that prompted the fashioning of art. Bergson's expansion of the realm of aesthetics to include any experience that enables a viewer or participant to see life more clearly is matched by the tendency of the period to see art in places seldom examined for it. The early twentieth century is notable for finding aesthetic experiences in the industrial squalor of cities, in factories and quarries, and even in the fires and trenches of war. Recognizing that art could be fashioned from things not conventionally thought beautiful helped to formulate a new, broader approach to aesthetics.[3] Bergson's aesthetic experience of all facets of life certainly contributed to this redefinition of aesthetics.

Along with the changing nature of art, Bergson's aesthetics addressed the issue of the artist's role. For Bergson, artists were not privileged creators of life; like any other group of sensitive people, artists were expected to use their perceptive abilities to present what these allowed them to see or experience. They were to discover what surrounded them and then present the surroundings in their chosen art form. Thus artists enter into an object or experience through the agency of Bergsonian intuition, and come to know the essential "thingness" of the object or experience under scrutiny. They then attempt to render accurately this so-called thingness. Since no perception is pure (all being tinged with memories of previous perceptions), artists can never duplicate the object or experience; however, they do attempt to recapture their experience. According to Bergson, just as artists use intuition to recreate the essence of the things studied, the audience (perceiver) uses its intuition to enter into the art object. Intuitively we, the audience, enter the poem, music, painting, sculpture, or moment of life and attempt to know its essence ("thingness"). By so doing, we are recreating the artists' experience, but also making it our own, since our interaction with the art is also tinged with our own previous experiences. This perpetual interplay of perception and recreation results in the immortality of the aesthetic experience, for as long as there is someone to enter into a relationship with art, art lives. It also means that all who encounter art or who have an aesthetic experience are artists, for we all help to fashion and refashion art. In essence, Bergson maintains that all people are capable of being artists, as long as they surrender themselves to the intuitive understanding of life around them and then school themselves to represent the experience in a viable art form. Bergson admits that the reason that not everyone is a practising artist is because most people do not use their perceptive faculties fully or properly. Those whom society calls artists are not superior beings endowed with measurably greater gifts; they just use their senses and minds more fully.

Bergson outlines three steps that are involved in the aesthetic experience and that explain the complicated relationship of artist – art object – perceiver (audience). He characteristically chooses dance, a *mobile* art form, to illustrate his theory. The steps are intuitively entering into the dancer's role; anticipating the movement of both the dancer and the sequence of actions, thus assuming the role as one's own; and feeling as if one is in control of the dance itself, as if one is the impulse within the creative activity.[4] In simple terms, Bergson is saying that the following occurs: an understanding of the object (through intuition); a re-creation of the object according to the perceiver's experience of it; and a final domination of the object by the perceiver, so that the object ceases to be part of the external world and becomes an intimate part of the perceiver's inner world. Thus the experience of art is highly personal, one in which the ultimate end is the appropriation of the art object into the perceiver's private world. In literature, this process is equivalent to the re-creation of a literary work in the reader's mind. In effect, readers first absorb the words of a text, and through them come to an intuitive understanding of the experiences that led to them, before recreating the experiences of the words, using their own lives to give the writer's experiences a place in their own inner lives. Thus a total involvement in the art object by the viewer is essential. For Bergson, then, art consists of the presentation of living moments in precise, ordered forms that will provoke individuals to respond from their own storehouse of experiences; because each reader is unique, texts may have different meanings for each reader.

According to Bergson, although the observer may work to recreate the aesthetic experience, the perception that initiates it can only come from an appreciation of how other things are structured and how they function. Bergson was particularly interested in how artists presented living moments in fairly structured ways. In literature this means an interest in language. In *Time and Free Will* Bergson wrote about the nature of language. He said:

[The] influence of language on sensation is deeper than is usually thought. Not only does language make us believe in the unchangeableness of our sensations, but it will sometimes deceive us as to the nature of the sensation felt … In short, the word with the well-defined outlines, the rough and ready word, which stores up the stable, common, and consequently impersonal element in the impressions of mankind, overwhelms or at least covers over the delicate and fugitive impressions of our individual consciousness. To maintain the struggle on equal terms, the latter ought to express themselves in precise words; but these words, as soon as they were formed, would turn against the sensation which gave birth to them, and invented to show that the sensation is unstable, they would impose on it their own stability. (*TFW*, 131–2)

Language, because it relies on analysing, organising, and spatializing experiences so that they might be communicated to others, cannot capture the flux of life. Language, however, is one tool which approximately conveys experiences to others. In this sense, Bergson believed that, short of intuitive interaction, language was the best means of communication available; he argued further that it was incumbent upon us all, and especially writers, to use language as effectively as possible. To illustrate the point above, Bergson said: "Now, if some bold novelist, tearing aside the cleverly woven curtain of our conventional ego, shows us under this appearance of logic [in language] a fundamental absurdity, under the juxtaposition of simple states an infinite permeation of a thousand impressions which have already ceased to exist the instant they are named, we commend him for having known us better than we know ourselves" (TFW, 133). Such a command of language is what the "stream-of-consciousness" writers aimed to achieve, and it is not hard to imagine Bergson commending them for "tearing aside" the conventional novel forms in order to render consciousness in a new manner.

Bergson believed that art, or the aesthetic experience, should startle people out of their daily lives. Ever the foe of habit and mechanical routine, he saw art as a way of prompting people to look at the world differently. Put another way, art functions as a guide into a new world; it also turns us back on ourselves, greatly enriching our inner worlds and prompting us to examine this existence too. Bergson's view of art's function is an unusual one: art is social because it may bring people together, forcing individuals and societies out of the their limited worlds; it is also non-utilitarian because its place in the world does not rely solely on its usefulness; finally, it is a bridge between artist and perceiver and between everyday life and *durée*. For Bergson, then, art is more than a simple expression of an artist's conception of beauty, society, or "reality"; it is also more than a beautiful object that is admired for itself. Art, he says, is the finest embodiment of life, and depends on both the artist and the perceiver for that status.

As is customary in Bergson's philosophy, his aesthetics rely on a duality for its form. He manages to combine the "expressive" theory of Romanticism with the more "objective" theory of later Modernism, thereby walking a fine line between nineteenth-century and twentieth-century aesthetics. The nineteenth century was coloured by Romantic aesthetic theory, which maintained, among other things, that art embodied the best of the artist's inner nature. Art was viewed as a unique, personal expression, capable of conveying its spiritual message intact to others. Wordsworth's statement about poetry – that it "is the spontaneous overflow of powerful feelings" (Wordsworth, 126) – conveys the idea that art is an inevitable expression of the artist's own self. In this theory, the perceivers' function is to recreate, as precisely as possible, the writer's actual emotion or state of mind; the perceivers are expected to leave aside their own emotions or reactions in their search for the creator's emotions and thoughts. Once they discover the creator's message, the perceivers are then expected to accommodate it to their own experiences. For nineteenth-century aesthetics, then, the first function is to establish what the creator wanted to say. Although the artist retains this central position in the twentieth century, the approach to art differs radically, having become what M.H. Abrams calls an "objective theory". Abrams defines this as that "which on principle regards the work of art in isolation from all these external points of reference, analyzes it as a self-sufficient entity constituted by its parts in their internal relations, and sets out to judge it solely by criteria intrinsic to its own mode of being" (Abrams, 26). This twentieth-century view of art, in contrast to the Romantic view, states that what is essential is not art's "spiritual" content, but the way in which its internal qualities interact with each other. The perceivers are expected to deal solely with the formal qualities of the text or art object since it is impossible to reconstruct the emotions or thoughts of the creator. Form or structure, in effect, become the real content or meaning of the work, and any attempt to claim that art has a social correlative or function is harshly treated.

Bergson's aesthetic offered a general approach to the problems of representation, perception, and beauty that fascinated and frustrated the artists of the period. Bergson's theory combines both the Romantic and modern views of art, thus reflecting the actual nature of the art of the period. Despite the many protestations of massive change made during this period, most people still clung to vestiges of the past in order to assuage the feelings of terror invoked by the chaotic present. This is certainly true in the arts, where the existing forms were only gradually replaced by more experimental ones and where, in almost every instance, experimental and traditional forms existed side by side in an uneasy alliance that most writers were unwilling to rupture. Bergson believed that the artist created both the art and the criteria by which it is judged; but he also believed that a central role must be given to the perceivers of the art object, for it was their responsibility to recreate the art form and to come to terms with what the artist had represented. Bergson's belief in coming to know something by entering into its internal world anticipates modern theorists. Late Modernist theory (it might be more accurate to speak of "New Criticism" which is not, strictly speaking, modernism as defined in this study) deviates from Bergson's notions by insisting that the internal elements should be isolated from the external world; that art should be valued for its own merits alone. This stance reached an extreme form in the critical tenets of Structuralism and Post-Structuralism later in the century. For Bergson, form and content are part of a unified whole and, while stressing the importance of internal awareness and analysis, he desires that every tool be brought to bear in an analysis of the aesthetic emotion evoked by the art work.

### BERGSON'S FALL FROM POPULARITY

Today it is extremely difficult to understand how Bergson, who was so immensely popular for the first decade and a half of the twentieth century, could fade into obscurity before the end of the third decade. Bergson's rapid demise from public prominence is often cited as proof positive that his impact on the intellectual world has been exaggerated – that it was at best temporary, and at worst an aberration rightly erased by succeeding generations. But none of this truly explains the Bergsonian phenomenon of early Modernism; nor does it take into account the ongoing, and now growing, interest in the role that Bergsonian philosophy, and the man himself, played in the redefinition of the world at the turn of the century. Although others have addressed this issue at length, it is necessary to touch here on Bergson's enormous fame and rapid demise in order to give an international context for the assertions made in the next two chapters – that Bergson's influence on modern British literature is every bit as significant as it was on French, American, or other literatures.[5]

Bergson was a cultural phenomenon: a large part of his popularity, as well as his subsequent obscurity, was caused by the way in which society outside the confines of academia embraced him. Bergson was seen by many as a champion of the spirit in a world where the spirit was sacrificed to the perpetual pursuit of material success and progress. Although this pigeon-holing may be partially ascribed to his association with the French Spiritualists, a link he never denied, it probably has more to do with the fact that his was one of the few academic voices that could still be heard asserting the role of the spirit in an era dominated by the material world. Bergson's charismatic personality, coupled with a straightforward, jargon-free speaking style that held huge audiences at his public lectures enthralled, meant that he conquered people easily. The vibrancy and attractiveness of a philosophy that advocated human control of the world and of individual behaviour also contributed to his almost cultlike popularity.

Bergson's growing interest in the state of the world outside academia also attests to his status as an eminent Frenchman. His election to the French Academy in 1914 (although accompanied by much controversy)[6] indicated that he had reached the pinnacle of his nation's intellectual world, while his later missions as ambassador extraordinary to the United States during World War I demonstrated the high esteem in which he was held by the leaders of both France and the United States. There has even been speculation that Bergson's conversations with President Wilson during his second American visit (June to September 1918) may have influenced the president's actions (Grogin, 202). After the war, Bergson involved himself in the cause of world peace, eventually becoming the first president of the International Committee on Intellectual Cooperation of the League of Nations. While all this public work raised Bergson's profile even higher, it meant that he neglected the original source of his position; moreover, he left himself vulnerable to the growing number of individuals who sought to criticize and undermine him and his work.

Bergson's difficulties can be traced, ironically, to the huge popularity of his philosophy. Despite the fact that it was based on a thorough understanding of previous philosophers and philosophical traditions, Bergson's own writings seem to pose fewer difficulties to non-expert audiences than other philosophical works. This is deceptive, for although one does need to have a sound philosophical background to understand Bergson's theories, the clarity of his language and the power of his rhetoric often led the general public to believe that they had grasped the nuances of his theories. This led to the rise of two distinct sorts of Bergsonian disciples: students and professional philosophers who were able to place Bergson's philosophy in a traditional context and were then able to study, attack, or accept the ideas based on their merit; and non-philosophers – intellectuals, writers, even society figures – whose grasp of Bergson's notions was less than perfect and often not very good at all. Nonetheless, this latter group embraced the philosophy for a variety of reasons, ranging from its growing fashionableness to the misplaced belief that Bergson articulated a philosophy that made human beings the central object of the universe and rendered unto them absolute control over their own fate as well as that of the world. In a world that seemed to demonstrate the reverse – an unseen set of natural forces controlling human destiny – this corruption of Bergson's ideas was especially welcome. The schism in the followers of Bergson resulted in two different versions of his philosophy: one that may rightly be called *Bergsonian* – consisting of the genuine students of the philosophy – and one that may be called *Bergsonism* – consisting of various corruptions of Bergson's ideas. Unfortunately for Bergson, and his future reputation, Bergsonism was the larger group, and the result was a widespread dissemination of ideas that resembled Bergson's and used the same catch phrases – *durée, élan vital* and so on – but that were confused and muddled in ways that the original philosophy was not. This popularity of Bergsonism was a two-edged sword. The corrupt versions of Bergson's ideas were sometimes more accessible to the public and thus became associated with Bergson, contributing to his public popularity. However, this same popularity prompted critics to address Bergsonism as the true version of Bergson's ideas, prompting misinformed censure and ridicule from his peers, particularly those politically opposed to him. Bergson's absence at crucial junctures during this period – which meant that his critics had nearly free rein in their attacks – coupled with Bergson's failure to publish any significant rebuttals resulted in a chipping away of his reputation. Added to this series of events was the fact that mechanism – in the guise of a variety of philosophies such as Logical Positivism, Formalism, and others – was consolidating its gains, while physical science was also making great strides in its task of demonstrating that man is at the mercy of physical forces.

In light of these events, it is possible to see why Bergson's philosophy fell out of favour. After the war, people were less interested in things that had been popular before it, regarding them as leftovers of an age that could not, and should not, return. Bergsonism thus became unfashionable. Moreover, Bergson suffered from crippling arthritis, which made it difficult for him to work from the 1920s on. Further, his absence caused him to be dropped by the very people who had made him popular in the first place – fashionable society and the intellectuals who dabbled in his works. Thus his name and ideas sank from public view. Bergson's name also receded in the universities, although less so in France (where he is still studied) than in the Anglo-American world (where much of the philosophy of this century has focused on the material rather than the spiritual). Plainly put, Bergson was labelled, unfairly perhaps, as a spiritualist. In an age in which the material is still emphasized, his philosophy was shunted aside.

Over the past ten or twenty years, an upsurge of interest in Bergson's work has occurred.[7] In the Anglo-American world the growth of this interest has been slower than elsewhere. Many recent studies of modernism have nevertheless paid close attention to Bergson, the charismatic French philosopher. Despite his rapid fall to obscurity during the 1920s and 1930s, the 1990s should see him restored to his proper position.

### CHAPTER TWO

# Bergson
# and British Culture

"In or about December, 1910, human character changed" ("Mr Bennett and Mrs Brown," 320). Virginia Woolf's remark, referring specifically to the first Post-Impressionist exhibition that opened 8 November 1910, accurately captures the enormous changes in English life that marked the years immediately prior to the World War I. These changes contrasted sharply with the insularity and feeling of cultural, even moral, superiority that had characterized the Britisher's sense of self in the latter years of Victoria's reign. As Samuel Hynes says, "No doubt a connection exists between England's imperial expansion at that time and the intensity of national insularity that accompanied it; as the British Empire expanded, England withdrew from political and cultural contact with other European nations" (Hynes, 307). Indeed, he goes on to say that "until 1910 there was little in English cultural life to suggest that contemporary Europe existed; the fine arts and literature were emphatically English" (Hynes, 313). The rediscovery of Europe, particularly in the last years of Edward VII and first years of George V, led to a "disordering of social and political systems and a radical revision of England's relations to the thought and life of Europe" (Hynes, 346). The way in which Bergson's ideas were greeted and discussed by an English audience illustrates just such a revision.

The period of 1909–1911 saw over two hundred articles published on Bergson in English journals, newspapers, and books. These ranged from philosophical treatises on his work – like those presented by Bertrand Russell and A. D. Lindsay, to mention two with distinctly opposite views[1] – to examinations of his mysticism[2]; his philosophy's impact on science, particularly on biology[3]; and the general impact of Bergsonian thought on English life.[4] This burst of interest in Bergson is only partially explained by the renewed interest in European culture and thought. In fact, three specific factors underlay this blossoming of Bergson's philosophy in England around 1910–1911.

The first factor was the widespread availability of English translations of Bergson's central works. *Time and Free Will* became available in 1910; *Creative Evolution* and *Matter and Memory* in 1911; and *Introduction to Metaphysics*, Bergson's most accessible work, in 1912.[5] While many would have had no problems reading Bergson's texts in the original French, the translations provided his philosophy with a much more extensive English audience. Reviews of the books were found in most major philosophical journals; they were also found in journals such as the *Lancet* and other more mainstream publications such as the *Athenaeum*, the *Saturday Review*, and *Nation*.[6] It is no surprise that his ideas became common currency when they were so widely available in translation.

The second factor was Bergson's visits to England in 1911. At Oxford on 26 and 27 May, he received an honorary degree and lectured at the examination schools to an audience of more than three hundred.[7] At Birmingham on 29 May, he gave the Huxley lecture. At University College London in October, he gave four public lectures. Contemporary testimony indicates that the lectures were successful social events as well as intellectual exchanges. A notice in the *Times* of 20 October reads: "No further applications for tickets can be entertained for the forthcoming lectures at University College by M. Henri Bergson. Persons to whom tickets have already been allotted and who find themselves unable to use them are requested to return them immediately to the secretary of the University College, in order that they may be re-allotted."[8] Members of the "very large audience" that assembled for the four lectures included the French Ambassador, M. de Fleuria; the First Secretary of the French Embassy; and Dr. Sadler, Vice-Chancellor of Leeds University. Indeed, the theatre audience for the final lecture is described as "filled to overflowing," with "Professor Dawes-Hicks, Chairman of the Board of Philosophical Studies ... in the chair" and the French Ambassador, the First Secretary of the French Embassy, and Sir Francis and Lady Younghusband in attendance. The fact that "this was Sir Francis's first appearance since his accident" lent the air of a society event to the lectures.[9] Bergson lectured in French and his audience was appreciative. The *Times* records that "Professor Bergson ... was loudly cheered on rising" and that his lectures were greeted with "Loud Cheers."[10]

These very popular lectures reinforced the impact of the translations. In Oxford, Bergson lectured on the nature of change and how our perspectives on change may resolve philosophical problems – a topic based on his central thesis about the nature of time, first articulated in *Time and Free Will*. At Birmingham, the lecture dealt with consciousness, life, and their relationship. Bergson examined evolution, the duality of mind and body, and the limitations of science and philosophy[11] – the underpinnings of both *Creative Evolution* and *Matter and Memory*. In London, where he dealt with the "Nature of the Soul" and examined how the actions of the mind operate on the body and how they should be represented, he rebutted scientific and philosophic opposition to his opinions. Drawn from his major works, these lectures amplified the essence of Bergsonian teachings. Of the three lecture series, the ones in London were the more accessible to a lay reader, their summaries in the *Times* being fairly easy to follow and the extensive *Times* coverage extending their reach to an audience well beyond the crowded lecture theatre. Nevertheless, the combined impact of the lectures and translations of his work, although it served to place Bergson near the forefront of the European invasion of England around 1910–1911, do not alone account for the popularity he enjoyed at this time.

At the risk of oversimplification, it seems likely that Bergson's popularity stems from the ways in which he engaged with the dominant issues of the day. His was a voice raised in many debates about the nature of life – both in the biological and the philosophical/spiritual senses. He articulated the fears of the time – that new discoveries in science degraded the position of humans as central forces in the world – and offered solutions to many vexatious questions. Indeed, by examining a few of the more central issues and charting Bergson's role in the English discussions, we may get some sense of how Bergsonian philosophy entered the discussions and assumed an important role therein. In the next chapter, I examine, at length, Bergson's impact on the literary world and on modernist aesthetics. In this chapter, I look briefly at three different areas of English intellectual life: scientific discussions, particularly those centered around evolution and physics; philosophical discussions, particularly those concerned with Bergson's alleged anti-intellectualism; and in a broad sense, the entry of Bergsonian ideas into the ongoing reformation of cultural norms and values. By this I mean to show that Bergson's ideas, as they did in France, provided fodder for those engaged in the massive redefinition of the English nation that occurred in the years leading up to World War I.

## SCIENTIFIC DISCUSSIONS

Early in his studies, Bergson encountered the work of Herbert Spencer and thus initiated a life-long interest in evolution. He absorbed from Spencer the deterministic account of evolution that is character-istic of the *First Principles*. He discovered, however, "that the more carefully he analyzed Spencer's commonsense, spatial concept of time, the less satisfactory it appeared" (Gunter, *Physics*, 7). Bergson's dissatisfaction with Spencer's spatial world view led him eventually to articulate his notions of *durée* and his own evolutionary force, the *élan vital*. Yet his debts to Spencer and other evolutionists – Darwin, for example – mark his work. His concepts are founded on a thor-ough knowledge of the debates of contemporary science; even though he rejected Darwin and Spencer's mechanism he deals at length with their propositions, if only to illustrate how wrongheaded they are. Bergson's dialogues with biology and physics are important features of his impact on British science.

Julian Huxley, writing of Bergson's *élan vital* and his theory of cre-ative evolution, noted: "To say that biological progress is explained by the *élan vital* is to say that the movement of a train is 'explained' by an *élan locomotif* of the engine."[12] Such skepticism was the norm in British science.[13] With the determinist legacy of Spencer and Darwin so deeply entrenched, Bergson's theories were hailed as "naive, if fascinating poetry" (Gunter, 15). But not all scientists dismissed Berg-son's ideas. Alongside the empirical or rational tendencies of science existed yet another – Vitalism. And as Burwick and Douglass point out, "There can be no doubt that, as the [nineteenth] century closed, the vitalist *tradition* was being powerfully reinterpreted by some of the most celebrated intellectuals of the West."[14] Bergson was at the forefront of this movement. His philosophy accentuated the process of becoming at the expense of the finished product; at the same time it insisted that physical matter was infused with a vital force that brought the matter to life. This duality marks Bergson's writings on the nature of life and how organisms function in their environment.

Bergson's philosophy was a direct challenge to the lingering En-lightenment notions of the power of reason and the primacy ac-corded the intellect. Bergson's reliance on intuition and his insistence that we cannot rationally explain the *élan vital* placed him at odds with scientists of the day, whose very existence was defined by the empirical mode of inquiry. The empiricists maintained that if we cannot measure something and divide it into its constituent ele-ments, we cannot know it. As Richard Lehan comments, "Bergson challenged at the outset the priority of a mechanistic, Darwinian evolution that robbed the universe of a creative unfolding and man of the corresponding creative power of a deep subjectivity within which the mythic, the primitive, and the intuitive could thrive" (Le-han, 307). Indeed, Bergson's ideas provided an opposing school of thought at the time and perhaps led other thinkers to reassess the received teachings and search out new ones. Biology was undergoing a tremendous upheaval with Dreisch's Vitalism, Mendel's work on genetics, and the ongoing study of life at a molecular level. Bergson's ideas, at the very least, prompted biologists to look outside traditional grounds of study. By arguing that the basic elements of life were subject to a vital force that propelled them toward adaptations that enhanced their viability, Bergson directly addressed the central argument of the day. By deviating from the deterministic theories of Darwin and Spencer, Bergson provided an alternative theory to examine and test. It is not of major importance that Bergson's philosophy ultimately fell by the wayside, for as Wolsky says: "It is not so much Bergson's ideas as he originally phrased them, but his concern that keeps us awake" (Wolsky, 169). Bergson's role here was one of agitator for reform.

Bergson's role in relation to physics is somewhat similar. In the introduction to *Bergson and the Evolution of Physics*, P.A.Y. Gunter claims: "From the beginning Bergson was not only thoroughly conversant with the outlook and the problems of physics – whose basic concepts he once studied with a view toward constituting a new philosophy – but also well aware, at a time when few possessed equal foresight, of impending crises in the 'foundations' of physical theory" (Gunter, *Physics*, 24). Bergson's excursions into the realm of physical phenomena started with his first work – *Time and Free Will* – where he postulated a view of matter as a stream of particles that are only made concrete by arresting their movement. He continued to study matter, most notably in *Matter and Memory*, where his central argument consisted of the notion that living beings are distinct from inert matter because of their continual motion in time. Humans, for instance, are constantly mobile and when they are made static by the intellect, they cease to be vital living beings. But perhaps Bergson's most notorious excursion into physics was his response to Einstein's theory of relativity – *Duration and Simultaneity*, published in 1922. As Gunter describes it, Bergson's central thesis was that "there is ... only one time-series in the universe – the qualitative temporal series which 'living and conscious' beings share in common. The plurality of times presupposed by the special theory of relativity must be construed as illusion or, rather, as the 'effects of perspective'" (Gunter, *Physics*, 123). The attack on Einstein's theory was assailed on all fronts, and as Einstein's ideas were increasingly championed, Bergson's reputation suffered accordingly. Although this is not the place to argue the merits of each man's case, it is important to note that the ferocious reaction was perhaps suggestive of the fear that Bergson's comments would undermine one of the most important scientific discoveries of the first years of this century.

It is in Bergson's theory of time and matter that we can detect a lasting influence. The physicist Louis De Broglie, in his essay "The Concepts of Contemporary Physics and Bergson's Ideas of Time and Motion" remarks:

We have been struck by the analogy between certain new concepts of contemporary physics and certain brilliant intuitions of the philosophy of duration. And we have been still more surprised by the fact that most of these intuitions are found already expressed in *Time and Free Will* ... [which] antedates by forty years the ideas of Neils Bohr and Werner Heisenberg on the physical interpretation of wave mechanics (De Broglie, 46–7).

Bergson's theories about the nature of matter and its movements evidently anticipated the discoveries of these physicists. Because quantum mechanics depends heavily on just such theories, it may well be possible to argue, as do Gunter and Milic Capek for example[15], that Bergson's influence lingers on in the physical sciences.

PHILOSOPHICAL DISCUSSIONS

Given that Bergson's impact on English philosophy has been the centre of much discussion, the arguments will not be replayed here. It is important, however, to establish the grounds of the controversy that Bergson's philosophy provoked. Although some English writers noted Bergson's work as early as the late 1890s, from 1909 onward Bergson's theories featured prominently in English philosophy. Every facet of his work was analysed and discussed in journals as diverse as *The Hibbert Journal*, the *English Review*, the *Monist*, *Science*, and *The Philosophical Review*. The discussions frequently centered around the issue of Bergson's perceived anti-intellectualism or, as others formulated it, his irrationalism. Some commentators, like H. Wildon Carr, embraced his philosophy enthusiastically, seeing in it an alternative to the prevailing empirical and rationalist philosophies. He wrote that "the philosophy of Bergson rests on the observation of a very simple fact. This simple fact is that true duration is known to us by a direct inner perceiving, an intuition, and not by an intellectual act such as that by which we perceive the object around us and the laws of their successive states. And the true duration which we know when we have this intuition is life" (Carr, 21).[16] Others, most notably Bertrand Russell, attacked the philosophy vigorously, accusing it of devaluing the place of the intellect at the cost of elevating intuition

and non-rational modes of inquiry.[17] Russell, like Bergson a philosopher with a strong foundation in mathematics, wrote of Bergson that
"in the main intellect is the misfortune of man, while instinct is seen
at its best in ants, bees, and Bergson" (Russell, 9). Russell criticized
what he saw as the anti-intellectual bent of Bergson's work; such criticism worked from the premise, stated or unstated, that reason or the
rational mind is the primary faculty and thus the privileged mode of
intellectual work. Bergson's philosophy was a direct challenge to the
lingering Enlightenment notions of the power of reason and the primacy accorded to the intellect.

At the turn of the century, English philosophy was dominated by
empiricism and rationalism; Positivism was to become central a few
years later. The leading philosophers of the day, men like Bertrand
Russell and G.E. Moore, had firm foundations in mathematics and
practised a philosophy that depended on the study and measuring of
sensory data. Moore's first major work, *Principia Ethica* (1903), had a
significant impact on thinkers of the time, particularly the members
of Bloomsbury, many of whom had been his students at Cambridge.
Moore went on to establish analytic philosophy. In Russell's first major work – *Principia Mathematica* (1910–1913), co-authored with A.N.
Whitehead[18] – his approach to philosophy at this stage was in concert
with that of logical Positivism, which assumed a dominant role in
British philosophy from the mid to late twenties on. Despite Bergson's own firm grounding in mathematics and science, his central
postulates depended less on scientific proofs and more on appeals to
common sense and intuition. And this is where Bergson's philosophy
falls under attack for being anti-intellectual; for if intuition, which
operates in a very different manner than intellect, is primary, then
Bergson's philosophy may be seen as anti-intellectual. Russell sum-
marized the position of a majority of the establishment philosophers
when he wrote: "Of course a large part of Bergson's philosophy, probably the part to which most of its popularity is due, does not depend
upon argument, and cannot be upset by argument. His imaginative
picture of the world, regarded as a poetic effort, is in the main not capable of either proof or disproof" (Russell, 346). What Russsell identified as the chief shortcoming of Bergson's work became the stick with
which Russell and others beat back Bergson's excursion into English
philosophy. And the fact of the matter is that Bergson's philosophy
never established itself on a firm footing among England's professional philosophers. Although American and European philosophers
were to remain engaged with Bergson's ideas long after World War I,
English philosophers dealt much less frequently with Bergson's ideas
after the late 1920s. Nevertheless, during the years before the war,

Bergson's philosophy consumed a fair amount of the intellectual efforts of English philosophers; whether they sought to refute it or embrace it, they were obliged to deal with it.

## OUTREACH

Bergson's theories reached beyond the rarefied worlds of philosophy and science to a broader audience, an audience that cut a wide swath through British life. As noted at the chapter's outset, his work was discussed in a wide array of journals and his London lectures were attended by society figures as well as students and other intellectuals. A man as eminent in English political life as Arthur Balfour wrote a knowledgeable essay on Bergson's central concepts.[19] T.E. Hulme comments on Balfour's "discovery" of Bergson in a sarcastic, but telling way:

Paris is only seven hours' journey from here, and there must have been quite a considerable number of people who for several years have known that Bergson was an important person, but it was necessary for Mr. Balfour to write an article, for him to become famous. Really this article has had some remarkable effects. It had produced four columns in the "Evening Times," references in the "Referee," and an article in the "Saturday Review." (*New Age*, 38)

For Hulme, an early champion of Bergson's philosophy, Balfour and all the others who commented less knowledgeably on Bergson than Hulme himself did were jumping on the bandwagon of rising popular support for Bergson, without quite knowing what the wagon was made of.

Hulme was quick to criticize the popularizaton of Bergson, but the strength of his attacks measures the growing popularity of Bergson among those Hulme called "ordinary persons." In the same *New Age* article, Hulme observes:

While the real influence of a philosopher must necessarily be very limited, he yet has a kind of spurious influence of a very widespread character. In his endeavour to state accurately his position a philosopher finds it necessary to create a certain special phraseology. The ordinary person reading his books retains only a vague feeling of excitement and the delusion that by repeating these phrases in an interjaculatory kind of way they are conveying over to the other person the kind of excitement that the reading of the book produced in them. It thus happens that all that survives as a rule in any system is a debris of phrases and catchwords which float down the floods of controversy for the next thirty years.

Something of the sort has already happened and is destined to happen still more here in regard to Bergson. One already meets people who, in arguments on all kinds of subjects, use phrases like "le continu," "élan vital," and "la durée réele." (*New Age*, 39)

Putting aside Hulme's obvious scorn for the "ordinary person" who adopts Bergsonism,[20] we can detect here a measure of Bergson's widespread influence. Hulme notes the process by which Bergson's ideas migrated from the worlds of philosophy and science to the realm of society figures and others with intellectual pretensions. Bergson's works may well have been read in just the manner Hulme intimates, and the ideas that were then passed as the philosopher's own may well have born little resemblance to what Bergson had written. But those who expressed their admiration of Bergson by un-knowingly corrupting his ideas were responsible for the popularity of Bergsonism. Indeed, the major force behind Bergson's popularity in England before the war was not the philosophers who debated his works, nor the scientists who poured over his theories; it was the in-dividuals who picked up some of his vocabulary and a piecemeal un-derstanding of his concepts and who then imported this language into their own discussions of the world around them.

Although many of these individuals were members of the literary world – they are discussed in the next chapter – some were simply amateur philosophers or individuals whose place in society revolved around their knowledge of the important movements, issues, and personalities of the day. I would put Balfour in the former category because he was not a professional philosopher and after he entered political life he merely dabbled in philosophy.[21] In the latter category, I would place society figures like the French ambassador and the Younghusbands who attended Bergson's London lectures. While I do not discount that such people had a genuine interest in Bergson's phi-losophy, I cannot rule out the possibility that their presence was simi-lar to that of society women in France, who sent their footmen down to the theatre to hold a seat for them at Bergson's lectures. Bergson was the flavour of the month and to be seen as socially aware, one must be seen at Bergson's lectures.[22]

What attracted "ordinary persons" to Bergson's philosophy was its way of dealing with the major social issues of the day. The years im-mediately prior to World War I were tumultuous in a way that often gets overlooked because of the greater tumult of the war. Hynes re-marks that "the Edwardian period was a time of undifferentiated re-bellion, when many rebellious minds seem to have regarded all new ideas as adoptable if only they were contrary to the old order"

(Hynes, 9). These rebellious minds were caught up in a number of debates. They questioned the established order of things – politically, socially, spiritually, and scientifically. New areas of thought began their rise to prominence during this time – psychology, anthropology and sociology, to name but three important ones. The established institutions came under attack and in many cases fought back with a vengeance. They were unable, however, to turn aside the rising tide of change. To quote Hynes again:

As the flood of radically new ideas entered England from the Continent, the pressure for intellectual and artistic liberation increased. But at the same time the counterpressure of conservative and reactionary elements also became greater, and more extreme and rigid in its expressions. As social unrest and political anxiety increased, so did the conservative will to suppress evident forces of change and to preserve by force majeure the stability of England. The result is that during these years the terms of liberation and control became more clearly defined, but as the terms of a sterile and debilitating stalemate. (Hynes, 348)

Entering this debate with what appeared to be fresh solutions to entrenched issues was Bergson. His picture of life as being a constantly changing process in which a creative element was established within the individual proved almost irresistible to those seeking a greater freedom of expression than afforded them by the conservative forces of English life. His major concepts – *élan vital*; *durée*; intuition; and the notion of a mobile, constantly changing self – attracted attention because they addressed the central concerns of the day. If a vital force existed that enabled humans to be part of a creative evolution rather than passive participants, or even victims, of a determinist evolution, then the human role was not degraded. Bergson's intuition allowed for a non-scientific understanding of the world, one which acknowledged that there are forces beyond empirical understanding that nonetheless help to explain the universe. In other words, if we know an object intuitively, we may say that the knowledge goes beyond the measuring of its shape and size and even its function. This was most useful in the new science of psychology, where empirical methods often fell short of explaining mental phenomena. Bergson became a rallying point for those who saw themselves as in the vanguard of social change. And for those who fought for the status quo, he became a compelling example of all that was wrong with the direction the country was taking. Whether the issue was the nature of *durée*, or the exact meaning of intuition, or even the prominence given to a French, rather than an English, philosopher, Bergson was a major presence in many different areas of English culture. His philosophy permeates the pre-war period in England much as it did the European continent early in the century. Ben-Ami Scharfstein neatly summarizes Bergson's position in this period when he says, "As Henri Bergson became the most famous philosopher in the world, he was welcomed with hosannas; and he was roundly damned" (Scharfstein, 3).

In a final analysis of Bergson's English adherents, it is likely that his popularity rests on his reception by the "ordinary people" to whom Hulme refered. The worlds of philosophy and science where Bergson's ideas were hotly debated did not reach the broader audience that created the Bergson mania of 1909–1911. The society figures used Bergsonisms as a kind of intellectual calling card: their use proved they were current with the ideas of the day; it also implied a certain amount of intellectual ability that set them apart from those less able to understand Bergson's ideas. Of course, these very same people were often guilty of just what Hulme alleges: absorbing the language without absorbing the ideas and then using the language as a private code that only the initiates could understand. It mattered little whether what they understood of Bergson bore any resemblance to what they presented as Bergsonism; simply having the language derived from Bergson's works set them apart from others, thus allowing them a measure of superiority. It is ironic that the same class of Englishmen and women who once claimed superiority simply because they were English were now appropriating the ideas of a Frenchman in order to claim their superiority over other English men and women. Times had certainly changed in less than ten years.

### CHAPTER THREE

# Charting Bergson's Theories of a Modernist Aesthetics

Many books have been written on the difficult topic of modern literature. Some very good books, such as Michael Levenson's *A Genealogy of Modernism*, restrict their focus to a narrow segment of Modernism, rendering an impressively thorough and coherent account of one aspect of it. Other equally good books, such as W.Y. Tindall's *Forces in Modern British Literature 1885–1956*, cast a broader gaze on the period and offer a more comprehensive, though less detailed, account of Modernism. This present study does not examine Modernism in a comprehensive way, nor does it trace only one or two variations of Modernism. Instead, it looks at those points where Bergson's philosophy, and particularly his ideas on art, intersect with the ideas put forward by a diverse spectrum of modernists.

## MODERNISM: A BRIEF OVERVIEW

In addition to the social, economic, and political forces that were prompting changes in society, modernist writers had to contend with specifically literary concerns. The formative period was 1908–1922: here most of the ideas underlying Modernism were hammered out, the works produced after 1922 reflecting the principles and methods distilled from the turbulent earlier years. Yet during this time, many different writers and works emerged that do not fall into what is generally called Modernism. The Georgians, for example, stand outside the parameters of most discussions of modernist literature. So what is it that separates modernists from others? In broad terms, the answer is straightforward – modernists were primarily concerned with new forms of expression and new subjects for literature. But this could apply to any movement emerging at any point in literary history. We need greater precision.

Modern literature was deeply affected by the growing uncertainty about meaning, and this forced writers to question the very nature of their art. The idea that there was no central or absolute meaning, no transcendent escape from the routine of life, touched Modernism in two basic ways. First, it shattered the traditional role of the writer as the scribe, or even conscience, of society. If there is no meaning, there are no universal truths to pass on; there is no longer much point to so-cial, moral, or ethical commentary because there is no "right" or "wrong." Second, if meaning was in doubt, so was language, that ar-bitrary system of symbols that is meant to convey meaning to others. These problems forced writers to reassess their own functions and forms; they also made it harder for the writers to follow the theories and practices of previous literary traditions. Unquestionably, these previous traditions had great impact on Modernism, but the writers of this period could not adopt any single one of them without altering it significantly to meet their new challenges. Instead, they attempted to devise ways of turning their problems into new literary practices. This involved a number of key elements.

First, modernists were concerned with the formal qualities of their art, and, inspired by experiments in other artistic disciplines, they questioned the nature of the form they used – language itself. By fo-cusing on *how* language functioned in poetry or prose, by refusing to accept that it held any absolute meaning in itself, by questioning its traditional uses, and by stretching it to the limits of intelligibility (and beyond), modernists shifted the emphasis away from "content" to "form." Formal aspects became content. Second, the vast social tapes-tries and the transcendent flights away from the earthbound status of human beings, so prominent in previous centuries, were rejected in favour of smaller subjects drawn from the daily life surrounding the writer. Third, the social, moral, or didactic function of literature was replaced by the belief that literature need not concern itself with any-thing other than the impressions of life that the writer recreates. This life need not be the material, external world of things. Instead, writers could focus on the inner world, depicting it according to their sense of it. Here writers could either become part of the expression, or with-hold their presence in an attempt to present life as they saw it, not as they lived it.

While all these ideas have counterparts of one sort or another in previous literary traditions – Romanticism, Classicism, Aestheticism, and Victorianism to name the most prominent – it is the way that the ideas are abstracted and altered to meld together into an unusual amalgam that brings about the literature characteristic of this period. The modernist approach to art conforms to the philosophical model already associated with Bergson. Modernists do not discard their pre-decessors – no matter how vociferously they claim to do so, careful study reveals ongoing interaction with the precursor they are actively denying – rather they unite aspects of each of the theories in their own approaches toward literature. What results is an uneasy union. Rarely is there a balance among the various forces; instead there is a constant tension, a constant movement back and forth to the forefront of aesthetic discussion. What is privileged depends on the issue being examined, the examiner, and the purpose of the study. For example, just as Bergson retains clock time in a fairly unequal union with *durée*, modernist writers hold Romantic ideals alongside their openly ex-pressed Classical beliefs. In this way, the general shape of Modernism takes on a Bergsonian cast, and by attempting to merge the dominant artistic forms of previous centuries and generations, modernist writ-ers emerge with their own characteristic aesthetics. Modernism is a mixing together of various ideas in order to hold off the chaos of the surrounding world. By so doing, the movement aspires to discover meaning in chaos. That modern literature persevered in the tradi-tional task of expressing people's thoughts and feelings about them-selves, their world, and their art attests to the impact that previous traditions had on early twentieth-century writers. But the adoption of Bergson's ideas and the role these play in the movement's develop-ment helped to make it distinct from these previous traditions.

One of the frequently used approaches to untangling modernist aesthetics is to focus on major figures or movements and to compare and contrast their positions on significant issues. Although this study will proceed in this fashion, I must start by qualifying my methods. First, Bergson's theories are pervasive in this period; one way of dem-onstrating this is to choose groups that were openly critical of each other and that claimed to hold opposite artistic views and then show how Bergson's ideas are common to both groups. If his ideas are present in such differing circles, they are a common thread in Mod-ernism. Second, I look at the two most important groups in the pe-riod: the Men of 1914 and the Bloomsbury group. Here it is important to emphasize that membership in these two groups was not formal-ized; rather it fluctuated, with individuals moving in and out of the circles that constituted the groups. Indeed, much of the debate about these groups has stressed the danger of assuming a cohesiveness in them that may not have existed. Having said all this, these two loosely formed groups played a major part in shaping Modernism and are necessarily a focal point in a study of modernist aesthetics. My examination of the Men of 1914 will be restricted to Ezra Pound and Wyndham Lewis. I start, though, by looking at T.E. Hulme, not strictly a member of the group but closely connected to it. Although others, such as Ford Maddox Ford, played prominent roles within this ill-defined group, my focus here will be on its leaders and those who can be tied most clearly to Bergson. For Bloomsbury, the focus will be confined to its later constellation – between 1909 and 1915 – when the power shifted away from Strachey, Leonard Woolf, and Keynes to the artists and Virginia Woolf. Two prominent individuals who provide a bridge between the two groups are examined the end of this chapter – John Middleton Murry, who flirted with both camps without belonging to either, and T.S. Eliot, who is often included as a member of the Men of 1914 though he was welcome at the Woolfs's home. Both these men provide clear examples of "high" Modernism. Eliot, who is of central importance to this study, occupies a good deal of space here. It is particularly crucial to pinpoint his Bergsonian borrowings because, as a leading modernist, he played an influential role in the subsequent development of literature in this century.

## THE MEN OF 1914

### T.E. Hulme

Critics did not fully appreciate T.E. Hulme's place in Modernism until after the posthumous publication of his writings in 1924 and 1929. Yet those involved in the literary scene early in the twentieth century knew of Hulme's importance; they were willing to listen to his theories on art and to accord him the privileged position of leader of a new movement. Hulme earned his position initially by his connection to the leading figures of the previous generation. As a member of the Poets' Club,[1] he came into contact with some of the leading literary men of the day, including Edmund Gosse, Henry Newbolt, Arnold Bennett, and Sturge Moore. Not satisfied with their approach to literature, Hulme and others seceded from the group and established their own informal gatherings that met in Soho on Thursday evenings to dine and discuss poetry. Included in this group were F.S. Flint; Ford Maddox Ford; and the American exile Ezra Pound, who eventually brought Richard Aldington and Hilda Doolittle (HD) into the fold. At the outset, the acknowledged leader of this little band of poets was Hulme, for even though he wrote little poetry his ideas on the subject dominated the group's discussions. Although Hulme had clearly been touched by the work of the poets of the 1890s, by Yeats, and by the French Symbolists, his predilection for philosophy meant that his approach to poetry was philosophical rather than practical. Because of Hulme's philosophical interests, it is not surprising that he was intimately familiar with Bergson's work; indeed, it is possible to argue that Hulme's greatest intellectual debt is to Bergson, and that his assimilation of Bergson's ideas led him to formulate ideas about poetry and art that were fresh and exciting and that eventually found their way into the works of those writers who were, in turn, influenced, at least in some measure, by Hulme.[2] Since this latter group includes Pound, the Imagists, and T.S. Eliot,[3] it is crucial to establish what elements of Bergson's theories found their way into Hulme's thoughts and writings on literature.

Hulme's actual output as a poet is slim (only five published poems), and his time as a literary figure was so short that it is difficult to determine how his critical thinking might have altered as he matured and was confronted by the postwar world that affected other prominent modernists. However, it is possible to discern three separate, but allied, phases in Hulme's abbreviated career.[4] The first phase, which lasts from about 1908 to 1911–1912, is notable for his devotion to Bergsonian philosophy. The second phase, which runs from about 1912 to 1914, is marked by his commitment to Classicism. The third phase, which extends from about 1914 until his death in 1917, is marked by an interest in religion and a markedly antihumanist stance. It is in the first phase that Hulme articulates an aesthetic that is centred on the primacy of the image in the poem, on the absolute importance of individuality in poetry, and on the precision and clarity of the language that accomplishes this.[5] Though Hulme moved far from his initial Bergsonian positions, it is arguable that the ideas he put forward at this time, both in print and in person to his circle of fellow poets, constitute his most influential legacy. After 1912 he turned to art criticism and wrote no more poetry or critical articles on literature. It is his literary activity during the period 1908–1912 that is crucial to the formation of modern literature. That his ideas are in many ways derivative of Bergson's leaves little doubt of the important role that Bergsonian philosophy assumes in British literature at this juncture.

Hulme's personal acquaintance with Bergson goes back to 1907; their relationship was friendly enough for Bergson to write to Cambridge on Hulme's behalf when Hulme attempted to gain re-admission (*Speculations*, x). Hulme's professional commentary on Bergson was extensive and favourable. It ranges from speeches, to numerous articles published in *The New Age* and other periodicals during the 1909–1912 period, to a series of lectures delivered in 1911, and to a full scale translation of Bergson's most accessible work – *An Introduction to Metaphysics* – in 1913. Although Hulme later performed a similar service for the German aesthetician Wilhelm Worringer, whom he sought to thrust onto the intellectual scene in Britain, his championing of

Bergson is more significant than just a young intellectual's passing fancy. From Bergson, Hulme gained a new insight into literature, and his subsequent approach to literature illustrates his enduring engagement with Bergson. Alun Jones, in his *The Life and Opinions of T.E. Hulme*, remarks, "Hulme's theory of poetry seems to demand classical restraint and impersonality on the one hand, and yet, on the other, concedes to the poet the power of individual creation" (Jones, 50). That is the same type of model that marks Bergson's general philosophical approach. The yoking together of opposites in an unlikely and uneven fashion characterizes both men's work and may, in fact, be illustrative of the depth of Bergson's imprint on the younger man. Clearer evidence of Hulme's Bergsonian borrowings, however, is found in the presence of two key Bergsonian ideas in Hulme's remarks about literature. The first is Bergson's notion of intuition; the second is Bergson's contention that art is the presentation of living moments in a precise, ordered form – requiring, in literature, a mastery of language.

Samuel Hynes writes: "Imagism is Hulme's application of [Bergson's theories] to the realm of language: abstractions and conventional locutions are 'approximate models', but images identify one with the flux. The former constitutes prose, the latter poetry" (*Further Speculations*, xvii). Poetry was Hulme's primary literary concern. He felt that the most important element in poetry was the way in which the poet could *directly* convey his experience to his audience. Direct transmission of the idea depends, he said, on clarity of image and language brought about through use of intuition. Remember here that Bergson's intuition involved an entering into another object, or self, for the purpose of apprehending its intrinsic qualities; and although intuition could not be defined in tangible terms, it was a quality of the mind that functions continually and is therefore constantly providing impressions and sensations. In "Notes on Language and Style," Hulme states: "A man cannot write without seeing at the same time a visual signification before his eyes. It is this image which precedes the writing and makes it firm" (*Further Speculations*, 79). By image, Hulme meant more than a visual awareness of an object (though he is more sensitive to visual stimuli than to aural or tactile ones); for him, "no image can replace the intuition of duration; many diverse images borrowed from very different orders of things, may, by the convergence of their action, direct consciousness to the precise point where there is a certain intuition to be seized" (*Speculations*, 143–69). In short, then, the image represents the artist's intuitive apprehension of the various elements of so-called real experience. Hulme's image is the concrete representation of this convergence of intuitive experiences – without the impressions provided by Bergsonian intuition there would be no image for Hulme.

Yet practice dictates that the expression of a poet's intuition must take place in a concrete, almost rigid, form – that of language. Language, both Hulme and Bergson thought, was an imprecise form of expression that frustrates the poet's attempts to relate his experience. Bergson's stance on language is stated in *Time and Free Will*:

> We necessarily express ourselves by means of words and we usually think in terms of space. That is to say, language requires us to establish between our ideas the same sharp and precise distinctions, the same discontinuity, as between material objects. The assimilation of thought to things is useful in practical life and necessary in most sciences. But it may be asked whether the insurmountable difficulties presented by certain philosophical problems do not arise from our placing side by side in space phenomena which do not occupy space, and whether, by merely getting rid of the clumsy symbols round which we are fighting, we might not bring the fight to an end. (*TFW*, xix)

While Bergson later reluctantly admits that language is necessary to represent the aesthetic experiences that a poet is trying to convey directly to his audience, he never loses his suspicion of language and its limitations, he never ceases to urge precision and accuracy. For Bergson, clarity of expression, brought about by correct word choice and vital expressions, helps to make language more precise and thus a better mode for representing experiences. Although Bergson looks upon language as a spatialization of *durée*, albeit a necessary one if we are to interpret our intuitions intelligibly, Hulme sees it as a special way of representing the elements that make up the *durée*. Thus, for Hulme, intuition may be embodied in language, the highest expression of which is poetry. He stresses that language should be vital and well chosen for its specific task. He says: "It is because language will not carry over the exact thing you want to say, that you are compelled simply, in order to be accurate, to invent original ways of stating things" (*Speculations*, 162), and again, "You get continuously from good imagery this conviction that the poet is constantly in presence of a vividly felt physical and visual scene" (*Speculations*, 164). In other words, language becomes the physical expression of the poet's deeply felt experience. Just as Bergson acknowledged the important role that spatial time played in man's representations of *durée*, Hulme acknowledges the importance of language in the representation of the poet's intuitive interactions with the world. For Hulme, the reader recreates the experience in its non-lingual terms from the language used by the poet to express the original experience. For this reason

Hulme demands that accurate language be used; he says: "You could define art, then, as a passionate desire for accuracy, and the essentially aesthetic emotion as the excitement which is generated by direct communication" (*Speculations*, 162–3). Hulme's subsequent move away from overt espousal of Bergson's philosophy did not affect these two fundamental issues of language and the poetic image. These ideas, in fact, were passed on by Hulme to his Thursday evening group and eventually found their way into the manifestos that outlined the nature of the Imagist movement. The prime mover behind Imagism was Ezra Pound, the American exile who held a prominent place in British letters at this time.

### Ezra Pound

The magnitude of Ezra Pound's contributions to modernist literature is difficult to gauge despite the many fine books written on the topic.[6] Part of the problem, as Humphrey Carpenter makes clear in his biography of Pound, is that Pound was something of a literary magpie; he borrowed ideas from a wide variety of individuals, frequently without acknowledging them openly, and fused them into his own highly idiosyncratic beliefs. At the same time, he often claimed great knowledge when he had only a slight acquaintance with the issue at hand. Added to this was Pound's tendency to self-promotion and his towering egoism. All this contributes to the very enigmatic figure that Pound presented both to his contemporaries and to subsequent generations. Yet few scholars argue against the notion that Pound played a central role in the evolution of Modernism, and that his actions around 1912–1916 were of particular importance. It was about this time that he helped to formulate the tenets of Imagism and then became entangled with Wyndham Lewis's *Blast* and with T.S. Eliot.

Pound's association with Imagism is a source of continuing speculation and disagreement. The main problems are Pound's claim to have invented Imagism, a movement that never really existed until after Pound announced the various poets' common poetic practices and ideals; and his failure to credit Hulme and other members of that circle properly for their contribution to the ideas that led him to gather, edit, and see published the poetry that illustrated the theories put forward in the manifestos that he largely authored himself. To untangle the situation a little, one needs to go back to Pound's early association with Hulme and F.S. Flint. Carpenter writes that Flint said that "Mr. Pound did not join us until the third evening" gathering of the young poets and that, furthermore, he " 'added nothing to the discussion' when they all talked poetry"(Carpenter, 116). The picture of

Ezra sitting quietly listening to Hulme and others discuss poetry is a little hard to accept, but there is something to the argument that Pound absorbed much of the contemporary literary scene by attending these Thursday evening soirées, where everything from French Symbolism to Bergson's ideas about aesthetics were being bandied about. Although Flint's claim that Pound "took away the whole doctrine of what he later called Imagisme" (Carpenter, 116) may be an exaggeration, Pound's encounters with this group were undoubtedly important in his own development as a player on the London literary stage and, to some extent, in his own development as a poet. One of the chief associations he made here was with Hulme, although Pound called his philosophical studies "crap" and was highly critical of Hulme's attachment to Bergson. (Carpenter, 114)

Dorothy Shakespear convinced Pound to attend one of Hulme's lectures on Bergson, from which, despite his dislike for the French philosopher, he came away with an idea that was to be crucial to his approach to literature. Carpenter describes this encounter in detail:

Ezra had no interest in Bergson – Dorothy had to drag him there – but he woke up when he heard Hulme saying that the artist does not *create* a truth but *discovers* it, picks out, "something which we, owing to a hardening of our perceptions, have been unable to see ourselves." The real challenge to a poet, said Hulme, was to satisfy this "passionate desire for accuracy".

Ezra thought about this all winter, and in February 1912 discussed it in an article which he contributed to *Poetry Review* under the mis-spelt title "Prologomena" (for "Prolegomena"). He said he believed in the need for "poetry which corresponds exactly to the emotion or shade of emotion to be expressed" and he made a forecast that twentieth-century poetry, at least during the next decade of so, would "move against poppy-cock," would be "harder and saner," would become "austere, direct, free from emotional slither." (Carpenter, 170)

This indirect encounter with the ideas of a man he openly despised was to lead Pound into creating a new kind of poetry, a poetry that was to emphasize precision and clarity; above all else, it was to allow him to develop the illusion of poetic impersonality that permeates his own work and that of many other modernists. Pound advocated a poetry that purported to present a simple, precise, hard image that the artist had captured by opening his senses to the world around him. Such poetry was devoid of personal emotion, indeed of the poet's personality, and meant to convey not some contrived social message to its reader, but rather a natural truth in a straightforward, but profound, manner. This is illusory, however, because Pound failed to see that in the very selection of images and their arrangements on the page the poet's personality was bound to be present.[7] Yet, despite the inconsistencies in theory and product, Pound's prediction did come true, largely because he set out to ensure that it did so. To achieve this, he first arranged for the publication of poetry that reflected this dedication to clarity and precision; he followed this up with a series of critical statements explaining the verses' merits. Thus was Imagism invented.

Leaving aside the wrangles over who first came up with the ideas presented as Imagist theory, let us look at what Pound and Flint actually wrote about the movement's poetics and see to what extent they are Bergsonian. The three points specifically named in 1913 by Pound as "Imagist" concerns were:

1  Direct treatment of the "thing" whether subjective or objective.
2  To use absolutely no word that did not contribute to the presentation.
3  As regarding rhythm: to compose in sequence of the musical phrase, not in sequence of a metronome. ("A Retrospective," 3).

To these he added three more in 1915:

1  To use the language of common speech, but always the exact word – not the almost exact one.
2  To create new rhythms. Free verse was encouraged but not required.
3  Absolute freedom in the choice of subject. ("Preface," 1)

He also described the image as "that which presents an intellectual and emotional complex in an instant of time." Pound argued that it "is the presentation of such a "complex' instantaneously which gives that sense of sudden liberation; that sense of freedom from time limits and space limits; that sense of sudden growth, which we experience in the presence of the greatest works of art" (*Poetry*, 199). While Pound had long struggled with the issues of language in his studies of Provençal poetry, the doctrines which he derived to explain the poetry of H.D., Richard Aldington, Flint, and others clearly show the influence of more recent thought. The ideas about language, in particular, are reminiscent of Hulme's statements and probably owe something to Bergson. The most Bergsonian statement, however, occurs in Pound's definition of the image. Its emphasis on the instantaneous nature of the experience of an image, its "freedom from time limits and space limits" and the fact that the image "presents an intellectual and emotional complex in an *instant of time*" (emphasis mine) echo the Bergsonian notions about life existing in *durée* and, most especially, the aesthetic experience at the centre of Bergson's art theory. The immediate interaction with the art object, in the case of Imagism with the image, the instant of time that this interaction takes, and the freedom from normal limits imposed by hardened habits of perception all have direct counterparts in Bergson's philosophy, as we have already seen. This cannot be dismissed as mere coincidence, particularly given the role that the Bergsonian Hulme played in the group's development and the encounters Pound himself had with Bergson's philosophy via Hulme. Whether Pound was aware that he had borrowed a central idea about the way in which the poet and the poem function is beside the point; the fact is that Bergson's ideas are present here and do shape Imagism's approach to poetry. Since Imagism, itself, has had a great impact on modern poetry, particularly in its definition of the form that poetry should take, Bergson's ideas have clearly been passed on to other poets. Imagism, however, held centre stage only briefly for Pound and for Modernism, for it was soon swept aside by the next "ism" to emerge – Wyndham Lewis's Vorticism. Lewis and Pound collaborated on the new movement in 1914, a collaboration that was to lead to the establishment of the Men of 1914 group.

### Wyndham Lewis

The direction of Modernism prior to 1914 was toward an art that was "anti-traditional, individualist, intuitive, expressive" (Levenson, 47). It celebrated the individual artist's unique vision, emphasized the importance of impressions to the creation of art, and excluded moral and social functions from art. At the same time it insisted on hard, precise forms of expression, and sought to eliminate excessive sentimentality. When Pound became involved with Wyndham Lewis's Vorticist group in 1914, the self-proclaimed spokesman for Modernism abruptly moved away from his positions about art.[8] Lewis's ideas became, at least for a time, Pound's, and together they set out to move the art world in a different direction. Although others also contributed to the changing atmosphere – Hulme was nearing the end of his second phase and was about to enter into his anti-humanist era, for example – it is Lewis who stands out at this point.

Lewis is as difficult to treat as Hulme, given the many transformations in his ideas throughout his long career. It is the Lewis who was dominant in the interlude between his break with Fry's Omega Workshops and his departure for the war in 1916, however, who is important here. This brief space of time was, arguably, his most important in terms of the influence he wielded on the course of British literature, for it is at this juncture that he made Vorticism into a vibrant, albeit brief, artistic force; it is here, too, that his collaborations with Pound were most intense. Indeed, the underlying role that Bergson played in Lewis's theories at this time is significant.[9]

During Lewis's continental wanderings of 1902 – 1908, his base was Paris, and while in Paris he attended Bergson's lectures at the Collège de France. Jeffrey Meyers remarks: "Lewis truly claimed that Paris was his university" and "Lewis found Bergson an excellent lecturer in philosophy, dry and impersonal" (Meyers, 15–16). The animosity to Bergson that emerges full force in 1927 in *Time and Western Man* does not seem to be in concert with his initially favourable reaction to the philosopher. In one way this is typical of the Lewis who routinely attacked his allies, friends, and artistic contemporaries and who often revised his ideas. In the revisions, former friends or colleagues became enemies and accounts of events were altered to fit the prevailing circumstances. Lewis's attitude to Bergsonian philosophy is symptomatic, then, of his failure to recognize the sources of his own inspirations. When he writes, "It is [Bergson] more than any other single figure that is responsible for the main intellectual characteristics of the world we live in, and the implicit debt of almost all contemporary philosophy to him is immense" (*Time and Western Man*, 166), he exempts himself from this influence by implicitly claiming to be outside the mainstream of society. Yet his concern with pointing out the dangers of Bergson's philosophy and his insightful Bergsonian readings of Joyce and the others indicate that he, too, is doubly indebted to Bergson.

First, his stature as an outsider depends upon his willful non-acceptance of Bergsonian ideas. By presenting himself as a non-Bergsonian modernist, he implicitly acknowledges the primacy of the Bergsonian inspired strain of Modernism. Bergson is mainstream Modernism – figures like Joyce and Proust were undeniably mainstream Modernism by 1927 – and Lewis is not. That Lewis insists that his is the "true" form of art and that Bergson is not matters little; Lewis's detailed and excoriating attacks in *Time and Western Man* prove the central position that Bergsonian philosophy held in Modernism, at least for Lewis. Second, and more germane to Modernism in 1914, are the Bergsonian undertones of the Vorticist ideas Lewis puts forward.

Vorticism is more difficult to define even than Imagism, but the Vorticist, in Jeffrey Meyers' words:

combined primitivism and technology; was fascinated with machinery, the city, energy and violence; was characterized by dissonance and asymmetry, iron control and underlying explosiveness, classical detachment and strident energy; reflected "steel and stone in the spirit of the artist"; and expressed dynamic emotion in abstract design. The Vorticist stood at the heart of the whirlpool, at once calm and violent, magnetic and incandescent: at the great silent radiant place where energy and ideas are concentrated, where (like a waterfall) form is created and maintained by force. (Meyers, 63)

The emphasis on movement, energy, and dynamism at the core of Vorticist beliefs is arguably Bergsonian, for in Bergson's theories *durée* is dynamic, mobile, and the source of energy. The concomitant belief in a still point at the heart of this dynamism and a structure for its expression is also Bergsonian: Bergson's claim that life exists fully in every moment of *durée* means that each moment is also a still point. By extension, each of Bergson's living moments is separate from every other moment, although we cannot see this because we are totally alive in this moment and it is only later that we see *durée* as a succession of moments. And again: while we are in the moment we are still, but the stillness is part of the overall dynamism of life. The Vorticist still point is not a moment separate from the dynamism surrounding it; it is the platform from which the dynamism is launched. Similarly, Bergson's moments are not separate from the flux; they constitute it. The picture of Vorticism – a maelstrom around a point of stillness – is applicable to Bergsonian *durée* because the moment we presently occupy is also surrounded by the flux of past and future moments. The emphasis on conciseness of form; clear lines and surfaces of art; and adjective-free, muscular literature is reminiscent of the ideas about language we have already seen and traced in Bergson. Finally, the growing assertion of the central authority of the artist which was later to be seen as Lewis's nascent Fascism, also has a Bergsonian counterpart.[10] Bergson's assertion that man was the architect of his own world and his own self – this is implicit in his doctrine of *durée* and explicit in his descriptions of the way the self operates – can be extended to the art world where the artist, and not the critic, determines what art is. Although Bergson would not have approved this use of his theory for he believed all people were potentially artists, it is possible to extract an elitist role for the artist from his ideas. This idea that Lewis and Pound jointly found so attractive, especially in light of their own difficulties with critics and the public, is central to the movement away from the ideas that had preoccupied Pound prior to 1914. Indeed, the artist as a supreme authority, separate from and above the common herd, was a comfortable position for modernist writers to adopt, allowing them to believe that their work was worthwhile even if others did not think so.

Lewis's relationship with Bergson is complex – it is overtly negative and covertly positive – but significant. Levenson, and others, are
right when they detect a change in the nature of Modernism around
1914; witness the rise of the Men of 1914, bringing about the form of
Modernism sometimes called "high" Modernism. Certainly its emphasis on classicism, poetic impersonality, tradition, and the authority of the artist take it a long way from early Modernism. But the
earlier ideas are not completely superseded: submerged in later modernist writings, they function in a subversive way, creating a tension
that is one of the characteristics of modernist literature. One of the
subversive elements that exists in later Modernism is Bergsonian philosophy. In Lewis's case, Bergson's ideas retain a complex function:
they become both the yardstick by which he measures what art
should not be and, because they underlie Lewis's own theories, they
subvert them.

## BLOOMSBURY GROUP:
## FRY, BELL, AND WOOLF

Today the name "Bloomsbury" conjures up images of a closed, snob-
bish, intellectual circle of privileged philosophers, writers, and artists
and, especially, of Virginia Woolf and her experimental writing style.
But the circle to which the name refers was not initially dominated by
Virginia Woolf, although she is, arguably, the most prominent writer
to emerge from the group that first met, in about 1905, at the
Stephen's residence at 46 Gordon Square, Bloomsbury. In addition to
Virginia and Vanessa Stephen, the group consisted mainly of Cambridge men – chiefly former members of the elite intellectual society,
the Apostles, which included Lytton Strachey, Maynard Keynes,
Leonard Woolf, and Duncan Grant – all of whom were very much
under the sway of the Cambridge rationalist philosopher, G.E. Moore.
Given Moore's repeated attacks on idealism and his persistent emphasis on logic and reason that directly opposed Bergson's writings,
we may assume that both at Cambridge, and later in the Stephens'
Bloomsbury salon, Bergsonian flux, intuition, and metaphysics were
attacked. Virginia and her sister, Vanessa, attended the group's discussions of life and art, where it is undoubtedly true that Woolf absorbed much, although the men frequently baited her because her
own notions were so often at odds with theirs. Indeed, the way Virginia Woolf's mind worked and the literature she produced were opposed to the Bloomsbury group's interests in rational thought, logic,
and the philosophy that dealt with these concepts. Roger Poole best
explains the gap between Woolf and most of her fellow Bloomsburies

when he writes: "Far from being the most brilliant adornment of Bloomsbury, Virginia Stephen, later Virginia Woolf, was working like an undercover agent in enemy-occupied country" (Poole, 62).[11] The initial dominance of Moore's disciples was disrupted in 1910 when Roger Fry entered the group, bringing with him his art theories. From this point until the war, when as Vanessa Bell remarks "Bloomsbury was killed"(Spalding, 173), the artists in the group dominate. Fry's Post-Impressionist Exhibition of 1910 was regarded as a turning point in modern art in Britain, and for Woolf it was also a crucial event. Although her first two novels are fairly conventional, it was this exhibition, as well as Fry and his ideas, which opened possibilities previously submerged in her. Perhaps Bloomsbury's insularity and snobbishness had prevented Woolf from fully appreciating the literary revolution that Hulme and Pound were attempting to unleash on London; through the influence of the artists in Bloomsbury, however, Woolf was about to unleash her own innovative literature. It is this element of Bloomsbury – literature that treats novelistic conventions experimentally, that is intuitive, expressive, and liberated from the rigid constraints imposed on it by rational, logical minds – that is responsible for the works now associated with the movement. Because it is this Bloomsbury that had a significant impact on the formulation of modern literature, it is this Bloomsbury we will be scrutinizing for Bergsonian influences. In this context, we will examine the art criticism of Fry, as well as that of his less accomplished colleague, Clive Bell, for its significant influence on Woolf. We then turn to Woolf's ideas about literature.[12]

### Roger Fry and Clive Bell

Roger Fry – like Hulme, Pound, Lewis and many other modernist figures – changed his ideas, often extensively, over the course of his career. In the late 1890s and throughout most of the first decade of this century, he made a name for himself in the art world as an expert on the Old Masters. Although his success elevated him to a lofty position within the art community – including posts at the Metropolitan Museum in New York and a well-respected career as an art critic – his real impact on British art is tied to the events of 1910. In 1910 Fry, in conjunction with Desmond McCarthy and Clive Bell, launched the first Post-Impressionist Exhibition at the Grafton Galleries. This exhibit was to have far-reaching effects. First, Fry – he had been brought into Bloomsbury just prior to the exhibit by virtue of a chance meeting with Vanessa and Clive Bell – was to become accustomed to the Bloomsburies and find an intellectual and social home among them just when he needed one most. Second, Fry's entry into Bloomsbury shifted the group's emphasis toward new approaches to art and helped to reinforce Virginia Woolf's latent tendencies towards intuitive, expressive, and non-traditional literature. Third, the 1910 exhibit, as well as the second Post-Impressionist Exhibition of 1912, established Fry as a champion of modern art and prompted him to move away from his previous field of expertise toward the field of contemporary art. Fourth, apart from developing theories about art that explained the work of contemporary artists, he established a Formalist school of art criticism and became one of the most influential figures in the art world. Clearly, 1910 was a crucial year for Fry.

Fry's sound education and wide travels brought him into contact with many of the era's prominent figures, and his own formidable intellect imbued him with a curiousity that did not limit itself to art. While at Cambridge he became a member of the Apostles, achieved a First in natural sciences, and participated actively in student life. It is probable that he encountered Bergson's ideas during his many trips to Paris in the first decade of this century; it is clear that he knew of them, for Frances Spalding remarks that in 1923, while on holiday at Vaison in France, he and his friends "went for picnics beside the river Ouze, discussed ants, crickets, Fabre, Bergson, Miguel de Unamuno and occasionally fell into violent arguments" (Spalding, 242). The casual circumstances of such a discussion underline Fry's breadth of knowledge and hint that Bergsonian philosophy was a topic he felt comfortable discussing some years after it had begun to wane in popularity. Regardless of how Fry became familiar with Bergson's ideas, the theories of art that he struggled to articulate in 1910 – precisely the time of Bergson's greatest prominence – contain Bergsonian echoes. Although Fry's ideas were not solely Bergsonian – to claim this would be a gross simplification of the many different factors that went into Fry's own intellectual development – the presence of Bergsonian ideas in Fry's work at this time is clear.

Roger Fry, and to a lesser extent Clive Bell, led the British art world in its rediscovery of the importance of form. They collaborated on the two Post-Impressionist Exhibitions and also defended the new art by writing explanations about what modern art involved. While Fry's articles were generally more difficult for the public to follow – he wrote mainly for fellow artists and art critics – Bell popularized modern art through his defenses of it in *Art*. His work is clearly indebted to Fry, and, indeed, Fry's ideas are fundamental to the arguments Bell put forward. It may well be fair to characterize their roles as follows: Fry's background and superior intellect made him the prime theorizer, while Bell acted as the popularizer of the theories. Both men admired the innovators of the continent so it is not surprising that their theories found inspiration and information from continental sources. For example, the works of the German aesthetician Wilhelm Worringer certainly played a part in the genesis of Fry's formalistic theories, and traces of Worringer's *Abstraction and Empathy* (1908) are evident as well. Indebtedness to Bergson is evident, too, in the Englishmen's work. Although this may seem unlikely – Bergson having often been called the Impressionists' philosopher,[13] and his notions of impermanence and flux seemingly at odds with the Post-Impressionists' emphasis on concrete form – one must not overlook Bergson's preoccupation with how the impressions of life are to be represented in the spatial world and his reluctant acceptance of the need to find adequate ways of spatializing *durée* in order to make it intelligible. Indeed, it might be fairer to align Bergson with Post-Impressionism, for the movement still privileges the experience of life that is central to art, while endeavouring to discover new formal means to adequately represent this dynamic world.

Bergson's notions about art found favour with Bell and Fry, whose ideas reflect significant parallels with those of the philosopher. Clive Bell, for example, echoes Bergson's discussion of the significance of dance when he writes: "Above all, let us dance and devise dances – dancing is a very pure art, a creation of abstract form; and if we are to find in art emotional satisfaction, it is essential that we shall become creators of form" (Bell, 284). He contends that the element setting art apart from other endeavours is its "significant form," by which he means the "relations and combinations of lines and colours" (Bell, 8) in visual art. Primitive art, which is almost exclusively forms and colours, is the highest art form, he argues, because, like free dance, it dispenses with attempts to be representational. By extension, then, vital, or representational, art is of lesser merit because it inevitably draws elements other than art into consideration of the work. Fry, too, believed that Primitive art was the highest form. He believed that good art was also "in the main self-contained – we find the rhythmic sequences of change determined much more by its own internal forces – and by the readjustment within it, of its own elements – than by external forces" (Fry, 6). Primitive art, by not attempting to imitate directly the external world in a representational way, captures far more readily the inner life and also prompts an intuitive response from the observer. Fry says this when he writes: "Art, then, is, if I am right, the chief organ of the imaginative life; it is by art that it is stimulated and controlled within us, and, as we have seen, the imaginative life is distinguished by the greater clearness of its perception, and the greater purity and freedom of its emotion" (Fry, 16). While the two disagree over the idea of significant form – Fry maintaining that it is "possible by a more searching analysis of our experience in front of a work of art to disentangle our reaction to pure form from our reaction to its implied associated ideas" (Fry, 87n), and Bell that it cannot be done – they agree on three basic points that are prominent in Bergson's aesthetics.

First, art, for Fry and Bell, was mostly self-contained; it need not rely on external elements for its significance, although it may interact with them. This does not mean that it is devoid of content; it means that the relations of the formal elements within the object are also its content. In other words, imitating nature is not adequate for a work of art; the formal elements in the object need to interact in order to capture the essence of nature, not its surface, and this essence is art's proper focus. Here we can see Bergson's notions about *durée* and spatial time in evidence; that is, spatial time allows us to put boundaries on the essence of life, but only imitates life, while life, *durée*, exists in the dynamic interaction of those boundaries.

Second, Fry and Bell believed that primitive art is the highest artistic achievement. Bergson insists that freeing individuals from habitual manners of perception enables them to discover the true nature of the world. In fact, Bergson's belief that we discover, not create, life underlies the emphasis on Primitive art in Fry and Bell's work. According to Bergson, the artists' senses are open to the world; perceptions and experiences derived from such sensory input become the foundations of art. Thus the artists "create" new forms, but new forms of artistic expression come about not because they create new life, but because they open themselves to experiencing life freshly through their own senses and not through the eyes of others. This is akin to Fry's notion that art is accessible to all who will open themselves to the experiences and impressions received when standing in front of an art object. Fry feels that if the observers dispense with the accepted opinions and wisdoms passed on to them and simply experience the object, they are creating a new art work – new for them at least. Fry's and Bergson's democratic ideas about art – both for artist and observer – are uncannily similar.

Third, Fry and Bell agreed that it is the perception of the emotions underlying a work of art that allows great art works to exist; they note that the perceived emotions alter little from century to century (in spite of changing fashions) and thus link the observer to the artist's initial aesthetic experience. Bergson's aesthetic experience – his observers reconstruct an aesthetic experience from the form when confronted with a work of art, the interaction between form and observer being an intuitive one – is similar to Fry's "imaginative life" and Bell's "personal experience." Fry distinguishes between what he calls "human life," which is "made up of ... instinctive reactions to sensible objects, and their accompanying emotions," and the imaginative life, where "no such action is necessary" and where "the whole consciousness may be focused upon the perceptive and emotional aspects of life" (Fry, 12). He further says: "Art, then, is ... the chief organ of the imaginative life, it is by art that it is stimulated and controlled within us, and ... the imaginative life is distinguished by the greater clearness of its perception, and the greater purity and freedom of its emotion" (Fry, 16). Fry's imaginative life is akin to Bergson's *durée*, in the sense that immersion in it heightens perceptions; moreover, the art produced from this imaginative life functions in a manner similar to Bergson's intuitive experience of art outlined in the previous chapter. Bell's personal experience of art involves the individual in the task of discovering what the art object's aesthetic expression is. He says: "The value of the greatest art consists not in its power of becoming a part of common existence but in its power of taking us out of it" (Bell, 266). Like Bergson, Bell argues that experiencing the essence of the art object, however loosely defined this may be, removes us from our habitual world and places us in a more vital, more important one. Bergson's intuitive interaction with the art object brings about just the same sort of thing – an awakening to the world around us that we do not see, because our perceptive abilities are imprisoned by the requirements of daily life.

An additional connection arises in the area of the aesthetic purpose. For Bergson, art, or aesthetic vision, successfully frees the individual from habitual conceptualizations of the world. Individuals, when confronted by a work of art or an aesthetic moment in life, see the world anew, and not as they do daily. Bell agrees with this concept, although he connects it with moral and spiritual "goodness." Bell echoes Bergson's belief that an aesthetic experience removes us from the confines of daily, habitual life. Fry, too, appreciates that the best artists of all periods attempt to find new methods of startling individuals out of routine life. His statement about French Post-Impressionists reflects this aspect of his theory and also agrees with Bergson: "[Post-Impressionism] is the work of highly civilised and modern men trying to find a pictorial language appropriate to the sensibilities of the modern outlook" (Fry, 156). All three men's theories thus express similar basic approaches to the arts. Of course there are differences; certainly Bergson's major interest was the aesthetic experience, whereas Fry and Bell's was the nature of art and the theory behind the new art produced during the second decade of this century. The fact that Bergson was primarily a philosopher and Fry and Bell artists and art critics helps to account for this. Nevertheless, it is important to stress the place of Bergson's ideas in their theories and to emphasize that these ideas had a great impact on future art and also on Virginia Woolf.

## Woolf's Aesthetic Theory

William York Tindall succinctly described the relationship of Virginia Woolf and Henri Bergson when he wrote: "Whether or not Mrs. Woolf read Bergson, she seems to have been familiar with him. Her novels reflect his hostility to concept, logic, character and external time, and his fidelity to flux" (Tindall, 202). Although Tindall is not necessarily correct in his assessment of the elements of Bergsonian philosophy that Woolf borrows, he is certainly correct in his assertion that her fiction is indebted to Bergson. While Woolf did not write a single, lengthy work on literary aesthetics, she left behind a massive amount of information in her diaries, letters, essays, and especially in her fiction. Her many comments therein on the nature of her art constitute a loose aesthetic theory, and it is here that we find traces of Bergson's ideas. Certainly, the best examples of Woolf's Bergsonian legacy are her experimental novels; these will be examined in part 2 of this study, while her non-fiction comments are discussed here.

The most characteristic expression of Woolf's literary ideas occurs in her famous essay "Modern Fiction." Here she attacks the fiction of Edwardians, Galsworthy, Wells, and Bennett, on the grounds that "these three writers are materialists" and "concerned not with the spirit but with the body" ("Modern Fiction," 147). According to Woolf, the greatest fault a writer could have was to concentrate on the external world at the expense of the inner. Here she echoes the aesthetic theories of Bergson, Bell, and Fry, saying that form should reflect the internal harmony of the artist and the subject, and that purely representational art devoid of such sympathy can not rightly be called art. Woolf advocates a fiction that portrays the inner life of an individual in all its multiple forms and yet is still encapsulated in a viable external framework. For her, "Everything is the proper stuff of fiction, every feeling, every thought; every quality of brain and spirit is drawn upon; no perception comes amiss" ("Modern Fiction," 154); moreover, fiction is free to chose its own subjects and is all inclusive. Here again, traces of the three men's ideas are evident. The description of Woolf's ideal fictional method is well known: "Let us record the atoms as they fall upon the mind in the order in which they fall, let us trace the pattern, however disconnected and incoherent in appearance, which each sight or incident scores upon the consciousness" ("Modern Fiction," 150). The seemingly haphazard inner world described here is a characteristic of most of her experimental fiction. But as later discussion of Woolf's novels will show, the impressions need to be carefully ordered and shaped, so that the formal interplay among them will achieve the desired effect of making the reader feel enmeshed in the chaos of life that Woolf claims is art's only subject.

Her emphasis on portraying the internal moment is not the only thing allying her with Bell, Fry, and Bergson. Her notion of "moments of being," those instants when the individual is forced outside the everyday world and into another that transcends usual limits, also provides a link. Some critics think of these moments as instances of frozen time, a notion contrary to Bergson ideas about time's constant flow. However, it would be more accurate to think of these moments of being as examples of *durée* that become spatialized because they are written down. Woolf's original moment is one in which time, as clock time, ceases to exist and time, as *durée*, takes centre stage. The raw experience of *durée* is shocking to Woolf, who always seeks to relate things to other experiences and who finds new experiences threatening. In "A Sketch of the Past," Woolf attempts to explain the impulse that makes her write. She says: "It is only by putting [experiences which shock her] into words that I make [experience] whole; this wholeness means that it has lost its ability to hurt me ... [this provides] the rapture I get when in writing I seem to be discovering what belongs to what" ("A Sketch," 84). Despite her fear of these moments, Woolf nonetheless attempts to integrate them into her fiction; they become the centerpieces around which she weaves her stories. In other words, her experimental fiction confronts her fear of moments of being; by solidifying them in words, she overcomes her fear. The fact that To The Lighthouse, Mrs Dalloway, and The Waves, the best of her experimental fiction, are built around such moments shows that her implied aesthetic explicitly relies on Bergson. Again, though Woolf's only comments on her moments of being are scattered throughout her diaries and autobiographical sketches,[14] the prominent place they hold in her fiction gives them a place in her unwritten aesthetic theory. Thus the form of her fiction – moments of being – as well as the subjects she tackles – the inner world and the perceptions and impressions of life – are central features of her work that have Bergsonian roots.

Let us turn now to two figures who, properly speaking, do not belong to either of the dominant literary groups, although they played major roles in the genesis of Modernism: John Middleton Murry who, though not much studied today, is an important representative figure of his day; and T. S. Eliot, whose name has become synonymous with Modernism.

### JOHN MIDDLETON MURRY

John Middleton Murry is much neglected in the literary studies of this period. Perhaps the reason for this can be traced to his frequent shifts in thought. Murry was guilty of changing his mind about issues and then letting the public know that he had done so. In effect, the ideas he held so firmly in 1910 – principally to do with humanism – differ greatly from those held in the 1930s – when he asserts a firm religious view of life and art. Despite his shifts, Murry remains one of the most influential figures of the 1910s and 1920s. As one critic remarks, "Between 1910, when he embraced the 'cause' of art, and about 1923, when his search for a 'credible religion' became his major interest, [Murry] took up the problems of poetry as one ultimately involved in their resolution. Only Eliot's or Pound's early critical writings as accurately reflect the concerns of the time, and it is doubtful whether either exercised more influence in the early part of this period" (Clements, 301). Murry, unlike most of his peers, appears incapable of finding and formulating his own aesthetic notions. Like Hulme and later Eliot, Murry's fervent, but temporary, embrace of Bergson's ideas was based on first-hand knowledge of his writings. He was in Paris in 1907 when he worked his way through Bergson's *Creative Evolution* in French – a daunting task since Murry's French at this stage was not good. His advocacy of Bergson in the 1910s is important: his numerous articles in journals such as *The New Age*, as well as his book reviews and editorship of *The Blue Review*, gave his ideas a good-sized audience and meant that his views on Bergson were widely circulated. Though he formally announced his rejection of Bergsonian philosophy in 1913,[15] all his early writings are influenced by Bergson's ideas about intuition and its role in art, as well as the nature of art. Murry's writings on language, often considered his lasting contribution to literary studies, also owe much to Bergson.

Murry's initial writings on art are in the Romantic tradition. He believes that art "is the revelation of the ideal in human life" (*Aspects*, 10), that "art is autonomous" (*Aspects*, 12), and that art occupies a position higher than either philosophy or science: "Philosophy and science seek the truth; but at the moment they apprehend it, they become art" (*Evolution*, 51). Bergson's doctrine of intuition becomes an aspect of Murry's literary theory. In one early essay, Murry wrote: "The world of the poet must be a continuation of the world of ordinary human experience. But that is not all. Poetry is also 'a submission of the shadows of things to the desires of the mind.' This 'imitation of emotions and actions' is only a means by which the profounder intuitions of the poet can be realised and made more communicable" (*Discoveries*, 41). He also remarked that "poetry is relative; but the intuition and the knowledge from which poetry is born is absolute" (*Discoveries*, 42). Murry wrote about the characteristic aim of the modern novelists as being "the presentation of his immediate consciousness" (*Discoveries*, 140). The idea that literature arises from intuitive experiences of objects or actions is, as we have already seen, central to Bergson's ideas.

Murry's works on style reveal another point of similarity in the two men's writings. He said: "For the highest style is that wherein the two current meanings of the word blend; it is a combination of the maximum of personality combined with a maximum of impersonality; on the one hand it is a concentration of peculiar and personal emotion, on the other it is a complete projection of this personal emotion into the created thing" (*Style*, 32). Bergson's aesthetic experience is conveyed through the work of art to the observer; in effect, the artist's personal experience is removed from the self and placed within the confines of the impersonal art object, where it is capable of being transferred to the observer. Here Bergson would acknowledge that the experience is never the same for observer and creator, just as Murry would admit that no two people would read the same word in exactly the same way. Nonetheless, the experience of each (observer and creator) approximates that of the other. A last point of similarity comes in the area of language itself.

Bergson disliked language because he believed it incapable of conveying internal life. Murry felt the same way. Murry writes: "Every work of enduring literature is not so much a triumph of language as a victory over language: a sudden injection of life-giving perceptions into a vocabulary that is, but for the energy of the creative writer, perpetually on the verge of exhaustion" (*Style*, 85). For him, finding vivid new ways of expression revives language and makes literature more powerful. Both men want language to shake its users out of their habitual life. This common interest provides the strongest suggestion of Murry's lingering debt to Bergson, for Murry's study of writing, *The Problem of Style*, is his major contribution to Modernism. With its emphasis on the constant need to improve style of expression and language usage, it clearly states the formal concerns of modernists. Murry's influence waned when he began to argue with Eliot over Classicism and when he began to consider religion as more valuable than art.

## T.S. ELIOT:
## CONSTRUCTION OF A POETICS

T.S. Eliot arrived in England to stay in 1914, having made a brief visit in 1911. He thus arrives after the Imagist upheaval had affected poetry and after the Post-Impressionist Exhibitions had altered the course of modern art in Britain. Within twenty years Eliot rose to the status of pre-eminent modernist, with his writings – both critical and creative – perceived as models of modernist literature. Eliot, who arrived in Britain, according to Ezra Pound's famous remark, already modernized, set about to make himself a name in London's literary world. In a short time, he managed to find his way into the leading literary circles, participating in their discussions and eventually publishing his own works alongside theirs. His collaboration with Pound is well known; his friendship with Lewis was lifelong despite numerous disagreements about art; and he was welcome at the gatherings of Bloomsbury. All of these people were to have a subsequent impact on Eliot's own writings. Because Eliot's influence on the writing of this century is incalculable, it is important to establish his mentors and models; by doing so Eliot and his legacy to this century can be better appreciated. Eliot's stature as a leading modernist makes necessary, too, a very clear understanding of his interaction with Bergson.

### Bergson's Role: The Critics' Assessment

It may have been possible to assess the importance of Eliot's link to Bergson in 1948, when Eliot remarked: "My only conversion, by the deliberate influence of any individual, was a temporary conversion to Bergsonism" ("Sermon," 5). That no study was undertaken at this point is puzzling, for despite Eliot's estimation that his time under Bergson's sway was "temporary," the fact that Eliot admitted to the philosopher's influence should have signaled to his critics that Bergson was important in Eliot's development. However, no significant work was published on this topic for almost twenty years after Eliot's statement, and no lengthy and detailed study occurred until 1986, almost forty years after his admission. In fact, Eliot's contemporaries accepted his statements at face value. For example, F.O. Mattheissen's comments on Eliot and Bergson in *The Achievement of T.S. Eliot* substantiate Eliot's claim that Bergson's influence was transitory.[16] Mattheissen is discussing *Burnt Norton*'s opening meditation on time when he remarks: "Some of the passages on duration remind us that Eliot listened to Bergson's lectures at the Sorbonne in the winter of 1911 and wrote an essay then criticizing his *durée réelle* as "simply not final." Other lines on the recapture of time through consciousness suggest the aspect of Bergson that most stimulated Proust" (Mattheissen, 183). Although he proceeds to discuss Eliot's treatment of time in the usual manner (pointing out the interplay between Eliot's awareness of the relative nature of time and the paradox of time embodied in Christianity that Eliot uses as a counterpoint to the first view), Mattheissen's comments, along with Eliot's own statement, exerted a very subtle, but significant, force on the critics' estimations of Bergson's role in Eliot's work. Together, they worked to block any pursuit of a closer link between Bergson and Eliot, for if the poet, himself, and one of his earliest and most perceptive critics denied Bergson a lasting role, who should argue with them? Fortunately, some did dodge the blockade erected by Eliot and Mattheissen, and more recent work has revealed how much Bergson did influence Eliot.

Many critics have noted the parallels between Eliot's early poetry, especially those poems composed around 1910–1912, and Bergson's ideas. Most dismiss this as a temporary thing, a phase that Eliot, like so many of his contemporaries, was passing through. Two critics, however, have argued for a much more significant place for Bergson in Eliot's career, contending that the philosopher's ideas are pervasive in Eliot's work both as critic and poet. The two are Philip Le Brun, who was concerned with Eliot's criticism, and Paul Douglass, who wanted to show the indebtedness of American modernists to Bergson and who used Eliot's relationship with him as the starting point for a discussion.

Philip Le Brun published two articles on Bergson and Eliot in the *Review of English Studies* in 1967. In them, Le Brun argues that "Eliot was greatly influenced by Bergson, in particular by Bergson's accounts of time, change, and the individual consciousness; influenced to such a degree in fact that, had he not known about Bergson's philosophical writings, Eliot's major formulations about poetry – about tradition, the associated sensibility of the artist, and the work of art as objective correlative – would have been different from what they are" (Le Brun, 149). In the body of the articles, Le Brun discusses the various stages of Eliot's relationship with Bergson; he also examines Eliot's critical writings, showing where they parallel Bergson's ideas and suggesting the various passages of Bergson's writings that are possible sources for these seminal ideas in Eliot's critical thought. Although the articles provide a good foundation for further explorations of the links between Bergson and Eliot, they are limited by Le Brun's dependency on others for certain vital information. He relies on Eliot's published comments on Bergson, primarily articles in which Bergson is mentioned in passing, and is apparently unaware of

Eliot's admission of his "temporary" conversion to Bergson's ideas. He also seems not to have had access to the unpublished materials that contain Eliot's comments on Bergson. Despite these shortcomings, Le Brun establishes a fundamental link between the two writers and demonstrates that many of Eliot's important critical concepts have their roots in Bergson's teachings, or at least in Eliot's understanding of Bergson's teachings. Le Brun's articles, while not having a great impact on other critics – possibly because they fail to demonstrate that Eliot's later negative attitude toward Bergson belied a lifelong debt to the Frenchman – in fact leave a tantalizingly speculative account of Eliot and Bergson's relationship. It was left to Paul Douglass, whose work clears away these difficulties, to establish that Bergson was a fundamental force in Eliot's development as critic and writer.

Paul Douglass's *Bergson, Eliot, & American Literature* (1986) rectifies previous scholars' neglect of Eliot's relationship with Bergson.[17] Although Douglass's stated purpose is "to revaluate Bergson's philosophy in relation to American literature" (Douglass, 1), he devotes almost half his study to establishing the ties that link Eliot and Bergson. In this effort he is aided not only by being able to refer to unpublished materials, but also by being able to publish portions of such work that fully supported his contention that "the practical effect Bergson had on Eliot's thinking was, finally, profound" (Douglass, 63). Douglass's detailed and convincing arguments demonstrating that Eliot was deeply indebted to Bergson will not be repeated here. The weight of direct and circumstantial evidence that Douglass presents is ample enough to convince even the most skeptical reader that Eliot's conversion to Bergson's ideas, although "temporary" to him, was in fact a lifelong engagement with the concepts central to Bergson's philosophy. As Douglass remarks,

Some of Eliot's most perspicacious critics have long acknowledged the broad parallels between Bergson and the poet/critic ... It would be well to say, at the outset, that while no single point in [Douglass's arguments] will convince overwhelmingly, the weight of the points taken together does convince, even if one allows for the fact that there are no new ideas under the sun, and that Eliot could conceivably have gotten some of them elsewhere or independently. (Douglass, 63–4)

This study will focus on those concepts identified as Bergson's lasting legacy to British literature – memory, consciousness, time, intuition, and language – that were as important to Eliot as they were to Bergson. It will place Eliot's use of them in a specifically British context, demonstrating that Eliot's own experiments with these concepts had a great effect on his peers and his successors. While this will involve some overlap with both Le Brun's and Douglass's studies, the frame of reference here is sufficiently different to engender something new to the debate.

First, Eliot was well versed in Bergson's philosophy. That he considered himself more than a disciple of "Bergsonism" is revealed in the breadth and depth of his knowledge of the intricacies of Bergson's works. He not only deals with the major works – *Time and Free Will*, *Matter and Memory*, and *Creative Evolution* – but also with the lesser known works, available at the time only in academic journals. The essay entitled "Life and Consciousness" in *The Hibbert Journal*, mentioned by Eliot in his unpublished "Essay" on Bergson, is an example of this knowledge. Although Eliot's subsequent turn away from Bergson's philosophy may have meant that he no longer ascribed to the theories articulated by Bergson, it does not mean that he forgot Bergson's teachings.

Second, Eliot, like many students, used his "attack" on Bergson's ideas to formulate his own notions on the same issues.[18] When Eliot talks about rewriting Bergson's theories, arriving at a "Bergson Resartus" in which "time would be the child of space" (Douglass, 61), he arrives at a vision of Bergson's philosophy to which the philosopher would rightly take exception. The points Eliot chooses to discuss reveal his own concerns, and his responses to Bergson's handling of them illustrate his own initial attempts to grapple with these issues. Here it is worth noting Eliot's remarks about *Matter and Memory*. He says, "This last part of M + M cap [sic] iv & conclusion – is a very remarkable and provocative – indeed tantalizing – piece of writing – I find one of the most interesting + most important parts of Bergson's work" (Douglass, 60). Significantly, the section to which he refers discusses imagery, perception, and matter. While for an aspiring poet, which Eliot clearly was at this time, the question of imagery would have been uppermost in his mind; for the sensitive young man searching for some meaning in the world, the issue of matter, in which Eliot detects a hint of an absolute, would also have proven interesting. His interest in perception, which is one of the essay's main themes, is indicative of both his philosophical training and his need to confront an issue central to his generation. Eliot questions the subject-object split that was a feature of both contemporary philosophy and art, asking if, indeed, perception could be resident external to, and also within, human beings, as he believes Bergson's theory unwittingly maintained. What the theory did, in fact, was bring about a radical undermining of the dualism that had asserted that there are things outside people that they know because they perceive them. It also questioned the split in terms of "man-Absolute," for if only the internal could be perceived, an absolute could only exist within, and not external to, a person. That Eliot focuses his argument on Bergson's contradictions in this area – illustrating that Bergson unwittingly appears to hold the contradictory position that perception is both external to people and internal, and that Eliot himself leans toward just such a union but cannot see how it may be possible – indicates how important this problem is to Eliot. Indeed, much of Eliot's later work revolves around just this question, his dilemma being that if we deny a subject-object split, we then deny the existence of an external absolute; on the other hand, if we accept the subject-object split, we then deny ourselves the prospect of knowing anything outside ourselves. Bergson does not deal with this question adequately for Eliot, and Eliot continues to gnaw on it, searching for a solution to a problem that he eventually recognizes he cannot solve. That he finds Bergson's handling of such issues "remarkable and provocative" hints at the degree to which these problems engaged him, and perhaps also aided him in reaching his own formulations.

Third, Eliot's conclusion that Bergson fails in his attempt to occupy "a middle ground between idealism + realism" (Douglass, 60) again says something about Eliot's own desires in this regard. Eliot is so strongly critical of Bergson's inability to find the middle ground because it is just the sort of territory that he would like to occupy. By finding a midpoint that allows the tenets of idealism and gives the individual mind the power of creation, and the tenets of realism that stress that objects exist separate from the consciousness that experiences them, Eliot, like Bergson, could have had the best of both systems. Whereas for Eliot the poet, this would mean that everything he experienced would be subject to the creating force of his own mind; for Eliot the man struggling to find meaning in the world apart from that which he could construct, this would invest his experiences with a meaning that he might not know directly, because its significance would depend on factors outside his own consciousness. In other words, this middle ground would permit Eliot to be a creator, but it would also allow him to be subject to another creative force, an Absolute to which he could defer. Eliot's harsh criticism of Bergson for failing to attain this middle ground suggests that he went to the Frenchman's philosophy in search of a viable middle ground and emerged disappointed. Nonetheless, Eliot removes from Bergson's work the sense that if the terms were correctly established and the arguments carefully constructed, this middle ground might be found.

Last, and perhaps most significant, Eliot's unpublished essay on Bergson demonstrates Eliot's interest in the process by which change occurs. Noting this point, Douglass quotes Elizabeth Schneider's perceptive comment on Eliot's preoccupation with change: " 'Change as process,' Schneider observes, 'may have engaged Eliot at a deeper level than did its content or result – deeper, that is, than the actual Christian view of life arrived at' " (Douglass, 63). Douglass does not expand on this comment; perhaps he feels that there is no need to do so. But such an important point needs some explication. What Eliot is reacting to in his essay on Bergson has less to do with the ideas with which he is engaged than with an unwritten, but central, feature of Bergson's philosophy. Bergson's philosophy privileges the concept of process. Each of his major theories may be reduced in one form or another to a basic set of propositions. The propositions include the following ideas: change is inevitable; without change there is no life; change is good; all living things are constantly in motion; all things strive toward a perfection of themselves as organisms; and individuals may only ever become aware of change when they arrest it, and in doing so destroy life. Implicit here is the notion that change is, in itself, the fundamental component of life. What is important is the process of living; not the attainment of perfection but the striving after it is the essence of life. If perfection were possible, change would no longer be necessary and life would cease. All of Bergson's major concepts – *durée, élan vital*, consciousness, memory, and free will – emphasize the process of living at the expense of the product of life. For example, the *élan vital* is a force that is always pushing individual organisms, as well as the whole of society, toward an improvement of itself. It has no set goal, apart from the pursuit of perfection; nor does it ever achieve a goal, for there is always something that may be improved. What is important, then, is the process of improvement and adaptation. Eliot's rewriting of Bergson is not compatible with the original philosophy and his "Bergson Resartus" is not really Bergsonian; nonetheless, he seems to absorb and understand the significance of Bergson's doctrine of process. Not surprisingly, the Bergsonian idea of constantly searching for perfection and recognizing that the process of searching is as important as the goal itself is not incompatible with the Christian beliefs to which Eliot ultimately turns. Perhaps because Eliot goes to religion knowing that it is filled with inconsistencies and paradoxes that cannot be resolved, he is able to accept what he could not accept in Bergson's attempts to grapple with the same issues. Although his later rejection of Bergson's theories hides the basic similarity of Bergson's "process" philosophy and Eliot's orthodox religious convictions, this early essay shows just how closely aligned the two are.

It is evident that Eliot's knowledge of Bergson's ideas was extensive. It is possible, too, to see just how deeply Bergson's ideas influenced him. Indeed, Eliot's criticism is imbued with these Bergsonian ideas, and a few others that Eliot did not treat in his essay. Here the work of Philip Le Brun proves to be as invaluable as that of Douglass.

Eliot's essay on Bergson demonstrates his deep interest in consciousness and change; thus, it should not be surprising that these same concepts are at the heart of Eliot's theories about poetry. Le Brun concentrates on three specific concepts, demonstrating the source ideas in Bergson's writings. While this is certainly valuable in establishing a link between the two men, we may be able to discern an even more important and fundamental link by first stepping back from specifics. After establishing this common ground, we can then trace Eliot's various critical concerns and their debts to Bergsonian philosophy in a way that adds to what both Le Brun and Douglass have already concluded.

### Nature of Existence

A good starting point is one already identified as a central question of the late nineteenth and early twentieth centuries – the nature of existence and the presence/absence of meaning. Although Eliot felt compelled to arrive at a new understanding of existence, he was uncomfortable about the absence of an Absolute in most of the systems proposed as replacements. Bergson's philosophy, especially its discussion of time, held a particular appeal for Eliot; it seemed able to embody the changes wrought by the widespread acceptance of evolutionary theory, while retaining a hint of the absolute Eliot wanted to preserve. Eliot's study of time leads to a series of contemplations about history, tradition, and art's role in the development of both. During the second stage of his explorations, Eliot sought to establish reasons for society's existence. The third stage of Eliot's journey focused on the creation of art and the function of language as a tool for conveying meaning. The final stage sees Eliot attempting to deal with the subject-object split; this ultimately results in his conversion to Anglo-Catholicism, which answered questions that Eliot himself could not.

Eliot's historical sense and his notion of tradition suggest a fundamental similarity between his and Bergson's approaches to the difficult question of existence. Although Eliot detected hints of an Absolute in Bergson's work, he still found *durée* an insufficient explanation for his own spiritual dilemma. He finally comes to terms with this problem when he turns to orthodox religion and its teachings.

Here the paradox that God is all things but not a physical object is central. In other words, Christianity insists that all things are made from God, but that God has no material form. We, who have great difficulty grasping this paradox, need to conceptualize God by making him in our own image. The story of creation, then, may be read in a reverse way, as one where we make God in our own image in order to create a concept with which our rational mind may cope. The Old Testament prohibitions on worshiping graven images and idols is rooted in this paradox about God's materiality. The writers of the Old Testament, aware of the danger of allowing God to become too human, walked a fine line: needing to make God more human and thus more understandable, they still needed to follow religious teachings that said that God was not matter but pure spirit. Since the existence of God was greatly in doubt by the end of the nineteenth century, other explanations for our life and our reality were sought. In Bergson's system, time occupies a role analogous to God's. *Durée*, like God, simply is. It is the condition of life that characterizes our existence, but paradoxically, it is not capable of a material existence. When *durée* is arrested, it becomes a conceptualization of existence and not existence itself. The Absolute that Eliot detects in *durée* is really the similarity of the nature of *durée* and the nature of God; both are built on a paradox which says that each simply is, and that we as human beings cannot understand the reality of either God or time unless we conceptualize them, thereby misrepresenting the true nature of each. In a sense, Bergson's God is time, so Eliot's apprehension of the Absolute in Bergson's theory is accurate. For Eliot, who could not accept such a radical world view (he preferred the tested and safer world of Christianity), Bergson's *durée* was "simply not final." However, *durée* did prompt Eliot to examine history and tradition.

Eliot forcefully states his idea of history and tradition in "Tradition and the Individual Talent." He criticizes the contemporary view of tradition with his statement: "If the only form of tradition, of handing down, consisted in following the ways of the immediate generation before us in a blind or timid adherence to its successes, 'tradition' should positively be discouraged" ("Tradition," 49). A proper sense of tradition, he claims, "involves, in the first place, the historical sense" which

involves a perception, not only of the pastness of the past, but of its presence; the historical sense compels a man to write not merely with his own generation in his bones, but with a feeling that the whole of the literature of Europe from Homer and within it the whole of the literature of his own country has a simultaneous existence and composes a simultaneous order. The historical sense, which is a sense of the timeless as well as of the temporal and of the timeless and the temporal together, is what makes a writer traditional. ("Tradition," 49)

Eliot's "historical sense" consists of an ability to experience all time at one moment; this is clearly similar to Bergson's view of *durée*. In religious terms, the "historical sense" becomes the sense of continuity of life, because of its identification with God's immortality. God exists both in time – each human is God – and out of time – God is not flesh and blood and is thus immortal. Eliot's view of history clearly depends on this implied religious view; it is also consistent with Bergson's view of time. Interestingly, Eliot was not at this point an Anglo-Catholic convert, though well read in theology; the source for his historical sense could as easily have been Bergson as the religious thinkers.

Eliot then talks specifically about the role of individual creative works in the larger tradition of literature. He echoes Bergson, who writes that the "supervening of each term brings about a new organisation of the whole" (*TFW*, 124), in his statement:

Existing order is complete before the new work arrives; for order to persist after the supervention of novelty, the *whole* existing order must be, if ever so slightly, altered; and so the relations, proportions, values of each work of art toward the whole are readjusted; and this is conformity between the old and the new. Whoever has approved this idea of order, of the form of European, of English literature will not find it preposterous that the past should be altered by the present as much as the present is directed by the past. ("Tradition," 50)

Eliot's statement adapts Bergson's original epistemological observation to the field of literary and cultural history. Bergson's idea refers to the way in which we acquire knowledge generally – the introduction of any new experience alters not only the knowledge of the present experience, but also the perception of past experiences. Eliot's statement indicates a similar approach to literature and cultural history: any new work of art, just like a new experience, affects both the understanding and acceptance of the present addition and the understanding of extant artistic works. In effect, the works themselves assume, in Eliot's view, the same place that Bergson assigns experiences. Art becomes an experience like any other of life's experiences, and as such it acquires a place in our individual and collective histories. Artists assume positions akin to philosophers and other thinkers, because their productions are of equal importance in the definition of culture. Eliot's notion of tradition, then, has a significance far beyond the worlds of literature and art.

Eliot uses his writings on literature to develop a model that explains existence. We can, says Eliot, arrive at an individual identity by placing ourselves within a known context; for example, we often test ourselves against others, for through this process we develop a sense of what is unique to us and thus of what constitutes that entity which we call "me." Eliot's writers do the same. By defining their work in reference to existing works, they develop an identity for themselves. That this process alters the perception of the existing works is a further stage in the manufacturing of an identity for the current artist. According to Eliot, the existing works do not so much change, as do the terms by which they are studied and judged. Moreover, since those terms are fashioned by the current artist, the altering of opinions about existing works says more about the artists than it does about the works. In other words, the framing of the dialogue is as revealing of the speaker as is the dialogue itself. Eliot is searching for meaning in a world that lacks it.

Eliot's attempts to define both the role of the artist in the creation of art and the artist's relation to the finished art work resulted in two of his best-known concepts: the idea of artistic impersonality, and the dissociation of sensibility. Eliot simultaneously seeks to invest and withhold from the artist the Godlike power of creation. Just as all people are made of God but God is never a material object, Eliot insists that artists create their art but the art is not the artists themselves. In "Tradition and the Individual Talent," Eliot talks about the artist's impersonality, saying:

The point of view which I am struggling to attack is perhaps related to the metaphysical theory of the substantial unity of the soul; for my meaning is, that the poet has, not a "personality" to express, but a particular medium, which is only a medium and not a personality, in which impressions and experiences combine in peculiar and unexpected ways. Impressions and experiences which are important for the man may take no place in the poetry, and those which become important in the poetry may play quite a negligible part in the man, the personality. ("Tradition," 56)

Eliot is separating the poet from the person by insisting that while an individual's experiences are important to the ability to write poetry, poetry is not simply a reflection of a person's experiences. He stresses the difference between poets and other people: a difference based on the implicit notion that writers create because they can detect patterns and connections in the surrounding chaos, while ordinary individuals fail to see anything but the stream of everyday experiences. He says:

When a poet's mind is perfectly equipped for its work, it is constantly amalgamating disparate experience; the ordinary man's experience is chaotic, irregular, fragmentary. The latter falls in love, or reads Spinoza, and these two experiences have nothing to do with each other, or with the noise of the typewriter or the smell of cooking; in the mind of the poet these experiences are always forming new wholes. ("Metaphysical," 287)

Clearly an ability to form wholes from all varieties of experience is a prerequisite for a poet. Although poets must do this while filtering the experience through their own personality, they must not allow that personality to dominate their expression of the patterns formed by the connection of disparate events. Here Eliot seems to be unaware of the contradiction that he is generating. If poets must use their personalities to "filter" the perceptions, then these personalities will invariably tinge those perceptions so that they are never really free of the poet's personality. The key here seems to be the degree of personality permissible in a poem. While full-blown presentations of the poet's undiluted emotions or perceptions were not allowed, the tinging of perceptions with the poet's personality was inevitable. Although Bergson would argue with Eliot's contention that an average person could not perceive the patterns in the surrounding chaos, he would agree that poetry results when the writer captures these patterns and places them on paper.

Eliot discusses the apparent gap between the metaphysical poets, whose poetic sensibility he lauds as ideal, and the many writers since who have failed to meet the necessary poetic requirements. Here he develops his theory of the dissociation of sensibility. Sometime late in the seventeenth century, we lost the ability to unify our experiences; our poetry ceased to reflect the whole range of human experiences; and the reconstruction of meaning which is possible only when poetry contains a unified, complete expression of the poet's experiences became almost impossible. Eliot frequently cited the metaphysical poets as examples of poets who had unified sensibilities. He remarks: "One of the characteristics of Donne which wins him ... his interest for the present age, is his fidelity to emotion as he finds it; his recognition of the complexity of feeling and its rapid alterations and antitheses. A change of feeling with Donne, is rather the regrouping of the same elements under a mood which was previously subordinate: it is not the substitution of one mood for a wholly different one" (Le Brun, 158). Metaphysical poets do not distinguish between kinds of experience or even qualities of experience; all experiences are necessary for an understanding of existence, so all experiences convey the nature of life. In poetry, this requires that both thought and feeling be used to recreate the poet's experience for the readers of the poem. All aspects of poets' personalities must be brought to bear during their creative endeavours. The dissociation of the poetic sensibility was brought about not only because society normally requires that experiences or phenomena be separated for analysis and classification, but because society functions better when things are presented in small conceptual chunks that explain phenomena difficult to grasp when taken in their totality. The poet's responsibility is to fight this process of conceptualization by reuniting those previously separate elements, and by then presenting this united sensibility to the reader. Here, again, Bergson's fundamental positions are evident: the world consists of both inner (experiential) and outer (conceptual) worlds, and good art needs to present a union of the two.

Eliot's championing of a unified sensibility should not be surprising in light of the underlying premise of his work. Poets, by unifying their sensibility, create works that mimic our struggle to create meaning in our society. By employing their total sensibility in a poem, poets recreate the experiences that were meaningful to themselves; by provoking a response from the readers that requires that they also use all their faculties to recreate the experience depicted by the poets, the readers gain access to the poets' own meaningful experiences. Eliot takes this same principle one step further, when he uses it to outline the poetic method.

### The Objective Correlative

One of Eliot's best known concepts is the "objective correlative."[19] In "Hamlet," Eliot defines this term: "The only way of expressing emotion in the form of art is by finding an 'objective correlative'; in other words, a set of objects, a situation, a chain of events which shall be the formula of that *particular* emotion, such that when the external facts, which must terminate in sensory expression, are given, the emotion is immediately evoked" ("Hamlet," 145). At first glance, this appears to be a straightforward continuation of his advocacy of a unified sensibility. While it is certainly this, it also suggests Eliot's concern with other artistic problems. The first is the problem of perception. Behind this definition lies Eliot's notion of the object, and his idea of how an object is perceived. Eliot defines an object in his thesis *Knowledge and Experience in the Philosophy of F.H. Bradley*: "Objects exist for us in two ways. As we *intend* an object, the intended object is so far real, and as we experience an object, it realizes itself, and comes to require a certain degree of fullness of relations before it considers itself an object" (*Knowledge*, 130–1). In other words, people only know an object when their senses perceive its external qualities and their intuition grasps its internal characteristics. Although Eliot's essay is on Bradley, the second process of knowing here requires an intuitive faculty akin to that of Bergson's intuition. In the process of writing poetry, then, poets must be aware that they need to capture not only the external qualities of the object (or experience) they are rendering, but also its internal qualities. Their objective correlative must trigger both a sensory response and an intuitive one in order to be truly successful. Eliot realizes this when he says that the "external facts" should "terminate in sensory experience" – knowing the object from the outside – and that this process prompts "the emotion [to be] immediately evoked" – the emotion contained within the sensory qualities of the experience provoking an intuitive grasping of the emotion.

The second concept behind Eliot's objective correlative is the familiar object-subject split. Eliot implicitly recognizes the gulf between the emotion experienced by the poet and the object created to represent it. The objective correlative is a device developed by Eliot to lessen the gap between the two. The subjective experience of the emotion is impossible to duplicate, simply because no two persons ever experience anything in the same way and therefore no two emotions are the same. The object created to represent this emotion may prompt a similar emotion in its viewer; the more carefully the object is structured and the greater the extent of agreement over the meaning of "a set of objects, a situation, a chain of events," the better are the chances of arriving at a similar emotion.

Eliot's objective correlative does not eliminate the gap between subject and object; not only did Eliot know that that was impossible, he also did not wish to do so. In the same essay, Eliot said: "The intense feeling, ecstatic or terrible, without an object or exceeding its object, is something which every person of sensibility has known … It often occurs in adolescence: the ordinary person puts these feelings to sleep, or trims down his feelings to fit the business world; the artist keeps them alive by his ability to intensify the world to his emotions" ("Hamlet," 49). Here Eliot acknowledges the importance of the gap between the object and the subjective experience of it; it is the emotion generated in the individual's experience of the object, says Eliot, that is the real target of the artist. The artist focuses on the object in order to generate an emotional response to it; indeed, says Eliot, the artist's true aim is to intensify this emotion. The subjective response of both the artist and the reader is the source of this intensified emotion. Thus Eliot is caught in his own apparent contradiction. Part of his theory calls for the narrowing, or even elimination, of the gap between subject and object; another part not only acknowledges that this narrowing is impossible, but also insists that the gap is a potent source of emotion and an important tool for the artist. Although it seems illogical, this contradiction is consistent with Eliot's overall approach to art and to existence.

While many of Eliot's contemporaries might have liked to eliminate the gap between subject and object, he could not eliminate the duality because it permitted him to hold on to a vestige of the former system and its absolutes. His subject-object dualism allows for an absolute – the object existing separately from the subject that apprehended it means that the object has an absolute, independent existence. This duality also allowed for the existence of God and for the survival of ethical, religious, moral, and social structures. By opting not to choose either one, Eliot, who was clearly torn between the two positions, makes an important statement and contribution to modern poetics. He contends that if both a monistic, subjective world and a dualistic subject-object world coexist, however shakily, then poetry is both part of the subjective world of its creator, and part of the broader world in which its creator is only one member joined with others in the search for meaning. Beyond its function of linking subject and object, the objective correlative conveys, or perhaps establishes, a network of experiences and meanings. Theoretically, at least, it should reproduce the same emotion each time the same set of stimuli are perceived. Here, again, Eliot seems to have appropriated Bergson's basic model of mediation between opposites that resulted in a discovery of a shaky middle ground. What links Bergson's theories to the specific concepts here is the similarity in Bergson's treatment of the subject-object split. As outlined earlier, he, too, balances a narrowing gap between subject and object in his theories of *durée* and intuition; in his insistence, however, that the inner world must interact with the outer world, he maintains a gap where absolutes may exist. Eliot's poetic technique, as described by this objective correlative, is also centrally concerned with the issue of establishing meaning in a chaotic world, as were his notions of tradition and history. The same basic premise is found as well in Eliot's approach to the medium of poetry, language.

## Language

Paul Douglass is astute in his description of the common bond that unites Bergson's and Eliot's interest in language. He writes of a shared theory in which

language has a dual source: It comes partly from the evolutionary heritage, partly from divinity. In this theory, language can be rejuvenated only by constant recurrence to the personal and unique. For this reason, Eliot, like Bergson, puts the poet in the roles of explorer and prophet, catalyst and vehicle. For Eliot, as for Bergson, language begins and ends not in the utilitarian concept of the 'message,' but in a dimly known realm of experience made available to us by intuition. (Douglass, 64)

Darwin's and other evolutionists' attacks on the Word (*Logos*) result in challenges to the capacity of words to convey meaning; words are a questionable means of conveying the deeply felt experiences of living. Words, language, are barely adequate tools for ordinary everyday experience; for any purpose of greater importance, they are completely inadequate. Words help us to grasp the external, but we must be able to see beyond, and into, the material to grasp the true essence of life. Poets who seek to revive language need to work with the words at their disposal; at the same time they should be aware that words are only concepts that hint at the nature of experience and the relation of things. In this theory, words do not themselves have any absolute meaning; constantly changing, they constantly need defining by context and by association. Yet words enable us to approach an understanding of the experiences they describe; by holding out the possibility of containing meaning, they may be seen as an equivalent to the spirituality embodied in the divinity of God. It is this dual nature of words – they are able to both reveal and conceal meaning – that has fascinated and frustrated modern poets and thinkers alike.

Wyndham Lewis comments characteristically on Eliot's approach to language when he says that Eliot "succeeded in instilling a salutary *fear of speech* – a terror of *the word*, into his youthful followers: they have not thought twice, but a dozen times or more before committing themselves to paper; and when they come to do so, have spoken 'neither loud or long' "(*Men*, 65). Eliot was clear when he wrote that "the poet must become more and more comprehensive, more allusive, more indirect, in order to force, to dislocate if necessary, language into his meaning" ("Metaphysical," 289). He thus concurs with Bergson, who says that "language is not meant to convey all the delicate shades of inner states" (*TFW*, 160). Bergson foreshadows Eliot's contention that language must be used effectively if it is to move beyond the level of the mundane when he wrote that "every language, whether elaborate or crude, leaves many more things to be understood than it is able to express. Essentially discontinuous, since it proceeds by juxtaposing words, speech can only indicate by a few guide-posts placed here and there the chief stages in the movement of thought" (*M&M*, 159). Bergson contends that, to guide readers effectively, words must startle them by appearing in unusual contexts and by performing unusual syntactical or conceptual functions. With new locutions indicating new directions in thought or emotion more clearly, poets trying to represent new experiences are obliged to twist language so that their readers will look beyond the extraordinary use of language and into the possible reasons for it.

Thus writing allows an intuitive understanding of the unspoken experiences that the words hint at and attempt to represent. Eliot wrote: "The music of a word is, so to speak, at a point of intersection: it arises from its relation first to the words immediately preceding and following it, and indefinitely to the rest of its context; and from another relation, that of its immediate meaning in that context to all the other meanings which it has in other contexts, to its greater or less wealth of associations" ("Music," 32–3). In other words, the music of poetry sometimes conveys the poets' experiences far more readily than their words. Translated into Bergsonian terms, Eliot is saying that the intuitive response to the various associative and contextual meanings of the words is as valuable a source of the emotion and experience of the poem as are the words themselves. Language, though it is a crude tool, is nonetheless the tool with which poet and philosopher must deal. The view of language shared by Bergson and Eliot is not a unidimensional one; both men accept that words have limits in their ability to convey the full experience of life, but both also argue that if we cease thinking of language as a purely conceptual device in which words stand for certain objects and only those objects, and instead accept that language is multidimensional and that words convey the nuances of experience through their contextual and associative meanings, then we will begin to see how language, in Douglass's words, "begins and ends not in the utilitarian concept of the 'message,' but in a dimly known realm of experience made available to us by intuition" (Douglass, 64).

Without wishing to belabour a point that must surely be clear by now, it is evident that Eliot joins the other modernists explored in this chapter in a common debt to Bergson's philosophy. Although the possible sources for Eliot's ideas are numerous, in light of his own remarks and the evidence provided by Le Brun, Douglass, and others,[20] it is possible to claim Bergson as one of the significant influences on Eliot's intellectual development. Indeed, given the extent to which Bergson's concepts have entered Eliot's ideas, as well as the communal pool of knowledge from which he drank at this time, it would be as difficult to argue against Bergson's role in Eliot's intellectual development as it would be to refute his role in the development of the Men of 1914, the Bloomsbury group, or Murry.

### CHAPTER 4

# T.S. Eliot: The Poet

Much of Eliot's poetry concerns itself with the clash between the rational mind's assertion that life is a fiction created by humans and the emotion's insistence that such a picture of life is insufficient. Throughout the verse, the terms assume different faces and different degrees of prominence; however, from his early poems to *Four Quartets*, Eliot creates an uneasy union of the two views. He handles the two in a way similar to Bergson's handling of them and, not surprisingly, employs many of the ideas absorbed from his study of Bergsonian philosophy. It is important to remember that although Eliot's poetry is very philosophical, he is not operating under the same constraints as a philosopher; thus he is able to take liberties with elements of Bergson's philosophy that its creator might not approve and might be unable to take himself. Nonetheless, a discussion of Eliot's poetry will demonstrate its dependency on Bergson's philosophy and will also illustrate how Eliot's gradual movement toward Christianity is foreshadowed by those elements Eliot borrows from Bergson's theories.

To examine all the poetry Eliot wrote would be a prohibitively lengthy task. Instead, I focus on three specific phases of his career: the major poems from *Prufrock and Other Observations*; *The Waste Land*; and *Four Quartets*. These have been selected for a number of reasons. First, they represent a good spectrum of Eliot's work, and all the poems discussed have been thoroughly analysed by others and judged as among Eliot's best and most characteristic work. Second, all the poems demonstrate Eliot's ongoing engagement with Bergsonian philosophy. Although the Bergsonian elements in some of the poems have already been noted, in others, the Bergsonian theories are less widely accepted as being important, prominent parts of the poems. And third, selecting poems from different stages of Eliot's career demonstrates that as Eliot's views of the world became clearer, Bergson's theories came to occupy a subtler but still significant place in his poetry. An examination of the poems for things such as consciousness, perception, time, the subject-object split, language, and meaning, allows Eliot's specific debt to Bergson to become manifest.

## EARLY POETRY

The major poems in *Prufrock and Other Observations*, with the exception of "The Love Song of J. Alfred Prufrock," deal with central Bergsonian ideas in relatively unsophisticated ways. For example, critics have frequently called "Rhapsody on a Windy Night" a Bergsonian poem because of its obvious Bergsonian treatment of time, while the other poems – "Preludes," "La Figlia Che Piange," and "Portrait of a Lady" – although less frequently associated with Bergsonian ideas, nonetheless may be seen as Bergsonian. "Prufrock" itself is also Bergsonian, but in a much more subtle way, one which foreshadows Eliot's later integration of Bergsonian ideas in his poetry.

These early poems, written around 1909–1912,[1] clearly illustrate Eliot's engagement with, but equivocal attitude toward, Bergson's temporal notions. The basic structures and underlying tensions of these five poems rely heavily on the Bergsonian idea of a conflict between two types of time. The experience of time in each poem results in a world the existence of which is defined by the individuals who inhabit it; this follows Bergson's idea about the relative nature of human existence. The underlying tone of all the poems, however, is pessimistic. We are caught in a world which has no meaning beyond that which we bring to it, and the bleak portrayal of this society suggests that Eliot rejects this world on an emotional level. The conflict underlying Eliot's most sophisticated musings about society is here presented on a fairly basic level. Eliot's pessimistic premise is that if humans live in a chaotic, relative world, then they alone bring meaning to it. And if humans cannot accept this premise, they either retreat into a faith based on emotion, not thought, or drift into the realm of madness. Eliot's harsh juxtaposition of two time worlds in the first four poems indicates that the option of faith is not yet viable: people must create their own world if they are to prevent a fall into the world of madness.

### Time

The time structure of "Portrait of a Lady," written in 1910–1911, is the least ambitious and most traditional of the five poems. The poem moves in a seasonal progression: from "the smoke and fog of a December afternoon" (*Poems*, 34); through to spring, "Now that lilacs are in bloom"; back to dismal autumn, "The October night comes down." Yet it is unconventional in its inclusion of a second type of time in the poem, the inner time of the blasé young man and the frantic middle-aged woman. Although their liaison lasts barely a year, the woman's feelings make the passage of time different for each. The young man's tedium is registered in phrases such as "Inside my brain a dull Tom-tom begins / Absurdly hammering a prelude of its own"; the strain under which the woman places the young man (or what he perceives as strain) makes life intolerable. For the woman, however, there is not enough time; the young man is slipping away from her: "You will go on, and when you have prevailed / You can say: at this point many a one has failed." Their different perceptions of the relationship create alternate time sequences: hers of time rapidly fleeing; and his of time almost standing still. Both are inner durations, and both are counterpoints to the clock time that overtly frames the poem. The bare juxtaposition of the two combined with the poem's pessimistic tone becomes a standard way for Eliot to deal with the issue of time. By counterpointing the two and leaving their clearly different stances unresolved, Eliot highlights the problem that modern notions of time bring to us as human beings. Not being able to resolve the dilemma results in a failure to get on with the more important question of the nature of life and the presence/ absence of meaning in the world; this in turn paralyzes us, rendering us incapable of existing on a level any deeper than the superficial social state that is the young man's in this poem. That he experiences inklings of another world also points to a deeper meaning; but until, or unless, he is able to resolve the problems created by his awareness of the coexistence of the two time worlds, he is doomed to remain locked in a superficial social world.

"Preludes" has a common Eliotic form: external time and internal duration provide a two-level framework. External time, clock time, is manifested by the lines that show the poem progressing from late one evening to early evening the following day. The first 'Prelude' takes place as "The winter evening settles down" (*Poems*, 22–3); the second moves toward dawn where "morning comes to consciousness"; the third occurs at dawn and after when "all the world came back / And the light crept up between the shutters"; and the fourth moves toward early evening "At four and five and six o'clock." The description of the street at different hours of the day reinforces the inevitable progress of time. On a second level, there is a timelessness. The eerie world exists today, as well as in the past and future. The last two lines imply just this sensation of flux: "The worlds revolve like ancient women / Gathering fuel in vacant lots." The "ancient women" are time present exhausted by past events, but they still gather fuel so they may live. The sordid real world of the poem, with its "burnt-out ends of smoky days" and its "faint stale smells of beer," exists simultaneously with the one alive in the mind of the poem's unnamed persona who is

> ... moved by fancies that are curled
> Around these images, and cling:
> The notion of some infinitely gentle
> Infinitely suffering thing.

This juxtaposition of present scene and fanciful world provides the poem's tension and also its cohesiveness. The persona remembers the woman "Sitting along the bed's edge where / You curled the papers from your hair"; and it admonishes the reader to "Wipe your hand across your mouth, and laugh" because the woman is part of the past, as the tense of "curled," "dozed," and "watched" reveals. She is also part of the present moment, his walk through the dark streets. Although all but the final three lines are either parts of the present moment, or the past, each contributes to the future – the final command of what should be done next. This second time level of "Preludes" is really a continuous moment of undefinable time, Bergson's *durée*. The bare juxtaposition of the time worlds, however, deprives the poem of a harmonious temporal world and makes the poem unsettling.

"Rhapsody on a Windy Night" has been widely regarded as Bergsonian.[2] It was started in Paris in 1911 and completed in Boston in about November of 1911 (Gordon, 40–1); as the dates indicate, it was written at the peak of Eliot's interest in Bergson. In "Rhapsody," one sees again the two-level time structure. Clock time is represented by the constant references to the hour of the day or night: "Four o'clock," "Twelve o'clock," "Half-past one," "Half-past two," "Half-past three" (*Poems*, 24). Each strike of the clock moves the "I" physically forward in external time, yet each also moves him backward in internal time. As the man moves down the street, images assault his mind, prompting his memory to become active. Memories in turn trigger other memories: "memory throws up high and dry / A crowd of twisted things." The actual passage of physical time, represented by the man's nocturnal stroll through the streets to his own lodgings, is juxtaposed with his duration, the wandering of his mind through past, present, and future life. Eliot underlines this conflict with his last line: "The last twist of the knife." In light of the poem's time conflict, this ambiguous line means that past time intrudes on present time – internal time on clock time – thereby creating a severe conflict. This poem illustrates the problems that arise when one unwittingly attempts to exist in a time-space midway between *durée* and clock time. The "madman" who "shakes a geranium" has already slipped into madness, perhaps because he cannot find meaning in this relativistic world. The persona in the poem has yet to follow the madman, because he is still attempting to reconcile the two time worlds; yet he too is near madness, because such a balancing act requires an implicit faith that doing it is worthwhile. The pessimistic tone of the poem suggests that even the persona is beginning to doubt the purpose for balancing the two; this in turn hints at a gradual decline into the sheer madness that lurks behind the poem's nightmarish world.

The time sequence of "La Figlia Che Piange" is interesting. In the first verse, the narrator issues a series of commands: "Stand on the highest pavement," "Lean," "Weave, weave," "Clasp your flowers," "Fling them to the ground" (*Poems*, 34). One discovers in the second verse that these actions occur only in the narrator's mind: "So I would have had her stand and grieve." The action he is discussing has presumably occurred on some past occasion. The third verse demonstrates that the action is indeed past: "She turned away," "Sometimes these cogitations still amaze / The troubled midnight and the noon's repose." The three verses, in fact, illustrate how the past impinges on the present, how it creates the present moment. The lines "And I wonder how they should have been together / I should have lost a gesture and a pose" also indicate how the past action, the lovers' meeting, impinges on a future action, the "I"'s image-making. Eliot creates one prolonged moment because all three divisions of time coexist. His more sophisticated treatment of time makes this poem different from the first two we looked at. This poem's narrator conceptualizes past life in order to understand it, but he is fully aware that he merely freezes moments and does not recapture them. The doubts expressed by the use of the verb "should" indicate that he is aware that he is recreating the situation for his own purposes and in his own way, while the lines that reveal how the past still preys on his present indicate that emotionally the re-creation of the painful event still carries powerful impact.

"The Love-Song of J. Alfred Prufrock" has attracted a great deal of comment; yet the Bergsonian aspects of it, including time, have received little attention.[3] "Prufrock" takes place on two time levels: clock time and internal time. The clock time of the poem is very brief; it is an afternoon that melts into an evening: "When the evening is spread out against the sky" indicates early dusk, while "And the afternoon, the evening, sleeps so peacefully" indicates that early evening has followed dusk. Its action takes place while Prufrock lies on the floor contemplating possible action, as the line "Stretched on the floor, here beside you and me" (*Poems*, 13–17) reveals. Although the real physical time of the poem is no more than a few hours, the mental time, or duration, is considerably different in scope and length.

Prufrock's inner duration ranges through his thoughts about the immediate experience he is missing, the tea party, to contemplation of both past events and previous eras, as well as to possible future events. The first element of his duration, preoccupation with the tea party, forms the bulk of the poem. Prufrock reflects on what it would be like if he were there:

> There will be time to murder and create,
> And time for all the works and days of hands
> That lift and drop a question on your plate;
> Time for you and time for me,
> And time yet for a hundred indecisions,
> And for a hundred visions and revisions,
> Before the taking of a toast and tea. (*Poems*, 15)

The emphasis on time underscores its centrality; time for all things exists, but time unceasingly flows, particularly where interaction with others or making decisions is concerned. This merging of moments is reinforced by the lines "For I have known them all already, known them all – / Have known the evenings, mornings, afternoons." Prufrock's sense of the past, when combined with the ruminations on time and on the probable outcome of events if he attended the tea party – "And would it have been worth it, after all" – demonstrates time's powerful presence. All of these speculations are internal; therefore, they express his *durée*, or his personal experience of time. Bergson says, in *Creative Evolution*, that "*the present contains nothing more than the past*" [author's italics] (*CE*, 15); Prufrock's reverie is ample evidence that this is true.

### Self

The self is another central feature of Eliot's poetry. He approaches it in two main ways in the early poems: through a dramatic monologue, or through an impressionistic collage of details that present an individual. The latter is particularly Bergsonian: it renders the self in a series of fragments which, when added together, give a coherent portrait of the self.

"Rhapsody on a Windy Night" and "Preludes" are the first important impressionistic renderings of self. In "Preludes" two selves are
described: the woman revealed through an accumulation of descriptions, and the man discovered by entering his mind as he walks
through familiar streets. Eliot's woman is a prostitute; she is vividly
described as someone who "lay upon [her] back, and waited" (*Poems*,
23) as day breaks. Brief lines such as "Or clasped the yellow soles of
feet / In the palms of both soiled hands" suggest a dirtiness about the
woman's physical and moral character. Eliot implies that the reader
cannot know what occurs in the woman's mind, that her real self is
unknowable because it is impenetrable. All that is left is for us to be
moved by her plight, moved by the "notion of some infinitely gentle
/ Infinitely suffering thing." Eliot shares with Bergson the belief that
one can never truly know another's internal self. The presentation of
the internal self in this poem is the exploration of the "I," the man
who only becomes visible in the last 'Prelude.' Eliot traces this man's
growth and his reactions to various situations, revealing in each 'Prelude' a new facet of the self, thereby implicitly demonstrating that
self has many elements. By the poem's end the reader is able to form
a mental picture of the "I"; a far more vivid one than the woman's,
because Eliot has rendered the internal world of the "I" together with
its external one.

In "Rhapsody" the same technique is employed. Several individuals are presented whose main role is to demonstrate the impossibility
of ever knowing another individual. There is "that woman / Who
hesitates towards you in the light of the door" (*Poems*, 24–6), as well
as the child behind whose eyes can be seen "nothing"; there are also
the "eyes" that are seen "in the street / Trying to peer through lighted
shutters." The "I" encounters all these figures but is separate from
them: their actions are strange, but somehow also familiar enough to
provoke a stream of memories. The reader, too, is separated from
them by Eliot, who underscores the futility of attempting to know
something by external appearances alone. The central figure is depicted through the things he selects as important in his wanderings,
the memories they provoke, and his reactions to both. There emerges
a picture of a man haunted by memories, yet aware that they are part
of his self. In fact, the creation of self depends on involuntary memory functioning in a Bergsonian way. The successive sections of the
poem function analogously to the principles of Bergson's memory.
The first three delineate pure perception and pure memory, their separateness in theory and their interdependence in fact; the last three illustrate how perception stimulates pure memory, which in turn
colours perception and then allows memories to form. The final line

of the poem emphasizes the Bergsonian notion, which Eliot also develops at length in "Tradition and the Individual Talent," that the past lingers into the present and that it, in fact, helps create the present moment.

The initial section of "Rhapsody" may be divided into two parts. The first seven lines establish the distinction between perception and memory, with "all its clear relations, / Its divisions and precisions." The second section, from the eighth line to the twelfth, places memory and perception on equal planes: "Every street lamp that I pass / Beats like a fatalistic drum" (perception), and

> And through the spaces of the dark
> Midnight shakes the memory
> As a madman shakes a dead geranium" (memory).

From this initial dualism Eliot expands his discussion in each of the next two sections. The second section, lines 11 to 22, illustrates perception. In lines 13 to 16, Eliot personifies a lamppost, turning perception of an object into a living force:

> The street-lamp sputtered,
> The street-lamp muttered,
> The street-lamp said, 'Regard that woman.

The second half of this section, lines 14 to 22, exemplifies pure perception. The woman, the object of scrutiny, is vividly described: "And you see the corner of her eye / Twists like a crooked pin." The third section treats pure memory. Its opening lines "The memory throws up high and dry / A crowd of twisted things" strike a keynote for the rest, which contains examples of images locked in the man's mind: "A broken spring in a factory yard," or "Rust that clings to the form that the strength has left." Although the poem's first three sections treat the dualistic aspects outlined in Bergson's theory, they erect a seemingly irreconcilable antithesis between pure memory and perception. In the final half of the poem, however, Eliot not only reconciles the two, but also illustrates their important function in the present moment.

Section four of the poem initiates the reconciliation; it may be divided into three parts. The first part, lines 33 to 37, is pure perception. Once again, the lamp functions as the observer: "The street-lamp said, / 'Remark the cat which flattens itself in the gutter." In lines 38 to 40, the perception of the cat prompts the man to remember a past event: "So the hand of the child, automatic, / Slipped out and pocketed a toy that was running along the quay." This memory leads to a more profound one, a 'pure memory,' in lines 41 to 45. Here the "I" remembers "eyes" which are "Trying to peer through lighted shutters" and "a crab" which "Gripped the end of a stick which I held him." The same pattern – pure perception, perception-memory, pure memory – is repeated in the poem's fifth section. The lamp commands, the man complies and is led to remember a woman; and finally memories are awakened of

> female smells in shuttered rooms,
> And cigarettes in corridors
> And cocktail smells in bars.

Thus Eliot demonstrates how pure perception leads to memory, which in turn leads to pure memory, thereby underscoring the interdependence of the two in an individual's mental process. The long final section of the poem repeats the pattern with one significant variation. Once again perception, "Here is the number on the door," prompts a memory, "Memory! / You have the key." In this section, however, rather than ending the moment with a pure memory, Eliot concludes it with an injunction to action: "The bed is open; the tooth-brush hangs on the wall, / Put your shoes at the door, sleep, prepare for life." He deliberately alters the pattern to emphasize the notion that past lingers into present – thereby, consciously or not, underscoring Bergson's theory. At the same time, the last line of the poem reminds the reader that present colours past as well, and that the two coexist in a delicate balance which, when broken, can be painful.

In the poems that assume dramatic (or partial dramatic) monologue form, Eliot gives more extended portraits of selves; yet even in these the reader receives only partial portraits. "The Love-Song of J. Alfred Prufrock" is a dramatic monologue: the narrator of the poem, the "I" of "Let us go then, you and I" (*Poems*, 13–17) is Prufrock. Readers are brought inside Prufrock's self and come to know the various aspects of this timid man. Although this proximity to Prufrock allows readers to believe that they know his essence, Eliot's belief in multiple finite centres prevents complete knowledge. Indeed, all of Prufock's selves are not manifest in the poem. Readers know the Prufrock who experiences uncertainty, fear, remorse, self-loathing, and false-hope, but they do not see the man who may exercise the decisiveness he so desires. Although Prufrock's characterization is incomplete from a narrative viewpoint, he is credible because his full self remains elusive. This poem exemplifies the subject-object split. If we feel that by working at the poem we can understand Prufrock, we admit that the object here – the poem and its central self – exists separately from us and that it contains some sort of definite meaning. At the same time, we cannot escape the fact that we participate in the discovery of Prufrock's inner self and by so doing we are an accomplice in his creation. In fact, the poem swings back and forth between these two approaches, and by so doing it attempts to find a middle ground between subject and object. Although Prufrock himself cannot escape the solitary world of subjectivity, Eliot tries to convince his readers that we can escape it through the belief that poetry, with its shared meanings, occupies a midground between the subjective and objective worlds.

"Portrait of a Lady" and "La Figlia Che Piange" are also dramatic monologues. Whereas in "La Figlia" the speaker is a third, unseen figure in the poem, in "Portrait" the speaker is the young man. The lines "Sometimes these cogitations still amaze / The troubled midnight and the noon's repose" (*Poems*, 34) from "La Figlia" give some idea of the reflective nature of the "I." They also throw a different light on the preceding lines, indicating that the whole poem is part of the "I"'s memory and that it is self-revealing. Again, as in "Rhapsody," memory is an important device in the "I"'s definition of self. The sad, lonely, occasionally haunted man is defined by his previous experiences in the same garden. Without the memory of those experiences, the man would not be able to compare his present persona with his past persona; without this comparison, his self would remain elusive. The young man's experience in "Portrait" reveals his complex nature: he is selfish about his desire to end his relationship with the woman, but sensitive enough to realize how the woman might feel about the breakup. The varying parts of his self are at war with each other: he is indeterminate and paralyzed; not only is he incapable of responding to the woman's gestures, he is also incapable of defining his own personality. In both poems the speakers are revealed as consciousnesses dependent on memory for their existence. As well, each depends on the accuracy of his perceptions for the construction of his self. The fact that the perceptions are less than accurate heightens the sense in each poem that the speakers' selves are not complete. Their incompleteness also tells the reader that Eliot was grappling with the very question of whether a self existed and if it did, whether it could be known beyond the boundaries of the individual. These two poems are unable to resolve that fundamental question and leave room to argue on either side. In *The Waste Land*, Eliot moves closer to an answer about the nature of consciousness, and its presentation in poetry.

## THE WASTE LAND

In *The Waste Land*, Eliot creates a new poetic form. Although the circumstances surrounding the poem's composition are familiar – Pound and Vivien Eliot's editing of the manuscripts, Eliot's mental collapse, the poem's reception by the press and so on – the one thing that has eluded many critics is Eliot's continued reliance on Bergsonian ideas. There are two primary areas where Eliot's debt to Bergson is undeniable: the poem's chaotic structure, and its presentation of consciousness.

### Structure

At first glance, the whole poem seems to illustrate a straightforward juxtaposition of Bergson's *l'étendu* and *durée*. However, recalling that Bergson maintained that both times were necessary for us to understand our lives may illuminate what Eliot is doing. He begins by showing the two in conflict and then spends much of the poem attempting to resolve it, by forcing the two to coexist. In the end, because he is not himself sure of the solution he suggests, he settles for an uneasy and ambiguous union. Eliot was still searching for a way of holding on to what his sense told him – that life was essentially a random, chaotic flow of events – and to what his heart wanted – a reason for these events that transcends the events themselves. *The Waste Land* attempts to fashion a middle ground. Each section of the poem reflects Eliot's experimentation with different ways of handling the temporal dilemma; each also works progressively toward Eliot's final statement, on combining the century's two prominent temporal modes.

Eliot's complex mythopeoic structure for this poem is perhaps the single greatest challenge for the critic. Although many studies have endeavoured to unlock the various myths and sources of allusions in this poem, I think there is a viable, additional explanation for Eliot's selection of such an allusive, discursive, all-encompassing framework. Eliot is working here with two separate notions of time. The first is the Bergsonian one of *durée*, which sees all events in history and all individual experiences as part of an endless flow of life. The flow does not just move in one direction, as Eliot realized from his study of Bergson; rather it holds within each moment every other moment. Although access to all the events of human time may be limited by inability to conceptualize them, this shortcoming does not mean that each moment does not contain all time. Eliot realized that if human beings had a means of tapping into the *durée* and then freezing it, they would be able to lay out all the events of generations past and generations to come. He therefore went to work fashioning a second level of time which does just that. In its actual structure of allusion and myth, the poem then presents this second level of time, freezing the *durée* in order to reveal its existence. In effect, Eliot's poem works out of the problem he felt Bergson had overlooked with *durée*: by its very nature as a flux of experience, *durée* does not allow us, as human beings, to conceptualize our own experiences, thus keeping us from establishing meaning for our life or our society. Eliot suggests that if we can conceptualize our experiences and place them side by side with the experiences of other cultures and generations, we may be able to find meaning in the seemingly random events of our life. The contrasting temporal worlds reflect his desire to move toward a union of the two – *durée* which is life and *l'étendu* which explains life – thereby providing a more satisfactory view of the nature of humans than either could alone. The obvious irony here is that Eliot arrives at the compromise that Bergson outlined in *Time and Free Will*; despite protestations to the contrary, the two works share this basic temporal structure.

In "The Burial of the Dead," the first eleven lines set up the time structure of the poem. They portray a seasonal progression: spring, "April is the cruelest month" (*Poems*, 61–80), follows winter, which "kept us warm, covering / Earth in forgetful snow." April is then "surprised" by summer. April is the pivot between the past – winter – and the future – summer – and contains bits of both, becoming an extended moment in time. With its promise of summer and its cruel winterish tendencies – "mixing / Memory and desire" – spring becomes the perfect symbol for *durée* because it shows how the two inevitably coexist in one season, or one moment. The next six lines reinforce the coexistence of past and present by placing the memory of winters spent with Marie and the archduke alongside the present custom of going south for the winter. The subsequent twenty-four lines continue to intermingle past and present. In them Eliot uses several voices. The first dozen lines refer to various Old Testament prophets. Ezekiel, Job, Isaiah, and the book of Ecclesiastes all question the existence of human beings and their perceptions of life: "You cannot say, or guess, for you know only / A heap of broken images." Here Eliot incorporates a universal, traditional, perhaps mythical, past into the poem. Already the contrast between localized time, April, and traditional time is underlined. Their coexistence in the one moment is highlighted by Eliot's juxtaposition of the various times in the next few lines. By alternating various times in an apparently random manner, Eliot suggests not only that the sequential nature of time is necessary so humans may order their experiences, individual or universal, but also that real living does not occur in such a neat tidy manner. The hyacinth-girl episode, a recurring motif in many of Eliot's poems, brings home this point. This episode contains a new voice talking about a personal experience: a past moment when a man failed to act and thus did not consummate a relationship. The man "was neither / Living nor dead," and he "knew nothing"; he was in a state of temporal limbo caused by the imposition of the past on the present. The Madame Sosostris episode, which occupies the next seventeen lines, represents the future. A fortune-teller makes predictions about the future, but the calculations are based on past and current knowledge. She predicts death: "Fear death by water," but she also sees life in the future: "I see crowds of people, walking round in a ring." Eliot lays the foundation for other sections of the poem here; the practical function thus mirrors its thematic consequences. The final twenty-six lines, the "Unreal City" section, tie together the various strands of time. The description of the city itself alludes to Dante's *Inferno*,[4] thereby combining present-day London and medieval Italy. The new persona travels throughout the city and, when he spies Stetson, joins past and present together. The reference to the corpse, "Has it begun to sprout?", is a question about some future action that depends on a past action. Past, present, and future are all combined in this one meeting. The whole first section of the poem is in fact an interplay of the three times. It represents a move from the experience of a fixed, ordered time – April – to the experience of a less well-defined, more ethereal time – that of the Unreal City.

"A Game of Chess" brilliantly juxtaposes past and present in its three sections. The first section, where Cleopatra's barge sails down the Nile in ancient Egypt, by alluding to a scene from Shakespeare's *Antony and Cleopatra*[5] which is itself based on historical events, not only places the action in the past, but also presents it as an already recreated past moment. This shows the way that past and present reshape each other: Shakespeare reshaping Cleopatra's history for his play and Eliot then reshaping Shakespeare's Cleopatra for his poem. The reader is sent further into the past by the reference to Philomel. The idea of past time is connected to present time by the seven lines that form the transition from the Cleopatra section to the neurasthenic-woman section. The image of "Other withered stumps of time" connects the transformed Philomel to the neurotic woman. The woman is old, "shuffled on the stair," but still vibrant and alive "her hair / Spread out in fiery points." Her age, however, forces her to adopt a restricted existence. She represents both past time, because of her age, and present time, because of her desire to live.

The next twenty-six lines present an interchange between two people: a neurasthenic woman and Tiresias, the poem's all-seeing narrator. Here the time contrast is between the present moment, as represented by the frantic woman, and the prolonged moment of universal time represented by the immortal Tiresias. The woman lives in a world fraught with worries: "What is that noise?", "What is that noise now? What is the wind doing?". Tiresias inhabits a far more ethereal world filled by different noises, "O O O O that Shakespherian Rag," and activities, "And if it rains, a closed car at four." As well, the contrast in the physical descriptions of the locale of this section, "I think we are in rats' alley / Where the dead men lost their bones," and the previous one calls attention to the different times – the opulent Egypt of the Pharaohs and the squalid London of the late 1910s.

The final section is a marvelously comical creation of a contemporary London pub. The time may be present – it is postwar – but the situation is timeless: Lil's best friend is trying to steal away her husband. The final lines, however, firmly tie the two times together, with the traditional closing call "Time, gentlemen please" being used, even today, to indicate a pub's closing time. This section extends the contrast between past and present to its breaking point; either clock time or duration must be the true temporal experience. But it also hints that no choice may be necessary: if the traditions of the past can be successfully adapted for use in the present, a way for both times to peacefully coexist may also be found.

The time structure of the "Fire Sermon" is not as clearly defined. It presents a much closer meshing of past and present. The lines alluding to Spenser's marriage song "Sweet Thames, run softly, till I end my song" and to Elizabeth and Leicester gliding down the Thames "Beating oars / The stern was formed" are past moments, coexisting with present ones: "The sounds of horns and motors" and "when the human engine waits / Like a taxi throbbing waiting." The overwhelming mood of this section is of an unstructured timelessness. One symbol of this is Tiresias: the "old man with wrinkled dugs" who has "foresuffered all" and who has also "Perceived the scene, and foretold the rest." He lives in all times and knows all times; he is timeless, yet he is in time because he assumes the shape of an aged man. In a way, as will be demonstrated shortly, Tiresias's position is like that of God, for he is simultaneously part of all people and also completely separate from them because of his immortality. Tiresias represents every person without being any specific individual; as such he embodies the essence of what Eliot seeks in this poem: a union of the flux and the absolute. The other central symbol of this section is the "Sweet Thames," which parallels Bergson's flowing river of flux. The river flows onward bearing no "testimony of summer nights," containing no litter of past times. Yet physically it links Elizabeth with the typist: past with present. The river is a symbol of the present, ever-changing moment, as well as a symbol of the absolute because it endures while other things around it change. This section, connected by themes and imagery to the previous two, continues and extends their search for the means of effecting a lasting and viable union between the two times.

The exquisite fourth section, "Death by Water," also advances the union of the two times. It is connected to the other sections by its central figure, Phlebas the Phoenician, who appears in the Madame Sosostris section and in "A Game of Chess," and by the image of water, which is central to "The Fire Sermon" and prominent in "A Game of Chess." Phlebas is dead, his fate that of any "Gentile or Jew" who plunges into "the deep sea swell." The water, a symbol of the continuity of life, has reclaimed him. Phlebas, however, is free from the wheel of life because he escapes the tyranny of time: his death brings freedom. His failure to locate his own duration, which resulted in his enslavement by time, is erased by his death. This section provides an obvious counterpoint to the last one, in which people enslaved by time failed to grasp the symbolic significance of the river and thus failed to find freedom in the flow of duration. Here water provides freedom, but Phlebas has mistaken its physical role for its symbolic function – a mistake which results in his "death by water."

"What the Thunder said" starts out in marked contrast to the previous three sections. The land is in the grip of a drought, "Here is no water but only rock." The absence of water indicates that time has ceased to flow. Instead, it has become fixed, rigid, and as a consequence, the population is suffering and the land is stagnant. The mythic structure here derives from the vegetation rites, in which the wasted land awaits the arrival of a saviour whose self-sacrifice makes the land fertile again. The cycle of birth, death, and regeneration links this section with the first one and also emphasizes the coexistence of all three times in one moment. However, the three are difficult to distinguish because there is no past, present, or future; there is only *durée*. Many of the images, personae, and themes of the previous four sections reappear – making this section both the resolution of the poem and a representation of *durée*, since it is an example of how one lives. When the Thunder speaks, its three commands lead humans into the discovery of the peace promised in the line "Shantih, Shantih, Shantih." The object of life is to live in this world of peace, and the poem seems to say that one finds peace by immersing oneself in *durée*.

These same lines, however, may be read as a cry for an experience of time as yet unachieved, a time in which *durée* is lived time but where we can understand the significance of each moment of our *durée* and, through this, find meaning in life. The ambiguity of the final lines underlines Eliot's continuing ambivalence toward Bergsonian *durée*. Throughout the poem *durée* and *l'étendu* have been presented as in conflict, but the promise of a resolution to the conflict has been held out as a possible solution to our problems. The poem's gradual progression toward a world in which *durée* appears to dominate is a clear representation of the world Eliot saw around himself and over which he despaired; what is difficult for Eliot is the fact that he needs more than just life; he needs to understand this life. *Durée*, Eliot implies, leaves us ultimately responsible for formulating our own world. In Section V, the Thunder presents Eliot's central problem with the Bergsonian world. The Thunder's three commands provide a structure upon which we may formulate reality; how we deal with these commands will determine the nature of our reality. A Bergsonian would internalize them, making them part of a personal world, while a non-Bergsonian would use them as external guides for conduct, in effect, as some communal code of behaviour. Eliot's decision not to choose between the two, attempting instead to effect an uneasy union, leaves the reader unsure of the poem's final meaning. Such an ending indicates Eliot's own inability to accept Bergson's theories and hints at his desire to turn away from a relativistic view of the world toward a more structured one. "Shantih, Shantih, Shantih" may in fact refer to the prospect of finding salvation through immersion in another, external form of time – a time that contains the absolute power to structure all other times and that also contains the answers to the questions that have haunted the speakers in the poem. The who am I, why am I, and what is life questions so central to the poem's personae may be answered if these people give themselves up to the everlasting peace of God. But even here, Eliot cannot decide. Thus the poem's ambiguous ending reflects his uncertainty about any form of union between *durée* and *l'étendu* and also an uncertainty about turning to any god – Christian, Hindu, Moslem, Buddhist, Greek, Roman, Egyptian, or any of the others Eliot has placed in this poem – as an answer.

### Consciousness

Eliot's continuing interest in the nature of individual existence – consciousness – prompts him to explore it fully in *The Waste Land*. He presents a tapestry of different consciousnesses: the little boy who goes for a sleigh ride with Marie, Madame Sosostris, the hyacinth girl, the typist, the young man carbuncular, the Phoenician Sailor, the currant seller, the merchant, and a host of others. How to deal with these many characters is problematic. No single character appears to encompass the wholeness of the individual that Eliot believed mirrored the wholeness of a society, an attainable state when we could both understand and live our experiences. Yet if Eliot was searching for a union of the temporal worlds that would allow us to understand our society and its place in history, in his treatment of consciousness he was searching for the same type of union, but between the different facets that constitute the individual. If one allows that Eliot's "Notes" to the poem provide pertinent information about it,[6] his note on Tiresias can be said to help explain how involuntary memory is used to establish a link between all the disparate consciousnesses in the poem. Eliot wrote:

Tiresias, although a mere spectator and not indeed a "character," is yet the most important personage in the poem, uniting all the rest. Just as the one-eyed merchant, seller of currants melts into the Phoenecian Sailor, and the latter is not wholly distinct from Ferdinand Prince of Naples, so all the women are one woman, and the two sexes meet in Tiresias. What Tiresias *sees*, in fact, is the substance of the poem. (*Poems*, 78)

This description of Tiresias's position as the poem's all-encompassing consciousness has long provided a point of difficulty. F.R. Leavis, for example, saw all the narrative voices encompassed within Tiresias's single, stable consciousness (Leavis, 103). More recently, Michael Levenson argued that Eliot attempts to 'dissolve the boundaries of the self' and that Tiresias provides only one of many points of view that attempt to achieve this (Levenson, 176–86). However, we must be careful here in our understanding of Tiresias's role. Leavis's view of Tiresias as a stable all-encompassing consciousness is too simple an explanation for the complex way in which each of the characters interact in the poem (Leavis, 103). Levenson's assertion that the poem's "characters are little more than aspects of selves or, in the jargon of Eliot's dissertation, 'finite centres' or 'points of view'," (Levenson, 190) points in a more fruitful direction. But Levenson does not push this observation to its logical conclusion. Surely the collisions of the many finite centres in *The Waste Land* are analogous to the clash of centres in an individual, which Eliot maintains is the process of self-definition. Since all the characters in the poem "meet in Tiresias," then in Bergsonian terms all of Tiresias's layers of self are merging and interpenetrating. Tiresias assumes the role of the poem's chief narrator because he is the superficial social self who provides the stability necessary to relate the poem. The many other voices that vie for prominence throughout the poem provide the subject matter of the poem, just as the layers of self that exist below the social self are ultimately responsible for its shape. Thus the tension (which Bergson and Eliot see as existing due to the collision of the various aspects of self) while providing a dynamic element in the poem, places these aspects within a superficially stable self (Tiresias) and gives the poem a semblance of stability. The complexity of Tiresias's role is, therefore, beyond what Leavis proposed, but within the bounds of Eliot's statement in his note to the poem itself.

Eliot's subtle use of Bergsonian involuntary memory heightens its importance because, though hidden from sight, it forms the very backbone of the poem. Bergson calls for involuntary memory to be "personal memory-images which picture all past events with their outline, their colour and their place in time" (*M&M*, 102). Reading Eliot's notes in Bergsonian terms, what we see in the poem are Tiresias's "memory-images," for if all the characters are embodied in him, then all the images from different places and times are also his. Hence the whole of the poem can be seen as one long sequence of memory-images and the poem as existing within the mind of Tiresias. Tiresias is looking over his life; although what he sees is the substance of the poem, in keeping with the ideas about memory and consciousness that Eliot found in Bergson, Tiresias can see only his own life and so all that he sees is Tiresias. Memory becomes the bridge between the various centres that constitute Tiresias and, by analogy, memory becomes the bridge that separates human beings from the different centres that form them at different moments in their lives. If readers will admit that they need a sense of identity in order to know who they are, then *The Waste Land* becomes a poem about searching for this identity and learning how to construct it. Here Tiresias really is the key, because he provides the model for self-definition. By gathering all selves into one, people can fashion an identity, but this requires that they exist both in the world of *durée*, where the many centres exist separately and clash to form new wholes, and in the conceptual world, where they can identify these selves and put them together. So the search for meaning at the individual level of this poem is duplicated, thereby forming the larger social level of the poem. In essence, although the same concerns propel Eliot forward and although the terms differ from society to individual, the answer – an uneasy union between the rational and the emotional – remains the same.

Although *The Waste Land* appears to be a dirge about the impossibility of ever finding meaning in this world and although it has often been called a vision of the belief of Eliot's generation that there is no meaning in the world, it may in fact be a great statement of the possibility of finding meaning and of the hope that such meaning can bring to a "lost" generation. Eliot is not certain of the solution he tentatively proposes, nor is he satisfied with it, but the fact that he centres his poem around the establishment of meaning and that he demonstrates one way of doing so indicates that he has not lost hope; he is still searching. Bergson's philosophy is a profoundly optimistic one; it contains the seeds for reinstilling hope for meaning in this world. Furthermore, although it changes the conditions and terms upon which this meaning can be found, it still provides something for those seeking meaning in the midst of chaos. Eliot is clearly clinging to Bergson's model in *The Waste Land*; but just as clearly, as shown by the poem's pessimistic tone and its ambiguous acceptance of the world it creates, Bergson's solution is not final for Eliot. Eliot's final solution is best displayed in his *Four Quartets*.

## FOUR QUARTETS

By the time Eliot composed the first of his *Four Quartets*, "Burnt Norton" (1935), he had undergone a tremendous personal change. In 1927 he converted to Anglo-Catholicism and in so doing he found a way to cope with the questions that pervaded his early poetry. His journey to faith was not an easy one; nor was it easy for him to sustain: he was still troubled by the fact that his belief in the absolutes that his religion demanded meant that he had to ignore, or at least rationalize, what his intellect told him about the world. For Eliot, the choice was painful but necessary. He could not exist in a world without absolutes; this much had been clear in 1912–1913 when he questioned the absence of an absolute in Bergson's work. Although his conversion did not necessarily answer all Eliot's questions about himself and the world, it did provide him with a framework in which the questions seemed less hostile, as well as a place where the questions seemed less important. Although it was impossible for Eliot to answer all the questions raised by the century's scientific studies and by its widespread skepticism, by posing the questions that were being asked and by showing the path toward religion as a way of answering the questions that we cannot answer ourselves, Eliot showed his contemporaries one way to combat and defeat the lingering doubts of modern society. In a way, *Four Quartets* may be read as a reenactment of Eliot's own spiritual struggle and as a paradigm of the struggle that Eliot believed we all must undergo before we can understand ourselves and our world. While many critics have read the poem in just this way, few have perceived Eliot's continued use of Bergsonian ideas.[7] In fact, to suggest that Bergson's philosophy, which so many regard as antithetical to traditional Christian beliefs, still held a prominent place in Eliot's own ideas seems to be contrary to Eliot's assertions and the fabric of the poem itself. Yet we need to remember that all the elements of Bergson's philosophy are built on the notion that process is more important than arrival at any fixed point. It is at this basic level that the fundamental link between Bergson and the Christian faith that Eliot so enthusiastically embraced is evident. Both writers maintain that human beings cannot know the direction in which their life will go and that they should concentrate on the process of living. For Bergson, this process meant understanding the nature of one's inner world and attempting to understand how it directs the search for the fulfillment of one's potential; for Christians, this means understanding that God's design for individuals or the world is not always clear, but that they are nonetheless to follow his teachings and attempt to live according to them in the hope that someday they will come to know God and his designs. Although the frameworks of belief are radically different, the methods involved are fundamentally similar; it is this similarity that is reflected in Eliot's continued engagement with Bergsonian ideas long after he formally renounced his conversion to Bergsonism. So while Bergsonian philosophy is very subtly present throughout the poem, it is nonetheless an important constituent; especially important is Eliot's lingering interest in the issues of time and memory.

*Time*

Recurring themes and symbols are cornerstones in the structure of the *Four Quartets*. Eliot discusses how such a method may give poetry form and meaning when he wrote, in "The Music of Poetry," that "the use of recurrent themes is as natural to poetry as to music" ("Music," 38). Time functions as a recurring theme throughout the poem; although the terms are somewhat different, this later poem joins his earlier works because it revolves around temporal conflicts. Here *durée* and eternal time are the opposites Eliot desires to reconcile.

The central theme of *Four Quartets* is time. Indeed, as Grover Smith says, the theme is the conflict of different times: "The central theme of *Four Quartets*, the union of the flux of time with the stillness of eternity (stemming from Eliot's earlier meditations on the disparity between the real and the ideal), involves several philosophical meanings of 'time'" (Smith, 253–4). The two major types of time are the flux, which corresponds to *durée*, and eternity. Throughout the poem, Eliot is concerned with effecting a resolution to the conflict generally found between these two.

Two epigraphs, drawn from Heraclitus, set the tone. The first, paraphrased by Smith as "Although there is but one Centre, most men live in centres of their own" (Smith, 255), expresses the conflict between the two types of experience implied by the two opposing times. The "one Centre" is eternity, while the "centres of their own" refer to the life we fashion from our *durée*. The second epigraph, "The way up and the way down are the same," implies that all time is the same. This notion unites the views of the "one Centre" and the "centres of their own." It is the epigraphs, then, that introduce the time conflict and also hint at how it may be resolved. In the Christian view of God, we find one answer to the riddle posed by the epigraphs: God is both the centre, for from him all things come, as well as the individual centres in which we live, because God dwells in all of us. Again, the paradox is that God is more than we humans; for us to understand God we must make him material, by conceptualizing and thus diminishing him. As already discussed, in temporal terms, the same argument is made in Bergson's notion of how time works. So while the epigraphs actually state the essence of the poem – the nature of life – at the outset, the rest of the 'Quartets' deal more fully with the questions of life and how one comes to know what life is.

The opening lines of "Burnt Norton" introduce the main temporal conflict. The first three lines present the very Bergsonian idea that all time is relative, that each moment contains all time:

> Time present and time past
> Are both perhaps present in time future
> And time future contained in time past. (*Poems*, 171)

The next two lines, "If all time is eternally present / All time is unredeemable," present the counterpoint of eternal time. Suggesting that all time is eternal, but that no time exists outside its proper place in the life of an individual, they indicate that there is a past, a present, and a future. The rest of the poem deals with each of these concerns in turn, developing each notion of time and extending the conflict. Lines such as the following emphasize the eternal nature of time:

> At the still point of the turning world. Neither flesh nor fleshless;
> Neither from, nor towards; at the still point, there the dance is,
> But neither arrest nor movement. And do not call it fixity,
> Where past and future are gathered. Neither movement from nor towards,

> Neither ascent nor decline. Except for the point, the still point,
> There would be no dance, and there is only the dance. (*Poems*, 173)

The "still point" is eternity, which gathers both past and future into it and without which there would be no existence, or "dance." Lines such as the following, which close the second section, reinforce the Bergsonian notion of time as flux:

> But only in time can the moment in the rose-garden,
> The moment in the arbour where the rain beat,
> The moment in the draughty church at smokefall
> Be remembered; involved with past and future.
> Only through time time is conquered. (*Poems*, 173)

Only by living in "time" – immersing oneself in *durée* – may "time" – eternity – be "conquered."

The poem ends with a hint of how the two times may be brought together. The first lines of Section V imply that the union of the two may somehow bring about an end to the conflict:

> Words move, music moves
> Only in time; but that which is only living
> Can only die. Words, after speech, reach
> Into the silence. Only by the form, the pattern,
> Can words or music reach
> The stillness, as a Chinese jar still moves perpetually in its stillness.
>
> (*Poems*, 174)

The moving life – "Words move, music moves" – exists within time, but is subject to time's limitations; it "Can only die." By finding a way to join with eternity – "the form, the pattern" – one may live forever as the Chinese jar does, moving "perpetually in the stillness." Here Eliot makes his strongest statement about the ability of art to act as an intermediary between the two worlds. Art is life, he says, because it is generated from the deeply felt experiences of an individual. It captures these experiences from the flow of the artist's life and freezes them. The art object becomes the repository of the experiences; it comes alive again when individuals enter into it by intuitively tapping into the artist's original creative impulse and transforming it into their own. Because once an object is finished it exists separately from the artists themselves, eventually existing in someone else's world, art is the perfect union between the world of flux and the world of absolutes. Having introduced the theme of time in its great complexity, Eliot proceeds in "East Coker" to treat it in detail.

Time in "East Coker" is defined as historical time. The name of this 'Quartet' refers to the home of Eliot's English forebears, a home they left in the seventeenth century for America and a place to which the twentieth-century Eliot returns. Immediately, the idea of succession is introduced as an aspect of temporal experience. The opening lines state what this poem will treat:

> In my beginning is my end. In succession
> Houses rise and fall, crumble, are extended,
> Are removed, destroyed, restored, or in their place
> Is an open field, or a factory, or a by-pass. (*Poems*, 177)

The conflict between time as a continuum, implied by the notion of succession, and time as something more infinite, implied by the line "In my beginning is my end," provides the motivation for this 'Quartet.' The final section of the poem emphasizes that our time as humans is most important, be it personal or universal. The personal aspect of *durée* is stressed in these lines:

> Home is where one starts from. As we grow older
> The world becomes stranger, the pattern more complicated
> Of dead and living. Not the intense moment
> Isolated, with no before and after,
> But a lifetime burning in every moment. (*Poems*, 182)

The more universal time is stressed in these lines: "And not the life-time of one man only / But of old stones that cannot be deciphered." The poem's final half-line, "In my end is my beginning," brings the treatment of historical time to a close. It also serves as a bridge to the next poem, "The Dry Salvages," with its implication of something more than a simple historical view of time, or even a view of time as *durée*. By changing the positions of the words "end" and "beginning" from their places in the first line, Eliot draws attention to the idea that beginning and end are contained in the same time.

The opening sections of "The Dry Salvages" present two seemingly opposing symbols: the river, which Eliot says "Is a strong brown god," and the sea. Each stands for one type of time: the river represents personal or human time which is always flowing, always changing; while the sea represents eternity. In this poem, the two are brought together: experiential time (*durée*) flows into eternity – "The river is within us, the sea is all about us." The image of the river clearly links Eliot's experiential time to Bergson's *durée*, both through the shared use of river as a symbol of personal time and because this time is inner time. Eliot rejects Bergson's time as insufficient, linking it instead with eternity. The two must somehow be combined so that a comprehensive picture can be developed, as this line emphasizes: "Time the destroyer is time the preserver."

Section V states the problem clearly and then provides a solution. The problem is how to unite these two times:

> But to apprehend
> The point of intersection of the timeless
> With time, is an occupation for the saint
> No occupation either, but something given
> And taken, in a lifetime's death in love
> Ardour and selflessness and self-surrender. (*Poems*, 190)

One achieves "the point of intersection," uniting *durée* and eternity, through the Incarnation:

> Here the impossible union
> Of spheres of existence is actual,
> Here the past and the future
> Are conquered, and reconciled,
> Where action were otherwise movement
> Of that which is only moved
> And has in it no source of movement –
> Driven by daemonic, chthonic
> Powers. And right action is freedom
> From past and future also. (*Poems*, 190)

Incarnation, the union of flesh and blood with God, unites temporal and eternal existences with another, more encompassing, one. As Grover Smith says, "There are many incarnations, many unions of matter and soul, of which Christ's is the only one reconciling time with eternity, for His Incarnation is the only one joining to the material flux absolutely pure form or actuality" (Smith, 285). In the Christian doctrine of Incarnation, Eliot found the resolution to his own conflicting ideas about time: God may be both flesh and spirit – Christ is both man and God – but through this capacity He can be both mortal and immortal, in time and out of time.

"Little Gidding" maintains the same high emotional and spiritual tones of the last section of "The Dry Salvages." It acts as a coda for the previous three 'Quartets,' restating and rephrasing the themes which the others have developed. Its opening meditation on time restates the essential conflict between *durée* and eternity: "Here, the intersection of the timeless moment / Is England and nowhere. Never and always." It proceeds to a more specific time – both the world of history and the present day world of London during World War II. It moves finally to the still point, the moment of Incarnation. The final section deals explicitly with the paramount importance of this time:

> The moment of the rose and the moment of the yew-tree
> Are of equal duration. A people without history
> Is not redeemed from time, for history is a pattern
> Of timeless moments. So, while the light fails
> On a winter's afternoon, in a secluded chapel
> History is now and England. (*Poems*, 197)

The moment of the rose – eternal life – and the moment of the yew-tree – experiential life – contribute equally to the true temporal experience, Incarnation. The final image of the poem underlines Eliot's belief that the true time is that which is united in God:

> When the tongues of flames are in-folded
> Into the crowned knot of fire
> And the fire and the rose are one. (*Poems*, 198)

Throughout Eliot's poetic career, the theme of time held a prominent position. His desire to understand time and to resolve its many conflicting forms provides tension in individual poems and also provides a thematic unity for his body of verse. The movement toward a Christian belief is a movement toward a view that allows him to resolve his temporal questions. It also involves a change in the terms of the discussion. Eliot no longer views *durée* as the incorrect representation of our time as humans; rather, he sees it as the true description of our existence when we are devoid of faith in God. *Durée*, for Eliot, is time without meaning or purpose. In his later poetry he contrasts that time with eternal time, God's time, and he restates his conflict as *durée* versus eternity. But as *Four Quartets* so amply demonstrates, Eliot is still preoccupied with the problem of closing the gap between the two temporal realities; although the terms may have changed and the solution may be different and more firmly accepted, the essential nature of the discussion is identical to the one in "Rhapsody on a Windy Night" and other early poems. The refined treatment of time in the poems – from the fairly simple *durée* versus clock time of the 1910–1912 poems, to the involved treatment of many times in *Four*

*Quartets* – and the accompanying change in tone and attitude reflect Eliot's greater ability to represent the temporal experience. But this does not alter the fact that Eliot, at the end of his career, was as obsessed with time as a key to understanding the nature of existence as he was at the beginning of it. Throughout, Bergson's theory of *durée* and his methods of using time as a model for existence fueled one side of the conflict facing Eliot. Bergson's most basic theory and most widely known concept had a profound effect on Eliot's own thought and approach to the most fundamental questions about the nature of life. But even more essential to Eliot's final position on the questions of existence and the nature of life is his presentation of memory as the chief factor for our self-knowledge. Time might help us to understand society; it might also help us to understand the Incarnation and its importance in our search for absolutes in the world; but memory allows us to understand ourselves. And for Eliot, understanding himself was as important as understanding his world.

Involuntary memory remains a prominent element in Eliot's later work, particularly in *Four Quartets*. Eliot's preoccupation with recapturing "the moment in and out of time," of finding once more the timeless moment, is a central example of the continuing presence of Bergson's involuntary memory in his work. One characteristic of twentieth-century literature, poetry and prose, is the centrality of the privileged moment. James Joyce calls his moments "epiphanies" and Virginia Woolf calls hers "moments of being"; although Eliot never labelled his, the whole of his later work revolves around certain central experiences or moments. Most commentators have noticed how a few images or moments recur in Eliot's work: recall, for example, the rose garden; or the image of the lost beloved, often a little girl, perhaps in a garden or associated with flowers; or the still-point, the timeless moment. Almost all the commentators have rightly mentioned the spiritual or religious significance of such a moment.[8] A small number have also recognized that these moments were the focus of earlier works, presented in different forms and apparently of little religious significance. Morris Beja, for instance, traces Eliot's use of the rose garden motif from "Dans le Restaurant" to *Four Quartets*, illustrating how the "moment of intensity or vision" (Beja, 67) is not only religious in quality, but also a product of secular memories. Beja argues that "the adult need never have undergone the experience to feel its effects" (Beja, 67), for involuntary memory will bring to mind the feelings experienced on another, more distant, occasion. Leonard Unger and Edith F. Cornwell also analyse the privileged moment, showing how particular moments pervade Eliot's poetry; unlike Beja they do not place Eliot's use of such moments in the same tradition as that of other twentieth-century writers.[9] Yet Eliot's use of involuntary memory places him firmly inside this tradition and connects him to Bergson via the agency of Bergson's intuition.

### Memory

Involuntary memory's role in the early poetry has already been noted; it also comes to the forefront in *Four Quartets*. Memory is introduced in "Burnt Norton":

> What might have been and what has been
> Point to one end, which is always present.
> Footfalls echo in the memory
> Down the passage which we did not take
> Towards the door we never opened
> Into the rose-garden. My words echo
> Thus, in your mind. (*Poems*, 171)

It is this failure to enter the rose-garden that provides one of the motivating forces of the poem. The regret over not having done something, "Down the passage which we did not take," assumes the form of a memory; images of things not done as well as things attempted spring to mind whenever an object reminds the poem's persona of past life. Eliot's privileged moment is often thought to occur outside time, and thus to be in opposition to Bergson's ideas that memory is what makes duration seem a part of physical time. The line "Only through time time is conquered" (*Poems*, 173), however, suggests an additional view. The timeless moment is an intersection of all other times – a time-filled moment – and only by living these times simultaneously will one find the moment that supersedes time. Only through the direct agency of memory can we connect other past times to present time and thus create this exceptional moment. Intuition, which allows us to have insights into other things and events as well as into our own inner world, provides the means that allow an individual to understand the significance of this moment. While "Burnt Norton" sets out all the arguments in Eliot's search for the timeless moment, a careful reader may also find some answers to these arguments in this 'Quartet.' Eliot added the other three 'Quartets' partly in an effort to amplify the arguments of the first.

"East Coker" is about the distant past and how it impinges upon the present: "In my beginning is my end." Eliot expands the scope of the poem dramatically in this section to include all people in a universal past that helps to determine a communal present life. The lines:

> The knowledge imposes a pattern, and falsifies,
> For the pattern is new in every moment
> And every moment is a new and shocking
> Valuation of all we have been (*Poems*, 179)

continue to insist that past is related to present. While Bergson says that the recollection of the past is coloured by present perceptions, Eliot, in "Tradition and the Individual Talent," makes the same point. Memory is the bridge between accumulated knowledge and new experiences; it helps to "falsify" experiences because nothing we do is free from the intrusion of memory. The more an individual experiences, the greater this burden of memory. In this 'Quartet,' Eliot suggests that because people carry within them the memory of all previous societies, not just their individual experiences, they are that much more burdened than previous generations. Yet this is also a positive factor: within their memories are the answers with which to solve current problems; all they must do is find the key to unlock those memories and bring the solutions to their problems to the forefront of consciousness.

"Dry Salvages" presents the more immediate past: Eliot spent childhood summers on the coast of Massachusetts where these islands are located. Although this 'Quartet' deals more with personal past and future than it does with the universal one, it attempts to place individual experience alongside communal experience:

> For our own past is covered by the currents of action,
> But the torment of others remains an experience
> Unqualified, unworn by subsequent attrition. (*Poems*, 187)

Since the only way we communicate with others is through common experience and since one person can never experience something in exactly the same way as another, communication, says Eliot, is never really complete. He suggests that a privileged moment, that time-filled moment that gives insight into both self and the world, is the only hope of communicating; but that "For most of us, there is only the unattended / Moment, the moment in and out of time," the moment provided by memory and experience. Incarnation is the goal that is never to be attained, but constantly striven for; the accent here is on the process of self-definition and not the attaining of the goal. Again, the terms are both Bergsonian and Christian – perhaps an unconscious, but important, use of both at this crucial juncture in the poem.

In "Little Gidding" the memory of the rose-garden resurfaces and its presence allows for a union of the two opposing times. This brings about one moment, the moment at which "the fire and the rose are one." Eliot alludes to air raids and also to ancient biblical stories, thereby combining the historical past and the vivid present. The spiritual union with God that he desires is a future action that is linked to the other two, thereby creating a multilayered time-filled moment. So it is the resonance of a memory that releases our understanding of our existence and also allows for the hopes of the future to take a prominent place on the poem's stage. Memory fulfills its role as bridge between the internal world, which is known, and the external world, which exists beyond us and which we someday hope to know. In this way memory becomes a powerful tool in the process of self-discovery, for it takes the individual from the known to the unknown and makes that new world familiar by relating it to past experiences. In effect, memory eliminates temporal boundaries; it allows past experiences to stand next to present ones and then defines these experiences. In the process, since we define ourselves by our experiences, memory helps us discover ourselves.

The poem, all four 'Quartets,' fits together as one unit because of the shared imagery and themes. Here involuntary memory has a secondary role as part of the framework; for example, the encounter with the rose-garden in Section V of "Little Gidding" is more meaningful because the reader's memory has recorded a similar encounter in "Burnt Norton." The reappearance of the same image thus acquires a greater impact on the reader. Other images – doves, fire, water – and themes – the inexorable process of time, the desire for redemption – function in a like manner, creating a series of echoes, the impact of which becomes cumulative. In effect, the poem is a physical representation of the process of self-discovery. Again, as in much of his early work, Eliot is using art as a model of how personalities function. Just as we search for our identity by accumulating and relating experiences, a long poem establishes its unity and identity by establishing the nature and relationship of its various parts – its images, metaphors, phrases, and words. As art's search for meaning is an extension of the artist's search for meaning, *Four Quartets* is a paradigm for Eliot's search for self.

Eliot is widely viewed as an important modernist; some would call him *the* major modernist poet. The real nature of his Modernism is found not in his prose pronouncement of what art should be, but in his poetic enactments of what art is. Bergson's ideas permeate Eliot's criticism as well as his poetry – from his earliest works to his mature masterpiece, Eliot grapples with the concepts central to Bergsonian philosophy. It is thus difficult not to conclude that Bergson profoundly influenced Eliot.

### CHAPTER 5

# Virginia Woolf: Bergsonian Experiments in Representation and Consciousness

Despite Leonard Woolf's claim that Virginia Woolf had not read Bergson's work nor even such secondary sources as her sister-in-law Karin Stephen's book on Bergson,[1] a survey of Woolf criticism reveals that many critics have noted a Bergsonian strain in her work. French critics were among the first to note the connection between the two. One of the earliest commentaries was Floris Delattre's article "La durée bergsonienne dans le roman de Virginia Woolf" published in 1932, which suggested that Bergson's work had had an impact on Woolf. Several English-speaking critics noted the possibility of Bergson's influence on Woolf, beginning with Winifrid Holtby in 1932, who said that he was not a significant force, and David Daiches in 1942, who claimed that Bergson must be placed along with Proust, Joyce, and Freud as a force in Woolf's writing.[2] By the mid 1950s and early 1960s, a few more critics had turned their attention to the issue of Bergson's role in Woolf's fiction. John Graham, for example, concluded that Woolf was not greatly influenced by Bergson, while James Hafley carefully charted the areas where their thought met.[3] And Jean Guiguet asserted that "Virginia Woolf's contacts with Bergsonism were on the one hand indirect, and on the other, inconsiderable."[4] It was Shiv Kumar's *Bergson and the Stream of Conscious Novel*, however, that became the first major study to examine Bergson's impact on Woolf in an extended manner. Subsequent criticism has generally dealt with Bergson vis-à-vis Woolf only in a passing manner, incorporating comments about him into arguments related to other concerns in Woolf's work.[5]

Although a quick check of the many studies on Woolf's output does reveal some mention of Bergson, most of the writers who explore Woolf's Bergsonian traits do so in a limited way. Hafley's comments that "Bergsonism is simply at times a practicable *tool* for the student of Virginia Woolf" and that his study is "an account … of

Virginia Woolf and not at all of Bergson, of art and not of pure philosophy"[6] show the restricted parameters of even a sympathetic treatment of Bergson and Woolf. It is puzzling, too, that no one has gone substantially beyond work done in the 1960s. In the almost thirty years since that time, Woolf scholarship has boomed, aided by the publication of her diaries and letters and by developments in literary theory that have changed the nature of a critic's role. Yet critics remain content to parrot the judgments of Kumar or Hafley (if they judge that Bergson did play a role in her work) or Graham (if they believe he did not). In this chapter, I go beyond the work of Kumar and Hafley, for I believe that Bergson was a strong force in Woolf's writing. My belief is that by restricting my discussion of Woolf to only those elements that are Bergsonian, I can update these studies.

## INITIAL EXPERIMENTS: TIME, INTUITION, AND MEMORY

Woolf continually experimented with the limits and possibilities of her art. Her particular preoccupation was with the issues of representation and the ways of dealing with the split between subject – the vital living aspects of the self or the artwork – and object – the static representation of the same things. She sought to close the gap between subject and object by depicting the process of living that occurs within her characters. But to establish a representational mode that would allow her to depict "real" life she had to develop a new writing style, one that would showcase the radically different underlying aesthetic. While Woolf certainly relied on some of her predecessors (Sterne, for example) and some of her contemporaries (Proust and the Russian novelists) for assistance in her struggles to redefine fiction and its methodology, she also seems to have incorporated three of Bergson's major ideas: time, intuition, and memory. Each of these assumes a central role in Woolf's literary aesthetics and practice, and each is employed in a manner so consistent with Bergson's articulation of them that they highlight Woolf's lasting debt to Bergson.

### Time

Shiv Kumar writes of Woolf: "Of all the stream-of-consciousness novelists, Virginia Woolf alone seems to have presented a consistent and comprehensive treatment of time. Time with her is almost a mode of perception, a filter which distills all phenomena before they are apprehended in their true significance and relationship" (S. Kumar, 64). Kumar is perceptive here; Woolf's characteristic mode of perception is temporally, not spatially, oriented. Life occurs fully in each individual moment; to represent life, therefore, one needs to represent the moment. Woolf's major concern is to capture not the external qualities of the series of moments that constitute a life, but to capture the invisible inner moments in which most important living occurs. To do this she developed a contrast between what she called "moments of being" and "moments of non-being." According to Woolf, the latter constitute the vast majority of our life; she referred to living in this state as being like "cotton wool" ("A Sketch," 84), something that muffles the senses and prevents a feeling of being alive. Moments of being are much rarer, said Woolf, and also much more valuable. During these brief moments one becomes alive: aware of one's immediate surroundings and also aware of one's place in history. As Woolf describes the moment, "It is a token of some real thing behind appearances; and I make it real by putting it into words. It is only by putting it into words that I make it whole; ... it gives me, ... a great delight to put the severed parts together" ("A Sketch," 84). These brief moments appear to arrest the flow of time, but they also bring about a conflation of times as each individual moment is related to previous moments that are resurrected almost instantaneously.

Far from being a moment out of time, Woolf's moments of being are instances of pure duration, moments during which past and present time not only literally coexist, but during which one is aware of their coexistence. In a Bergsonian sense, these are moments of pure *durée*. They are moments when we leave *l'étendu* and enter into an intuitive relationship with the essence of ourselves or those things that spark the moment. By penetrating to the level of *durée*, Woolf seeks to depict life as it occurs on a temporal, rather than spatial, level. Even more crucial, Woolf provides an artistic model of a process that revolves around fluidity and impermanence. While Woolf's moments might appear to contradict Bergson's insistence that life is vital only in its flux and not when it is static or spatialized, Bergson accepted that representation meant a spatialization of flux. As noted in chapter 3, Bergson believed that "speech can only indicate by a few guide-posts placed here and there the chief stages in the movement of thought" (*M&M*, 159). He insisted that a representation that could provoke an intuitive interaction between object and perceiver brought about a renewal of the initial "moment of being" that had first provoked the artist. And it is in just this way that Woolf's moments of being act. Each is a brief, sharp representation of a clear, extraordinary experience. Adding such moments together creates a sustained moment of being that, for example, may encompass a lifetime in one day of a character's existence (*Mrs Dalloway*), or the combined lifetimes of several characters as revealed by the intersection of selected moments in their individual lives (*The Waves*).

Despite the spatializing hazards involved in narratives, Woolf's experiments in form and subject matter are an effort to prove "that one's life is not confined to one's body and what one says and does; one is living all the time in relation to certain background rods or conceptions" ("A Sketch," 84). The background against which Woolf lives her life is the sense that "behind the cotton wool is hid a pattern" ("A Sketch," 84), a pattern consisting of time-filled moments of being.

In order to capture these moments, Woolf manipulates traditional narrative form. Such novels as many of her contemporaries were writing – Wells, Gissing, Bennett, or Galsworthy, for example – would not allow her to present moments of being. She set out to develop new narrative strategies to show the conflation of time into one time-filled instant, and to show that this moment is a profound inner experience that is every bit as important as the more public events of the external world. The resulting style, labeled stream-of-consciousness[7], was Woolf's solution. Although she did not arrive at a satisfactory form immediately (her first two novels were fairly conventional), we can detect the initial stages of her refashioning of prose narratives in the short stories that form *Monday or Tuesday.*

*Monday or Tuesday,* published in 1921, was viewed by critics as a series of highly experimental "sketches" that challenged traditional narrative structures.[8] Three of the stories – "Kew Gardens," "Monday or Tuesday," and "A Haunted House" – illustrate Woolf's first steps toward a Bergsonian fiction.

"Kew Gardens" plays with the nature of a fixed or relative perspective. The fixed perspective – a solid centre from which a narrative can be viewed – is the flower bed that people pass during their walk in the gardens. Above and around it people wander, preoccupied with their own concerns and conversations. The flower bed thus becomes a fixed point in the life that flows around it, for we only hear snippets of conversations and get brief glimpses of the people who pass by our narrative watching-post. However, Woolf undermines the bed's fixity by placing a snail in it. The snail cautiously navigates the landscape, labouring "over the crumbs of loose earth which broke away and rolled down as it passed over them" (*Shorter Fiction*, 91). Thus the apparently fixed viewpoint of the snail in the flower bed is mobile as well. So there is no stable centre in this story; there is only a relative sense of the universe. The snail's is the world of "brown cliffs with deep green lakes in the hollows, flat blade-like trees that waved from root to tip, round boulders of grey stone, vast crumpled surfaces of a thin crackling texture" (*Shorter Fiction*, 91–2). The human world revolves around love – the two lovers who stand in front of the bed – metaphysical discussions – the older man who talks about the spirits – and tea – the "ponderous" woman who "ceased even to pretend to listen" (*Shorter Fiction*, 93) to her friend and thought only of her desire for tea. This juxtaposition of different realities underscores the relative nature of the world and this, in turn, underscores Woolf's continuing concern to represent this relative flux in a spatial form – prose.[9]

"Monday or Tuesday" and "A Haunted House" reflect Woolf's growing desire to dispense with more traditional narrative forms. Each is a short impressionistic account of a brief moment, and in their mode of expression they reflect a Bergsonian concern with the temporal nature of existence. The focus on time-filled moments rather than a more conventional relating of events in a sequential manner requires a new form. One is tempted to call these stories Post-Modern in their blurring of the line between story and essay. In "Monday or Tuesday" the heron's flight over the church unleashes a meditation on truth that ceases when the heron comes back into sight. Time collapses as the narrator ranges over time and place – venturing from "Miss Thingummy drink[ing] tea at her desk" to the world where "from ivory depths words rising shed their blackness, blossom and penetrate" (*Shorter Fiction*, 137). In "A Haunted House," Woolf fixes the perspective in the physical object of a house. She conflates time by placing the perceptions of a ghostly couple who wander – "from room to room they went hand in hand, lifting here, opening there" (*Shorter Fiction*, 122) – next to those of the current inhabitants who track the ghosts' process by the noises the house makes. The narrator awakens from sleep at the story's end – "Waking, I cry 'Oh is this *your* – buried treasure? The light in the heart" (*Shorter Fiction*, 123). The dreamscape of the story incorporates three times – the time when the ghost couple lived in the house, the current owner's time, and the time of the house itself. The first two are clearly fixed – the first couple died; the narrator will die, too, eventually. The house's physical time seems eternal in comparison, for its existence encompasses both the ghosts and the dreamer. Since the house is haunted by the past, though, the past lingers into the present moment, thereby circumventing clock time and enabling the moment when the dreamer awakens to rise above clock time and reach the realm of *durée*. These three stories show Woolf experimenting with time sequences as well as with the formal elements of fiction. This experimentation was to carry over into Woolf's next novel – *Jacob's Room*.

On 26 January 1920, Virginia Woolf wrote in her diary that she had "arrived at some idea of a new form for a new novel." She describes this form:

Suppose one thing should open out of another – as in An Unwritten Novel – only not for 10 pages but for 200 or so – doesn't that give the looseness & lightness I want: doesn't that give the speed & enclose everything, everything? My doubt is how far it will <include> enclose the human heart – Am I sufficiently mistress of my dialogue to net it there? For I figure that the approach will be entirely different this time: no scaffolding; scarcely a brick to be seen; all crepuscular, but the heart, the passion, humour, everything as bright as fire in the mist. Then I'll find room for so much – a gaiety – an inconsequence – a light spirited stepping at my sweet will. Whether I'm sufficiently mistress of things – thats the doubt; but conceive mark on the wall, K[ew]. G[ardens]. & an unwritten novel taking hands and dancing in unity. What the unity shall be I have yet to discover: the theme is a blank to me; but I see immense possibilities in the form I hit upon more or less by chance 2 weeks ago. (Diary 2, 13–14)

The novel about which she was writing was *Jacob's Room*, and it did break new ground. Yet it is not entirely satisfactory in its attempts to present the pattern behind the cotton wool, nor does it really succeed in dispensing with the "scaffolding" or the "bricks" that hold together more traditional narratives. What makes the novel so important is what Woolf attempts, as well as the lessons she learns, which in turn push her toward a radically new form. Her halting manipulation of the temporal and spatial aspects of the novel is perhaps its most important facet, and also its most clearly Bergsonian aspect.

The narrative sequence of *Jacob's Room* is an uneasy union of a conventional, linear narrative and an unconventional, fragmented discontinuity. The novel wants to do two things: tell a fairly straightforward tale of the life of young Jacob – his schooling, his loves, his senseless death at the battlefront of World War I – yet at the same time subvert this conventional narrative presentation – with its excessive fragmentation and discontinuous narrative, and its many gaps that are not completely resolved by the novel's end. The fact that these two almost contradictory impulses do not complement each other actually contributes to the novel's lack of unity. Woolf's outright juxtaposition of what is essentially Bergsonian *durée* (the fragments of moments of being in Jacob's life) and *l'étendu* (the underlying conventional narrative structure of the novel) lacks polish; it fails because she does not develop a representational mode that would allow them to coexist. One primary reason for this failure is that Woolf does not fully capitalize on the roles of both intuition and memory when linking the two views of time.

## Intuition

We have seen that Bergson's intuition is an important component of his philosophy; he defines intuition as "the kind of *intellectual sympathy* by which one places oneself within an object in order to coincide with what is unique in it and consequently inexpressible" (*Intro*, 6). However, the reason for applying this theory to a fiction that seeks to abandon the traditional narrative structures is quite apparent. If a writer dispenses with, or even simply alters, the sequence of a narrative, readers will have much greater difficulty comprehending the traditional aspects of the novel: things such as plot, characters, and themes. When the onus for reconstructing the novel's aspects is placed at the readers' door, the readers must become part of all the narrative aspects. In other words, the various elements must be identified and put in some sort of relationship to each other. One of the easiest ways of doing this is to enter into the novel's elements intuitively, to "see what is unique in it and consequently inexpressible" and then to render this intuitive experience in concrete terms. Hence writers infuse the artwork with their experiences and readers reconstruct them in order to arrive at some insight that satisfies their curiousity about other things or lives. It is essential, then, that the readers not only carry out this intuitive action, but also *want* to do so.

The latter point hints at one of the problems in *Jacob's Room*. Woolf depends on her readers' ability to put together the fragments of the narrative and also to discern the difference between important moments of being and the less important moments of non-being; however, she fails to provide her readers with a character about whom they will care enough to want to use their intuition. Jacob is too diffuse, too poorly differentiated to care about enough to want to discover his uniqueness, to determine how he works and what his essential being is. Moreover, the novel's texture is not as carefully woven as in later novels. The echoes of words and images give the later novels a unity that is missing here. This is not to say that there are no echoes in *Jacob's Room*; there are, but they are not fused together well enough to provide a seamless whole. In addition, Woolf's less than skillful handling of the novel's competing time structures makes it difficult to know which moments are important enough to enter into intuitively and which are essentially moments of non-being that will not reward the reader with a unique, informative insight into the character. Intuition is a valuable tool; although Woolf does not use it to the fullest in this novel, she does use it more effectively in later writings.

Despite the relatively rough juxtaposition of *durée* and *l'étendu* in the novel, Woolf almost succeeds in her quest for a new novel form because of her understanding of how memory works. Woolf's sense of how memory works is uncannily similar to Bergson's. For Bergson, memory allows the linking of current and past experiences in such a fashion that the two reflect upon each other: the present experience is rendered comprehensible by comparison with a previous experience, and the past is renewed and altered by its contact with the present. Memory allows for the time-filled moment of being. On the purely textual level, then, Woolf uses memory to join the two opposing narratives.[10] She achieves the union largely through a series of images – leaves, waves, colours, voices (or noises), and such personal items as Jacob's shoes – which join the linear narrative to the fragments of Jacob's life that the reader shares, even though these fragments must be imagined since access to them is denied. When a particular image reappears, as do the leaves in the following passages, the subtle alterations in their representation demonstrate how memory links the two times. The first passage comes from the opening of the novel, while the second comes from the novel's close:

The wind blew straight dashes of rain across the window, which flashed silver as they passed through the light. A single leaf tapped hurriedly, persistently, upon the glass. There was a hurricane out at sea. (*JR*, 10)

Engines throbbed, and carters, jamming the brakes down, pulled their horses sharp up. A harsh and unhappy voice cried something unintelligible. And then suddenly all the leaves seemed to raise themselves, "Jacob! Jacob!" cried Bonamy, standing by the window. The leaves sank down again.(*JR*, 290)

Although the leaf in the first passage foreshadows Jacob's death in the war ("hurricane"), we miss the importance of this imagery if we do not see the patterns it creates and the way it links the two apparently opposed times in the novel. Woolf expects an affective aesthetic response from her audience and plays upon this by making them use memory to retain the elements of the novel and the subsequent transformation of early events (objects) by later ones.

In *Jacob's Room* Woolf does not destroy the barrier between subject and object (presenting the heart, not the bricks or the scaffolding), because the novel form does require some bricks – no matter what shape the author chooses to make them. However, the importance of this novel lies not in what it accomplishes but in what it contributes to the process of redefining the novel form that Woolf had embarked upon. Woolf continues her experiment in her next novel, *Mrs Dalloway*.

On 30 August 1923, Woolf wrote: "I should say a good deal about The Hours [*Mrs Dalloway*], & my discovery; how I dig out beautiful caves behind my characters; I think that gives exactly what I want; humanity, humour, depth. The idea is that the caves shall connect, & each comes to daylight at the present moment" (*Diary* 2, 263). She has in mind a refinement of what she attempted in her previous novel. She provides more information about her characters (the "caves") and shows more explicitly the links between the novel's alternate time structures. The novel's greater success suggests that Woolf was beginning to come to grips with her new methods.

The backbone of *Mrs Dalloway* is the union of the two times which she was able only to juxtapose in *Jacob's Room*. *Durée* and *l'étendu* are both prominent in this novel. The latter accounts for the novel's outer shape – one day in the life of the London society-hostess Clarissa Dalloway – while the former supplies the novel with its "humanity, humour, [and] depth." The outer shape of *Mrs Dalloway* is that of a conventional novel: the reader sees Clarissa's preparations for the party she is giving, and comes to know her and some of the characters surrounding her in the course of her tasks during the day leading up to the party. Introducing Septimus Warren Smith creates a parallel plot. He represents aspects of Clarissa's character that she denies but that are necessary for her to recognize if she is to achieve self-knowledge. His death, the success of her party, and her gradual awareness of her own nature and mortality fill out the rest of the novel. Alone, this level of the novel would be satisfactory: it presents characters who evolve in the course of the novel and also demonstrates the conventional unity of time. But Woolf transforms the convention through the inclusion of the novel's second level, its *durée*, which contributes not only to the development of the various characters but also to Clarissa's complex process of self-discovery. Woolf's caves contain the motivations, explanations, and possible resolutions for Clarissa's (and the others') actions. Woolf wrote: "It took me a year's groping to discover what I call my tunneling process, by which I tell the past by installments, as I have need of them" (*Diary* 2, 272). An incident sparks off a memory of the past which, in turn, brings about a fresh understanding of the present. This continual mixing of different times results in the novel's sense of timelessness, as if all of Clarissa's life existed simultaneously. The "tunneling process" does not just provide background information; it knits together present actions and choices with the elements that led the character up to the moment of action. The depth and continuity of life that was missing in *Jacob's Room* is evident in this novel, for Woolf is able, by joining the two modes of existence, to fashion a rich and complex reality.

Far from making this novel an apparent series of frozen moments recaptured by the gradually awakening Clarissa, the intermingling of moments results in a single, continuous *time-filled* moment – one in which Clarissa finds solutions to her present problems by coming to see how her past provides the answers. In discussing the novel's conclusion, Woolf wrote: "It is to be a most complicated spirited solid piece, knitting together everything and ending on three notes, at different stages of the staircase, each saying something to sum up Clarissa. Who shall say these things? Peter, Richard, and Sally Seton perhaps" (*Diary 2*, 312). This occurs in the novel's final version. Clarissa's distant past combines her present and her possible future in one single, prolonged moment of insight into herself. In effect, the novel's close becomes its supreme moment of being, by virtue of its conflation of Clarissa's life into one time-filled moment.

Woolf's increasingly skillful treatment of intuition and memory is an important facet in the success of the novel's time structure. The novel makes intuition an explicit feature through its clear doubling of Septimus and Clarissa and its less prominent doubling of Clarissa and the old woman in the room across the street. Clarissa never actually meets either of her doubles, though she sees both of them; nevertheless, she is able to enter into their lives and learn from them something that allows her a greater degree of self-knowledge. If Bergsonian intuition involves the ability of discerning what is unique and inexpressible in another, then Clarissa more than any other character in the novel possesses this ability. More than Dr. Bradshaw, Clarissa experiences Septimus's pain and visualizes his suicide and how he must have felt. Her reaction initially seems resentful. She thinks:

What business had the Bradshaws to talk of death at her party? A young man had killed himself. And they talked of it at her party – the Bradshaws talked of death. He had killed himself – but how? Always her body went through it, when she was told, first, suddenly, of an accident; her dress flamed, her body burnt. He had thrown himself from a window. Up had flashed the ground; through him, blundering, bruising, went the rusty spikes. There he lay with a thud, thud, thud in his brain, and then a suffocation of blackness. So she saw it. But why had he done it? And the Bradshaws talked of it at her party! (*Dalloway*, 163)

Yet she also thinks: "Death was defiance. Death was an attempt to communicate, people feeling the impossibility of reaching the centre which, mystically, evaded them; closeness drew apart; rapture faded; one was alone. There was an embrace in death" (164). As she works her way through her reaction, she decides: "She had escaped. But that young man had killed himself. Somehow it was her disaster – her disgrace. It was her punishment to see sink and disappear here a man, there a woman, in this profound darkness; and she forced to stand here in her evening dress" (164). She absorbs Septimus's actions, and they make her aware of her own fragility and loneliness. But she is stronger than he is and she survives while he dies.

She is able to make this affirmative decision when she finally understands the significance of the elderly woman who lives across the street. Clarissa's last encounter with the woman occurs after she has worked her way through her reaction to Septimus's suicide. She observes the woman:

She parted the curtains; she looked. Oh, but how surprising! – in the room opposite the old lady stared straight at her! She was going to bed. And the sky. It will be a solemn sky, she had thought, it will be a dusky sky, turning away its cheek in beauty. But there it was – ashen pale, raced over quickly by tapering vast clouds. It was new to her. The wind must have risen. She was going to bed, in the room opposite. It was fascinating to watch her, moving about, that old lady, crossing the room, coming to the window. Could she see her? It was fascinating, with people still laughing and shouting in the drawing-room, to watch that old woman, quite quietly, going to bed alone. (*Dalloway*, 164–5)

This incident – combining as it does Clarissa's renewed awareness of the natural world with her intimation of her own mortality, because of her intuitive sympathy with the old woman – is crucial. It pushes her back into life, but she re-enters her world wiser and more self-aware. Outside her house the wind blows, the moon rises, and old women go to bed alone. But Clarissa is not alone, for she feels a kinship with life outside her house and her circle of friends; this gives her strength to live fully. More than simply possessing the ability to enter into intuitive relationships, Clarissa is able to act upon the knowledge gleaned from her encounters. Again this is explicit in the novel, for as Clarissa prepares to re-enter life and to confront her problems, the narrator tells us: "But she must go back. She must assemble. She must find Sally and Peter. And she came in from the little room" (*Dalloway*, 165). The little room, possibly a symbol for the twilight world between life and death in which Clarissa had existed, is left behind as she re-enters the party, confronts her past – Sally and Peter – and embraces life. Intuition is the faculty that permits self-knowledge, but

Bergson would insist that self-knowledge is useless unless we are prepared to act on it; Clarissa is a very Bergsonian figure in her acceptance of the actions that intuition permits her to take.

### Memory

Memory, which plays such a prominent role in Woolf's novel, occupies two distinct positions. The first is as a part of Woolf's tunneling process. Memory functions as the bridge between the past at Bourton and the present in Mayfair, just as it functioned as a bridge between Jacob's past and his present. Although the reader is required to make the connections between the two times, the effort here is more rewarding: the novel's real tension does not revolve around a resolution to the characters' problems or relationships, but rather around the process of relating different segments of one's life to each other and arriving at a coherent whole. A good example of how the novel shifts between Bourton and the present moment occurs when Peter Walsh finds himself in Regent's Park. The passage starts in the present and moves to the past, returning finally, some pages later, to the present. Only the first part of this passage will be quoted so as to illustrate the easy transition from present to past:

So the elderly nurse knitted over the sleeping baby in Regent's Park. So Peter Walsh snored. He woke with extreme suddenness, saying to himself, "The death of the soul." "Lord, Lord!" he said to himself out loud, stretching and opening his eyes. "The death of the soul." The words attached themselves to some scene, to some room, to some past he had been dreaming of. It became clearer; the scene, the room, the past he had been dreaming of.

It was Bourton that summer, early in the nineties, when he was so passionately in love with Clarissa. There were a great many people there, laughing and talking, sitting round a table after tea, and the room was bathed in yellow light and full of cigarette smoke. They were talking about a man who had married his housemaid, one of the neighbouring squires, he had forgotten his name. He had married his housemaid, and she had been brought to Bourton to call – an awful visit it had been. She was absurdly overdressed, "like a cockatoo," Clarissa had said, imitating her, and she never stopped talking. On and on she went, on and on. Clarissa imitated her. Then somebody said – Sally Seton it was – did it make any real difference to one's feelings to know that before they'd married she had had a baby? (In those days, in mixed company, it was a bold thing to say.) He could see Clarissa now, turning bright pink; somehow contracting; and saying, "Oh, I shall never be able to speak to her again!" Whereupon the whole party sitting around the tea-table seemed to wobble. It was very uncomfortable. He hadn't blamed her for minding the fact, since in those days a girl brought up as she was knew nothing, but it was her manner that annoyed him; timid; hard; arrogant; prudish. "The death of the soul." He said that instinctively, ticketing the moment as he used to do – the death of her soul. (*Dalloway,* 53)

This passage is very Bergsonian in the way its movement is determined by the random memory of the key phrase – "The death of the soul." Involuntary memory swings into action when prompted by the phrase and suddenly the whole scene returns in all its vividness. By shifting the focus away from resolution and on to process, Woolf foregrounds memory's role in the conduct of life.

The second position that memory assumes in this story is found in Septimus's life. His inability to make his memories join with his present life results in a fragmented existence. When Rezia and Septimus are in the park, his inability to reconcile memories and present life provokes a memorable scene. He is initially aware of his surroundings: "He strained; he pushed; he looked; he saw Regent's Park before him" (*Dalloway,* 62). But he crumbles when overwhelmed by memories:

The word "time" split its husk; poured its riches over him; and from his lips fell like shells, like shavings from a plane, without his making them, hard, white, imperishable, words, and flew to attach themselves to their places in an ode to Time; an immortal ode to Time. He sang. Evans answered from behind the tree. The dead were in Thessaly, Evans sang among the orchids. There they waited till the War was over, and now the dead, now Evans himself –

"For God's sake don't come!" Septimus cried out. For he could not look upon the dead.

But the branches parted. A man in grey was actually walking towards them. It was Evans! But no mud was on him; no wounds; he was not changed. I must tell the whole world, Septimus cried, raising his hand (as the dead man in the grey suit came nearer), raising his hand like some colossal figure in the desert alone with his hands pressed to his forehead, furrows of despair on his cheeks, and now sees light on the desert's edge which broadens and strikes the iron-black figure (and Septimus half rose from his chair), and with legions of men prostrate behind him he, the giant mourner, receives for one moment on his face the whole. (*Dalloway,* 63)

The man in grey, Peter Walsh, passes the pair and observes their acute distress with some sympathy. Unlike Peter, who is able to keep memories in their place and insert them into his present life with some sort of order, Septimus is overcome by his memories and loses his grip on the present moment and thus on himself. By bringing Septimus and Peter face to face, Woolf underlines the power of memory and its role in forming the present life. The fragmentation that was the hallmark of *Jacob's Room* becomes the nightmare world in which Septimus lives and which eventually prompts his death. Memory unassimilated with present life is seen as the source of madness; this hints at a central aesthetic concern of this novel as well as later ones. The "pattern behind the cotton wool" which Woolf wants to capture, and which she sees as the basis of all art and the unifier of humanity, is not found at the end of a story or life, but is glimpsed periodically throughout the whole work or lifetime; memory, by bringing together these various moments at intervals, permits glimpses of the pattern. It is imperative, then, to have a memory faculty that is capable not only of storing experiences but also of relating them to current life. By having Septimus die because he lacks this ability, Woolf powerfully suggests the centrality of memory to the aesthetic process and to life itself.

### THE EXPERIMENTS CONTINUE: SUBJECT-OBJECT

*To the Lighthouse* continues the process of experimentation with the novel's form. In *Mrs Dalloway*, Woolf had been able to balance the two time worlds yet still present an interesting and viable story, largely because she restored some of the conventional narrative elements absent in *Jacob's Room*; but she still had to eliminate the gulf between the subject of her writing (the inner life) and the object created (the characters). In *To the Lighthouse*, Woolf renews her efforts to achieve a form of representation that would accomplish this. She focuses more on the nature of the characters and makes a greater use of symbolism to eliminate, if possible, the barrier between her subject and her object. She continues to play with the narrative sequence, again attempting to vary it in order to create the impression of life's chaos bounded by the restraints imposed on it by the rational mind.

The novel's well-known structure – two sections, each consisting of no more than a few hours in duration, bracket a section that contains the events of ten years – is its most obvious Bergsonian feature. Certainly the middle section, "Time Passes," is representative of *durée*, in that much happens yet little is seen by the reader. Indeed, all the actions in the middle section are assigned less visibly important places than the events of a few hours on either side of this section. It is almost as if the necessary living that enables the characters to make the changes and choices they do in "The Lighthouse" section is invisible, because the living happens in the rapid movement of "Time Passes."

In this way Woolf's second section is similar to the flow of life that goes on beneath the events of daily life; that is, although constant change and growth occur in *durée*, they are not necessarily visible until they affect some action in the everyday world. Without this evolving and chaotic inner life, however, there would be little change in the more stable external world; just as in this novel the insights that Lily and Mr. Ramsay reach might never occur. Recalling Bergson's assertion that both *durée* and *l'étendu* are necessary for an integrated life allows for an even better appreciation of how Bergsonian this novel is; by balancing the middle section with the two that surround it, Woolf implicitly represents Bergson's ideal situation.

The chaotic appearance of the novel's middle section is also an advance for Woolf in her attempt to represent "real" living, for if life occurs primarily at the level of *durée*, then Woolf should represent this world. Stylistically, the flux of this inner world is approximated by the fluidity and obliqueness of the prose. For example, the death of Mrs Ramsay in chapter 3 of "Time Passes" is only obliquely presented: [Mr Ramsay stumbling along the passage stretched his arms out one dark morning, but, Mrs Ramsay having died rather suddenly the night before, he stretched his arms out. They remained empty] (*TTL*, 120). The emphasis in the rest of the chapter that precedes this parenthetical statement is on seasons and the different types of night. This underscores the primacy, as well the ravages, of time. Placing Mrs Ramsay's death in parentheses makes this central event in the novel only one incident in the unceasing flow of life. Death, birth, autumn, spring – all come in their turns; it is only when events are vested with significance by humans that they transcend the flux of time. In other words, we as humans create significance; nature holds all events and creatures as the same – transient and insignificant. In "Time Passes" all the events that we would construe as important – Andrew's death, Prue's death in childbirth, Mr Carmichael's publication of his first volume of verse – are presented in parentheses, subordinated to the descriptions of the house's decay, the passing of the seasons, the flux of time. Just as the novelist consciously fashions events and characters when writing a novel, we fashion our random experiences, perceptions, and interactions with others in order to make some sense of life. The real living is chaotic and continuous; ordering it makes it inert, but intelligible.

Here Woolf is on the verge of achieving both her goals: developing a new mode of representation and breaking down the subject-object split. The reader must enter the text intuitively in order to grasp the reality represented by Woolf's juxtaposition of times and her redefinition of character as a function of time and not space. By tying the

many actions of the middle section to the journeys of Lily and Mr.
Ramsay, Woolf welds the specific moment to the broad spectrum of
moments that constitute life.

The important feature in the journey to the lighthouse of the first
section is the reaching of the structure itself; in the third section, the
actual voyage to the lighthouse is the important thing, for it is here
that James, Cam, and Mr Ramsay experience their own individual
moments of being. In "The Window," James's initial emotion at the
thought of going to the lighthouse is joy: " 'Yes, of course, if it's fine
to-morrow,' said Mrs Ramsay. 'But you'll have to be up with the
lark,' she added. To her son these words conveyed an extraordinary
joy, as if it were settled the expedition were bound to take place, and
the wonder to which he had looked forward, for years and years it
seemed, was, after a night's darkness and a day's sail, within touch"
(TTL, 9). It is the prospect of what he will see and do at the lighthouse,
as well as seeing the structure itself, that is important. As important is
the fulfillment of his dream; the end is important, not the getting
there. Yet this trip is called off by Mr Ramsay, who fails to see his
son's pain and is just as oblivious to the demands he places on his
wife and all those around him. In a sense, his behaviour reflects his
ambition to succeed in his philosophical endeavours – the end is
important, not the process.

In contrast, the emphasis in "The Lighthouse" is not on achieving
the goal – the reader only sees them land, not reach the structure or
their activities while there – but on the journey there. Here James
looks for and finally wins his father's approval. Cam's comments
illustrate this:

"Well done!" James had steered them like a born sailor.

There! Cam thought, addressing herself silently to James. You've got it at
last. For she knew that this was what James had been so wanting, and she
knew that now he had got it he was so pleased that he would not look at her
or at his father or at anyone. There he sat with his hand on the tiller sitting
bolt upright, looking rather sulky and frowning slightly. He was so pleased
that he was not going to let anybody take away a grain of his pleasure. His
father had praised him. They must think that he was perfectly indifferent. But
you've got it now, Cam thought. (TTL, 189–90)

James's spiritual journey in the novel reaches a new stage; the possibility that he may new begin a closer relationship with his father overshadows the purpose of the physical journey, reaching the lighthouse.
What had been important to the boy is now much less so, for time
and a succession of "nights of darkness" had led to a new beginning,

a new understanding. For his father, too, a profound change is brought about by this long-delayed trip. For Mr Ramsay the trip, the process, is important because it makes him aware of those around himself – most notably his son's great need for his approval. Ramsay has grown from a figure fixated on the ends of actions, to one who acknowledges the importance of process. Again, it is the process of time and living that is foregrounded in a Bergsonian way, but what makes this novel's treatment of the issue so distinctly better than in Woolf's previous attempts is the subtlety of her presentation of both.

Lily's painting functions in much the same way as Mr Ramsay's journey, although the actual painting assumes an aesthetic significance not granted the lighthouse. Lily's powers as a painter are intuitive; she does not seek to recreate the rational surface of life, but to depict its hidden depths. She looks at her painting, in "The Window," and thinks:

She could have wept. It was bad, it was bad, it was infinitely bad! She could have done it differently of course; the colour could have been thinned and faded; the shapes etherealized; that was how Paunceforte would have seen it. But then she did not see it like that. She saw the colour burning on a framework of steel; the light of a butterfly's wing lying upon the arches of a cathedral. Of all that only a few random marks scrawled upon the canvas remained. And it would never be seen; never be hung even, and there was Mr Tansley whispering in her ear, "Women can't paint, women can't write ..." (*TTL*, 48)

She sees things differently because she sees the essence of them, but she does not know how to represent this. Nor does she know how to cope with the censure of individuals like Tansley, who fail to see the depths of life and ridicule her efforts to represent them.

At the end of the novel, Lily finally does finish her painting. Here the resolution of an aesthetic problem is symbolic of Lily's resolution of her own emotional turmoil; it is also representative of the general emotional turmoil of the novel, since by this stage Lily has come to represent all the forces that assail the characters. Her thoughts reveal the balance that she has achieved: "Quickly, as if she were recalled by something over there, she turned to her canvas. There it was – her picture. Yes, with all its green and blues, its lines running up and across, its attempt at something. It would be hung in the attics, she thought; it would be destroyed. But what did that matter? she asked herself, taking up her brush again" (*TTL*, 191). She sees her creation wholly new, as if for the first time. She knows that its importance is not physical – its presence and its merit as art are ephemeral – because it is the journey she has taken to get to this point that is important. As it is for

James, Cam and Mr Ramsay at the lighthouse, it is the journey inward that permits the growth and new vision that is essential. To finish the painting, to create a monument to her knowledge, is less important than the acquisition of the wisdom that living according to her sense of the world is more important than conforming to its external rules.

Lily's thoughts at the end reveal the pattern developed by Woolf over the course of the novel, which is only fully revealed when Lily can push aside the "cotton wool" and see the pattern behind it: "With a sudden intensity, as if she saw it clear for a second, she drew a line there in the centre. It was done; it was finished" (*TTL*, 192). The "it" is more than her painting; "it" is her journey of self-discovery, Mr Ramsay's journey, and also the novel itself. The rich intermingling of the symbols adds depth and complexity to the novel and serves as a counterpoint to its unusual time structure.

The structure of Woolf's next novel, *Orlando*, is not as overtly experimental as that of *To the Lighthouse*. Indeed, she viewed the book as an exercise that would remove her from the experimental novels she had been writing. She writes:

For the truth is I feel the need of an escapade after these serious poetic experimental books whose form is always so closely considered. I want to kick up my heels & be off. I want to embody all those innumerable little ideas & tiny stories which flash into my mind at all seasons. I think it will be great fun to write; & it will rest my head before starting the very serious mystical poetical work which I want to come next. (*Diary 3*, 131)

Serious fiction or not, Woolf continued her struggle with representations of the moment of being.

The book's central conceit is that it spans three hundred years while following the life and fortunes of the main character, Orlando. Orlando's own transformation – from boy to man and then to woman – destabilizes the sense of continuity suggested by centring the novel around one character. The multiple selves that Orlando reflects in these transformations function in a very Bergsonian way. Bergson believed that each individual consists of multiple selves, with a superficial surface self that presents itself to the world while others, existing below the surface, constantly mesh and change and have an impact on which superficial self is displayed at any one moment.[11] Woolf makes clear Orlando's sense of self near the end of the novel, during Orlando's musing about the nature of herself:

For if there are (at a venture) seventy-six different times all ticking in the mind at once, how many people are there not – Heaven help us – all having lodgement at one time or another in the human spirit? Some say two thousand and fifty-two. So that it is the most usual thing in the world for a person to call, directly they are alone, Orlando? (if that is one's name) meaning by that, Come, come! I'm sick to death of this particular self ... But it is not altogether plain sailing, either, for though one may say, as Orlando said (being out in the country and needing another self presumably) Orlando? Still the Orlando she needs may not come; these selves of which we are built up, one on top of the other, as plates are piled on a waiter's hand, have attachments elsewhere, sympathies, little constitutions and rights of their own, call them what you will (and for many of these things there is no name) so that one will only come if it is raining, another in a room with green curtains, another when Mrs Jones is not there, another if you can promise it a glass of wine – and so on; for everybody can multiply from his own experience the different terms which his different selves have made with him – and some are too wildly ridiculous to be mentioned in print at all. (*Orlando*, 192–2)

The Bergsonian nature of this idea about self is clear.

A second Bergsonian feature of this novel is the way in which Woolf handles memory. Woolf writes:

Memory is the seamstress [of our experiences], and a capricious one at that. Memory runs her needle in and out, up and down, hither and thither. We know not what comes next, or what follows after. Thus, the most ordinary movement in the world, such as sitting down at a table and pulling the inkstand towards one, may agitate a thousand odd, disconnected fragments, now bright, now dim, hanging and bobbing and dipping and flaunting, like the underlinen of a family of fourteen on a line in a gale of wind. Instead of being a single, downright, bluff piece of work of which no man need feel ashamed, our commonest deeds are set about with a fluttering and a flickering of wings, a rising and falling of lights. (*Orlando*, 49)

Orlando's life reflects this shifting, almost random, sense of how memory works. He/she careens from one adventure to the next, but rather than consigning events to a storehouse memory from which they seldom emerge, memories bubble to the surface when least expected and play a role in the current moment. For example, near the novel's end, Orlando finds herself in Marshall & Snellgrove's department store. A sound sets off a train of memory:

Orlando stood there hesitating. Through the great glass doors she could see the traffic in Oxford street. Omnibus seemed to pile itself upon omnibus and then to jerk itself apart. So the ice blocks had pitched and tossed that day on the Thames. An old nobleman in furred slippers had sat astride one of them.

There he went – she could see him now – calling down maledictions upon the Irish rebels. He had sunk there, where her car stood. (*Orlando*, 190)

This functioning of memory is similar to Bergson's sense of it. Involuntary memory is the type of penetration of the past into the future that results in a time-filled moment, a moment of being.

As Woolf was composing *To the Lighthouse*, her mind had already begun to generate ideas for an even more experimental novel. The writing of *Orlando* provided her with the distraction that was necessary to let the ideas for the new novel ferment. In her diary, where she records what she wanted to tackle, she wrote: "I am now & then haunted by some semi mystic very profound life of a woman, which shall all be told on one occasion; & time shall be utterly obliterated; future shall somehow blossom out of the past. One incident – say the fall of a flower – might contain it. My theory being that the actual event practically does not exist – nor time either." (*Diary 3*, 118). This describes the Bergsonian notion of time perfectly. Future does come out of past time: the minute one stops to analyse a present moment, that moment becomes part of the past and its impact is felt not on the present instant but on the moments that follow the present. In this way, time – as in the actual moment of living – seems to disappear or become "obliterated." So one isolated incident might release all sorts of recollections of past events, thereby creating a time-filled moment that supersedes the sensations of the present moment and overshadows the event that initiated the recollections. Bergsonian memory plays a role in Woolf's process of obliterating time, as does intuition, which helps the observer to enter into the event in order to initiate the recollective process. Here, whether Woolf had read Bergson's philosophy seems beyond the point, for she echoes his ideas.

### THE EXPERIMENTS MATURE

*The Waves* is a Bergsonian work. It completes the melding of the two time structures – *durée* and *l'étendu* – held together, with varying degrees of success, in an uneasy union in the previous novels. Woolf achieves this interpenetration of times by deviating sharply from standard narrative conventions. She creates the impression of timelessness by bracketing her prose passages with poetic ones that describe the ceaseless rhythm of life: while the progress of the sun through the sky represents the daily pattern of individual lives, the waves breaking on shore represent eternity – the passing of time through generations of life. Although the actual events of the work occur in the intervening prose passages, Woolf here provides only moments of being in the lives of her six characters: Bernard, Louis, Neville, Susan, Rhoda, and Jinny. Discarding the other moments as less significant, she presents highly charged emotional scenes in which the characters' basic natures are revealed either directly or through recollections. But even though the prose passages follow a rough chronology – from childhood to death – they do not really constitute a conventional linear narrative because so much is omitted in the telling of their stories. Woolf weaves together the prose and poetic passages by having both share the same imagery – waves and light primarily – thereby creating a prolonged moment of being that captures the characters' lives, the life of their era, and all of history. In doing this she is Bergsonian.

When Woolf was beginning to conceive *The Waves*, she outlined the thought behind what she was trying to do:

The idea has come to me that what I want now to do is to saturate every atom. I mean to eliminate all waste, deadness, superfluity: to give the moment whole; whatever it includes. Say that the moment is a combination of thought; sensation; the voice of the sea. Waste, deadness, come from the inclusion of things that dont[sic] belong to the moment; this appalling narrative business of the realist: getting on from lunch to dinner: it is false, unreal, merely conventional. Why admit any thing to literature that is not poetry – by which I mean saturated? Is that not my grudge against novel[ist]s – that they select nothing? The poets succeed by simplifying: practically everything is left out I want to put practically everything in; yet to saturate. That is what I want to do in The Moths. (*Diary 4*, 209–10)

Woolf tells the stories of six characters by including only the important moments and through their lives she manages to tell the story of the main figure of this work – Percival. Although each character is intuitive, some are more able to enter into an "intellectual sympathy" with others and their environment (Susan and Bernard are particularly intuitive); all, however, can sense the others' presence and essence at some point in the novel. The ability of each character to enter intuitively into each other's life allows them all to become part of the stream of humanity which, at first glance, seems to be absent from the novel. By splitting the various emotions and social personae among the six characters and allowing them to live within each other's selves, and by then allowing them all to combine in the figure of Percival, Woolf creates a society that resembles the world outside the novel in its apparently conventional social roles and interactions. Yet it contains Woolf's own vision of a reality in which everyone is mutually dependent and responsible for the generation and preservation of society. She herself said to Leonard Woolf that the "*dramatis personae* were meant to be 'severally facets of a single complete person.' "[12] The image that best captures this completion of life by the union of fragments within a single shared vision is that same image of the flower, which she had earlier recorded in her diary. Bernard, the narrative voice in much of the novel, states Percival's role in the others' lives, as well as in the novel's representation of society, when he says: "The red carnation that stood in the vase on the table of the restaurant when we dined together with Percival is become a six-sided flower; made of six lives" (*TW*, 154). Percival is the stem, the source of nourishment, order, and purpose for the six; as such, it is he who is the unspoken focus of the work. But he remains unseen throughout the novel, his character being relayed through the others. Here again, Bergsonian memory assumes a prominent role.

The recollections of the six are used to recreate Percival and the events of his life, as well as their own. Woolf sets internal monologues next to each other; each character has a distinctive voice so that the reader can identify who is speaking. A succession of individual thoughts and emotions must be collated by the reader in order to understand each character, Percival, and the novel itself. A brief example of Woolf's method is difficult to give because the characters' speeches are generally long, so excerpts of Neville, Bernard, and Rhoda's reactions to Percival's death will be given here. In the novel they form one continuous section of ten pages; each speech flows into the next one. Neville speaks first:

"He is dead," said Neville. "He fell. His horse tripped. He was thrown. The sails of the world have swung round and caught me on the head. All is over. The lights of the world have gone out. There stands the tree which I cannot pass.

"Oh, to crumple this telegram in my fingers – to let the light of the world flood back – to say this has not happened! ...

"I will not lift my foot to climb the stair. I will stand for one moment beneath the immitigable tree, alone with the man whose throat is cut, while downstairs the cook shoves in and out the dampers. I will not climb the stair. We are doomed, all of us. Women shuffle past with shopping-bags. People keep on passing. Yet you shall not destroy me. For this moment, this one moment, we are together. I press you to me. Come, pain, feed on me. Bury your fangs in my flesh. Tear me asunder. I sob. I sob." (*TW*, 101–3)

Bernard speaks second:

"Such is the incomprehensible combination," said Bernard, "such is the complexity of things, that as I descend the staircase I do not know which is sorrow, which is joy. My son is born; Percival is dead. I am upheld by pillars, shored up on either side by stark emotions; but which is sorrow, which is joy? I ask, and do not know, only that I need silence, and to consider what has happened to my world, what death has done to my world ...

"But now I want life around me, and books and little ornaments, and the usual sounds of tradesmen calling on which to pillow my head after this exhaustion, and shut my eyes after this revelation. I will go straight, then, down the stairs, and hail the first taxi and drive to Jinny." (*TW*, 103–17)

And Rhoda's is the last voice in the section:

"There is the puddle," said Rhoda, "and I cannot cross it. I hear the rush of the great grindstone within an inch of my head. Its wind roars in my face. All palpable forms of life have failed me. Unless I can stretch and touch something hard, I shall be blown down the eternal corridors for ever. What, then, can I touch? What brick, what stone? and so draw myself across the enormous gulf into my body safely? ... Now I will relinquish; now I will let loose. Now I will at last be free the checked, the jerked-back desire to be spent, to be consumed. We will gallop together over desert hills where the swallow dips her wings in dark pools and the pillars stand entire. Into the wave that dashes upon the shore, into the wave that flings its white foam to the uttermost corners of the earth, I throw my violets, my offering to Percival." (*TW*, 107–11)

The voices of each character offer varied perspectives on Percival's death, but each is devastated by it. The underlying principle is that because events are felt and perceived differently, their representation must somehow capture the multiplicity of possibilities. Woolf links the speeches subtly through imagery. Stairs are prominent in Neville's speech, as they are in Bernard's. Pillars are important in Bernard's thoughts, while Rhoda ends her speech wishing to find pillars, and Percival, in the desert. Other images work in a similar way, linking speakers together, amalgamating them thereby into one whole and at the same time building unity in the novel's disparate voices and lives.

When novelists create a story they compose and order events with the intent of arriving at some vision or statement that explains, or at least conveys, a certain sense of their reality. Woolf's attack on this presumption is the same as Bergson's; they both think that there is no single reality because all representations of experience are subjective and therefore open to interpretation and criticism. By having the six characters participate in the construction of Percival's life (and in each other's lives), Woolf demonstrates that all pictures are valid and necessary in the portrait of this one character. Percival, like the novel and Woolf's view of life, is a composite of the many moments of being that are shared by all of the novel's participants (writer, characters, reader); they constitute a reality as viable and valid as that found between the pages of any other novel or in life itself. Woolf would maintain that *The Waves*, devoid as it is of anything but the stuff of life, is a more accurate representation of life than other novels and that it successfully breaks down the subject-object barrier because the reader must be immersed in the process of creating reality in order to read the novel. The novel also comes close to attaining the style of representation that Woolf sought, because she believed "real" life occurs only in the exquisite "moments of being"; hence a novel that only depicts these moments and does so in a startling way fulfills her methodological desires. She admitted her satisfaction with the novel's presentation of her vision when she wrote: "I think I am about to embody, at last, the exact shape my brain holds. What a long toil to reach this beginning – if The Waves is my first work in my own style!" (*Diary 4*, 53).

*The Waves*, a high point in Woolf's narrative innovations, is her most experimental published work. Its debts to Bergsonian philosophy are evident. If Woolf really did believe that this novel embodied her own literary style, we can conclude that Bergson's place in Woolf's writing was extensive and pervasive. Although the final two novels – *The Years* and *Between the Acts* – continue to explore the possibilities of the novel form, their Bergsonian elements are muted. In fact, *The Years* retreats from the "mystical poetry" of *The Waves*[13] and from its Bergsonian structure.

It must be evident by now that once the focus is shifted – away from attempts to detail direct links between Woolf and Bergson and on to the degree to which their approaches to common issues are similar – the echoes of a similar philosophy in the fiction and its underlying aesthetic become clear. While it may never be possible to prove that Woolf read Bergson, her ongoing experiments with the conventions of fiction and with the problems of narration and representation reflect the same concerns Bergson had with the nature of art and language, in particular. Bergson was the most articulate spokesman of the many in his age who explored the same problems; that both he and Woolf arrive at similar answers, although in different mediums, is surely more than just the coincidence of a shared *Zeitgeist*. That Woolf's works move progressively toward a vision of reality that is Bergsonian in its representation of the nature and process of life suggests that she found this vision to be reflective of her own sense of things. Woolf had many ideas from which to choose – the period is replete with competing aesthetic and philosophic ideas – but she chose to write about the inner life; to depict this as fluid, chaotic, and continually mobile; to insist that real living occurred in extraordinary moments of being in which time was conflated and all moments existed simultaneously. Such agreement in principle on these fundamental issues surely forges a strong intellectual link between the two.

### CHAPTER SIX

# James Joyce: Fiction as the Flux of Experience

Wyndham Lewis, James Joyce's contemporary, who devoted much of *Time and Western Man* to a discussion of Joyce's Bergsonian tendencies, concludes: "Mr. Joyce is very strictly of the school of Bergson-Einstein-Stein-Proust. He is of the great time-school they represent" (*Time*, 89). He says of Joyce's *Ulysses*, in particular, "I regard *Ulysses* as a *time-book*; and by that I mean that it lays emphasis upon ... the self-conscious time-sense, that has now been erected into a universal philosophy" (*Time*, 84). While Lewis's attack on Bergson is complex in origin, he is nonetheless accurate when he points out Joyce's affinity with Bergson's time theories. That Joyce knew Bergson's work first-hand is highly likely. Indeed, Richard Ellmann, commenting about the contents of Joyce's library, remarks, "He had a spotty but not unimpressive group of books on philosophy, including Aristotle, Marcus Aurelius, Bergson, Berkeley, Bruno, Hume, Nietzsche, Russell, Schopenhauer, Thomas Aquinas."[1] Ellmann also notes that *Creative Evolution* was on a list of books sent to Joyce by a bookseller in 1913–1914.[2] Joyce himself makes two references to Bergson in his work. The first is in the notes to the play *Exiles*, where Joyce comments that "all Celtic philosophers seemed to have inclined towards incertitude or skepticism – Hume, Berkeley, Balfour, Bergson" (*Exiles*, 174). The second comes from *Finnegans Wake* where, as Dominic Manganiello points out, Joyce uses his narrator's attack on Professor Jones to rebut Lewis's attacks on Bergson.[3] Jones's speech is worth quoting at length:

So you think I have impulsivism? Did they tell you I am one of the fortysixths? And I suppose you heard I had a wag on my ears? And I suppose they told you too that my roll of life is not natural? But before proceeding to conclusively confute this begging question it would be far fitter for you, if

you dare! to hasitate to consult with and consequentially attempt at my dis-
posale of the same dime-cash problem elsewhere naturistically of course,
from the blinkpoint of so eminent a spatialist. From it you will here notice,
Schott, upon my for the first remarking you that the sophology of Bitchison
while driven as under by a purely dime-dime urge is not without his cashcash characktericksticks, borrowed for its nonce ends from the fiery good-
mother Miss Fortune (who the lost time we had the pleasure we have had our
little *recherché* brush with, what, Schott?) and as I further could have told you
as brisk as your D.B.C. behaviouristically *pailleté* with a coat of homoid icing
which is reality only a done by chance ridiculastion of the whoo-whoo and
where's hairs theorics of Winestain. (149)

Jones's derision of Bitchison's (Bergson's) time theory as "a dime-
dime urge [which] is not without his cashcash characktericksticks"
echoes many of Lewis's charges from *Time and Western Man*, most no-
ticeably Lewis's contention that "this psychological time, or duration,
this mood that is as fixed as the matter accompanying it, is as romantic and picturesque as is 'local colour' and usually as shallow a thing
as that. Some realization of this is essential. *We can posit a time-district,
as it were, just as much as we can a place with its individual properties*"
[author's italics] (*Time*, 101).[4] But the Joycean context results in a privileging of Bergson and Einstein (Winestain) because the pervasive
irony suggests that Jones is wrong in his attack. Jones, the "eminent
spatialist," attacks Bitchison because his philosophy is popular – "not
without its cashcash charackterterickstick" – but this only underscores
the opportunism of Jones's attack, making it ironic that Jones seeks
his own fame on the back of Bitchison. The more derisive the comment – Bitchison's philosophy is "sophology" – the greater the underlying irony and the stronger the vote of confidence in Bergson and
Einstein.

Many commentators have followed Lewis's lead and examined
Joyce's Bergsonian notions of time. W.Y. Tindall, in one of the more
perceptive early analyses of Joyce and Bergson, writes: "Like Bergson
and Proust in this one respect, Joyce found the absolute in time and
thereby reconciled it with eternity. He found eternity in the historical
pattern, the family, and man. Above all these, he found eternity in
art."[5] Other early, major studies of the 1950s noted Joyce's Bergsonian
sense of time as well. While Hans Meyerhoff and A.A. Mendilow discussed Bergson in relation to time and literature, Melvin Friedman
dealt more extensively with Bergson's impact on the development of
the stream of conscious novel.[6] And as noted earlier, in the 1960s Shiv
Kumar dealt with Joyce and Bergson, in his *Bergson and the Stream of
Consciousness Novel*, though Kumar characteristically retreated from

asserting a strong link between the two. Indeed, Kumar writes, "Although Joyce, unlike Virginia Woolf, was directly acquainted with Bergson's thought, it does not necessarily imply that his literary experiments show the influence of the philosopher's theories" (S. Kumar, 106).[7] Margaret Church's *Time and Reality: Studies in Contemporary Fiction* provides perhaps the most thorough discussion of Joyce and Bergson published to date. She concludes: "In a final evaluation of the influence on Joyce's sense of time, one may see, as the titles imply, *A Portrait of the Artist as a Young Man* as chiefly Bergsonian, *Ulysses* as chiefly Jungian, and *Finnegans Wake* as chiefly Viconian" (Church, 65). Bergson's theories remain evident in later works, however, as Church herself notes when she says: "But Bergson's influence is still apparent in *Finnegans Wake* in the stream-of-consciousness technique and in the recognition of the existence within the individual of his own past" (Church, 63).[8] What discussions there are of Joyce and Bergson have focused almost exclusively, then, on temporal issues. In this chapter, although I, too, comment on Joyce's temporality and Bergson's *durée*, I will also trace other Bergsonian elements – memory, theories of self, and intuition.

### TIME, SELF, MEMORY

Like Virginia Woolf, Joyce's fundamental orientation was temporal and, like Woolf, Joyce's central interest was to devise a narrative that would reflect the primacy of time over space. Although Joyce's variation on stream-of-consciousness fiction achieves this goal, it was, as with Woolf, his early experiments that laid the foundation for *Ulysses* – so aptly described by Lewis as a *"time-book."* Unlike Woolf, who was preoccupied with the opposition of *durée* and *l'étendu*, Joyce's interest in time centres around the exploration of character and how to represent life's fluid inner world. Witness Shiv Kumar, who, though timid in his treatment of Joyce's relationship with Bergson (refusing to state Joyce's debt directly), does understand that Joyce's borrowings from Bergson are central to the development of his unique treatment of characters in fiction. Kumar writes: "The development of James Joyce as an artist can be understood in terms of his increasing awareness of the free creative evolution of personality unimpeded by any utilitarian interests. His preoccupation, therefore, with tides, waves and river-flow, suggested in pictorial or auditory images, is Bergsonian in character" (S. Kumar, 107–8). Kumar continues: "In presenting life as a stream 'never the same', and personality as a process of dynamic blending of physic states, Joyce comes nearest to the Bergsonian flux" (108). Two Bergsonian ideas are prominent here: the notion of *durée*, and the allied notion of self. Joyce's fictional worlds are very much based in *durée*, because his primary focus is the inner world, and the main subject in his work is the self and its evolution and changes. Bergson's concept of the self, however, is based on viewing *durée* as "real" time; his sense of self is inextricably bound up with the other major points of his philosophy, self being best understood in relation to them.

As we have seen, Bergson said that the *élan vital* pushes both body and mind together toward adaptations; that the self consists of many layers that all interpenetrate and are also the whole self at any one time; and that intuition allows us to know both ourselves and other things much more fully than intellect – it "pierces the darkness of the night in which the intellect leaves us" (*CE*, 282). Bergson says, too, that our view of self reveals an essential split between inner and outer worlds. He divides his inner world into two further categories: the outer, social self – which he perceives as "a crust solidified on the surface" – and the inner self – which, he says, exists below the crust of the social self. Bergson claims that the social self, although useful for our interaction with others, is no longer vital because it has solidified. Rather it is the vitality of the inner self – indefinable and seldom known because of its states that continually evolve and merge with each other – that forms our total self. Such a constantly changing, constantly growing self resembles Joyce's own fictional portraits and is, in addition to time, one of Joyce's three principle Bergsonian inheritances. The third legacy involves the way in which Joyce uses memory to provide a narrative structure for his novels, a structure that relies on "epiphanies" for its form.

Joyce's epiphanies have been the subject of much debate, but perhaps the best place to go for a definition of Joyce's meaning of the term is *Stephen Hero*, where he has Stephen define it for us. Stephen is out walking with Cranly when he undergoes an experience that he calls an epiphany; he tells Cranly what he means by the term: "By an epiphany he meant a sudden spiritual manifestation, whether in the vulgarity of speech or of gesture or in a memorable phase of the mind itself. He believed that it was for the man of letters to record these epiphanies with extreme care, seeing that they themselves are the most delicate and evanescent of moments" (*Hero*, 188). Church comments that for Stephen "epiphany is a moment of heightened awareness in which time rather than being rejected is seen subjectively in terms of his own relation to it" (Church, 35).[9] This is precisely what Bergson has in mind when he discusses immersion in *durée*.

Morris Beja, in *Epiphanies in the Modern Novel*, provides a comprehensive study of the different manifestations of Joyce's epiphanies.

He analyses Stephen's definition and places Joyce within a tradition of using such moments, but he also shows how Joyce goes beyond the bounds of this tradition. He examines Joyce's manuscripts and notebooks for the original epiphanies, discussing how they translate to the novels and stories themselves. Neither Beja's work nor that of others will be duplicated here; instead, the discussion follows a line that Beja mentions but never pursues. Beja wrote: "A more imperfect, elusive, and also more significant revelation through 'a memorable phase of the mind' is the one that arises from memory. There are in Joyce several hints of recaptures of the past" (Beja, 76–7). Beja is reluctant to pursue this thought, however, perhaps because he believes that such moments are uncommon and that other forms of epiphanies are more numerous and thus more deserving of discussion. Instead he pursues what he calls "retrospective epiphanies," those occasions when "an event arouses no special impression when it occurs, but produces a sudden sensation of new awareness when it is recalled at some future time" (Beja, 15).

Both epiphanies, however, are similar in their dependence on memory. In Bergsonian memory, the recollection of the past moment illuminates both the previous experience from which it comes and the present experience that prompted the recollection in the first place. Joyce's epiphanies depend on just such a faculty of memory. Epiphanies occupy the same role as Woolf's moments of being because Joyce, like Woolf, centres his work around them. Starting with *Dubliners*, in which short stories present individual epiphanies, and culminating in *Ulysses*, in which the entire novel revolves around a few central epiphanies, Joyce challenges conventional prose forms by dispensing with the usual narrative structures and replacing them with an inner world.

Having laid out the grounds upon which Bergson and Joyce meet – time, self, memory (epiphany) – it is time to examine Joyce's work for these three elements. Again like Woolf, Joyce experimented extensively in his first few works, trying to discover the form that best suited his needs. Like Woolf, and most other modern writers, Joyce was fundamentally concerned with the question of representation and the subject-object split in art. Unlike Woolf, Joyce seems to have worked with a consistent underlying idea about what he wanted his work to say about both these issues. Rather than simply discovering the answers to his aesthetic problems in the process of his writing, he uses his early works as preliminary sketches for *Ulysses*; there he brings together the ideas and forms that he had refined and polished in *Dubliners*, *Stephen Hero*, and *A Portrait of the Artist as a Young Man*. However, the experiments of the early work are interesting for themselves, as well as for what they tell us about *Ulysses*.

DUBLINERS

The collection of fifteen stories that make up *Dubliners* is important because they are all constructed around central epiphanies. Each presents epiphanies in the lives of ordinary Dubliners, showing how each life is filled with extraordinary moments and also commenting on how such moments may encapsulate and define the lives of the individuals who experience them. Although the stories vary in form and in the way they depict their central epiphany, they all involve a significant "showing forth" of an individual. The central Bergsonian element in these epiphanies is memory. Three of the fifteen stories – "A Little Cloud," "A Painful Case," and "The Dead" – make extended use of memory to create epiphanies. In these three, a Bergsonian-like involuntary memory brings about a sudden insight into life, thereby prompting the main characters to change their manner of life or to see themselves anew.

In "A Little Cloud," Little Chandler's past and future, embodied in the form of his old friend Gallaher and his baby son, assault his present world. Gallaher represents part of Chandler's past, inasmuch as they share many memories of student life (as is revealed over their whiskies at Corlesse's). He also represents the path that Chandler did not take, a future life passed up in favour of his present dreary existence. Chandler has a steady, if dull, job; a home; a wife; and a child. But the dreams of his youth remain unfulfilled. Compared to Gallaher's more glamorous life as an international journalist, Chandler finds his life inadequate. As Chandler attempts to recover part of his past by reading Byron, the baby's crying brings him out of the past into what he sees as the unpalatable present. His emotions spill out uncontrollably: "It was useless. He couldn't read. He couldn't do anything. The wailing of the child pierced the drum of his ear. It was useless, useless! He was a prisoner for life. His arms trembled with anger and suddenly bending to the child's face he shouted: 'Stop!'" (*Dubliners*, 84). This vehement reaction is out of proportion to the provocation; Chandler is screaming not at his son, but at his own longings for a life that can never be. His past is bathed in a golden glow, especially now that he realizes how unhappy he is. His epiphany is very painful and depressing.

"A Painful Case" employs memory in a number of different ways. For example, it is used for straightforward narration: over the course of a few pages, Mr Duffy's life is revealed – his habits, career, education, and personality. The story's central moment is set up by an incident that involves Duffy's recollection of events that had presumably been safely consigned to the past. Some months after the termination of an affair with Mrs Sinico, ended when she expressed a desire to move on to the physical level, Duffy comes across a paragraph in the newspaper relating the circumstances of her death. The article upsets him and initiates a prolonged reflection about her conduct and their relationship. The more Duffy thinks, the more he becomes buried in the past and the more distraught he becomes: "As the light failed and his memory began to wander he thought her hand touched his. The shock which had first attacked his stomach was now attacking his nerves" (*Dubliners*, 116). Leaving the restaurant, Duffy wanders aimlessly, his memories prompting him to re-evaluate his life and actions. He finally realizes that his life has been empty and futile and that she was the only thing to have brought him joy. In Duffy's despair, he felt "that he was alone" (*Dubliners*, 117). The images of past life provoked by the article prompt the recall of vivid, harsh emotions and cause a re-assessment of his life; the moment therefore becomes a significant epiphany. It is an epiphany dependent on memory. The chance nature of these devastating recollections mirrors Joyce's assertion about the nature of the epiphany – "a sudden spiritual manifestation" – for, despite Duffy's attempt to ignore or forestall the consequences of the memories, they take over his present life in much the same way that Bergson says recollection does. Duffy's recollections of Mrs Sinico are also tempered by the circumstances surrounding them; his feelings of guilt over her death result in a distorted memory of their relationship, one based on his fear that his actions led to her apparent suicide. The complexity of his epiphany and the resultant impact on his life thus depend on having a memory that functions in precisely the way that Bergson's involuntary memory does.

"The Dead" is the longest, most complex, and most critically acclaimed story in the collection. It contains many elements that Joyce was later to use in more extended works, as well as a very good example of a memory-based central moment. This important epiphany occurs after the evening's entertainment, when Gabriel and Gretta have retired to their hotel room. Gabriel, flushed by the success of the party, is in an expansive mood; Gretta, in contrast, is quiet and withdrawn. She finally explains the reason for her mood, thereby undergoing a moment of such emotional distress that Gabriel is startled out of his complacency into self-reflection. Gretta's is the original epiphany: she has heard a familiar song that has revived the memory of her first love, Michael Fury, who died, she believes, because of his great love for her. This recollection affects her deeply and in turn prompts her husband, Gabriel, to examine his own past and present in order to see if he is capable of such great love for another. His conclusion, "He had never felt like that himself towards any woman, but he knew that such a feeling must be love" (*Dubliners*, 223), leads him to think about how he might reorder his own life so that he, too, might experience love. Gretta's epiphany causes Gabriel to experience one that then helps him to determine a future course. Although this is a Proustian method of recollection – a recollection brought to present life prompts another that then alters future life – it is also Bergsonian, because it shows how memory impinges on present life and is, in turn, altered by this relationship. Even if Michael Fury's death was not caused by his trip to Gretta's home during a storm, Gretta, possibly disappointed in her marriage to Gabriel because it lacks the great passion she thought love entailed, chooses to explain Michael's death as a result of his love for her. The events of the past assume a significance that may in fact be distorted but they, in turn, prompt both Gretta and Gabriel to reassess their present lives. Joyce uses this type of moment repeatedly throughout later works.

### STEPHEN HERO

*Stephen Hero*, or the remaining fragments of it, contains important statements about art and the creation of art that hint at what Joyce was to attempt in later novels; moreover, as stated earlier, this work contains Joyce's definition of the epiphany. One also finds two epiphanies using memory to create important moments that prefigure his later use of this technique; the second epiphany also serves to introduce one of his important comments about aesthetics.

The first, very brief epiphany occurs at Isabel's death. Stephen, brought face to face with her mortality, remembers her short life and reflects that she really had never lived. He thinks that "the spirit that dwelt therein had literally never dared to live and had not learned anything by an abstention which it had not willed for itself" (*Hero*, 149). Stephen goes through the mourning process mechanically, becoming increasingly aware of the hypocrisy of those who mourn the death of someone they neither knew nor loved. His reflection on her past life allows him to see the mindlessness of following tradition for its own sake. This crystallizes his intention to leave Dublin. The second epiphany immediately precedes the definition of the term. As Stephen thinks about the epiphany, he recalls his first such experience. It was during a walk in Eccles Street when "a trivial incident set him composing some ardent verses which he entitled a 'Vilanelle of the Temptress'" (*Hero*, 188). The incident – he overhears a conversation between a young man and a woman – causes him to recall his feelings for Emma Clery, which prompts him, in turn, to reflect about this and what it reveals about himself. The key to the insights that

Stephen gains from both epiphanies is memory, because memory provokes them, extends contemplation of the past into the present, and provides a store from which Stephen may draw his ideas.

After this second epiphany, Stephen outlines to Cranly the constituents of his aesthetic theory, the highest level of which is revealed by an epiphany: "First we recognize that the object is *one* integral thing, then we recognize that it is an organized composite structure, a *thing* in fact: finally, when the relation of the parts is exquisite, when the parts are adjusted to the special point, we recognize that it is *that* thing which it is" (*Hero*, 190). Memory thus has a role in the discovery of the "thingness" of objects or states of mind, because it pieces together all the observations and perceptions concerning the thing in question. Bergsonian intuition is evidently an important part of this aesthetic. Implicit in Stephen's statement is the idea that the process involved in recognizing the thingness of other objects (and presumably people or events) requires a discarding of traditional approaches to art, particularly the dominant spatial mode of perception and representation. By recognizing that the significance of the object derives from understanding the internal relations of the various parts of the object, one can realize that the external shell holding these parts in a static, spatial arrangement reveals little of importance for any "real" knowledge of the object. Entering into the object to discover its thingness means discerning its essence, which in turn means experiencing it on a temporal as well as a spatial level, for the parts are constantly changing in relation to the other parts with which they are compared or contrasted. This aesthetic is similar to the affective one implicit in Woolf's work, where the onus is placed on the perceiver to recreate the essence of the art object. It is also similar to Bergsonian aesthetics, in its insistence that the importance of art is found in the essence of the object, and in its privileging of the process of creation and recreation over the finished art work. While *Stephen Hero* itself does not demonstrate these aesthetic principles, it does present a clear statement of those that Joyce will employ in his subsequent works.

### A PORTRAIT OF THE ARTIST AS A YOUNG MAN

In *A Portrait of the Artist as a Young Man*, Joyce makes his first fullfledged attack on the conventional novel. His main deviations involve the narrative structure of the work, which is essentially an assemblage of several epiphanies, and the characterization of Stephen Daedelus. Interestingly, Joyce chooses to attack the conventions of the novel from within one of its most traditional forms, the *Bildungsroman*. His own attempt, however, varies significantly from those of other writers such as Fielding (*Tom Jones*) or Dickens (*David Copperfield*). For example, no attempt is made in *Portrait* to provide the reader with a well-delineated, chronological account of Stephen's growth. Instead, one is thrust into various moments of his life, viewing Stephen and his world from his perspective: from babyhood, "Once upon a time and a very good time it was there was a moocow coming down along the road" (*Portrait*, 7); through to early adulthood, "Welcome, O life! I go to encounter for the millionth time the reality of experience and to forge in the smithy of my soul the uncreated conscience of my race" (*Portrait*, 252–3). Readers, immersed in the main character's *durée*, see Stephen's consciousness grow in front of them. Thus the outer world is understood only in terms of the inner one; reality becomes dependent upon understanding the inner world of self.

Joyce tears down the barrier between reader (subject) and Stephen (object) in two essential ways. First, at intervals throughout the novel, the reader enters directly into Stephen's world. Although Joyce prevents a complete immersion in Stephen's consciousness by retaining an intrusive narrator, he creates the illusion of an end to the split between object and subject by occasionally permitting a closer identification. An example of this is not hard to find. In chapter 3, for instance, Stephen is overwhelmed by his sense of sin:

The ache of conscience ceased and he walked onward swiftly through the dark streets. There were so many flagstones on the footpath of that street and so many streets in that city and so many cities in the world. Yet eternity had no end. He was in mortal sin. Even once was a mortal sin. It could happen in an instant. But how so quickly? By seeing or by thinking of seeing. The eyes see the thing, without having wished first to see. Then in an instant it happens. But does that part of the body understand or what? The serpent, the most subtle beast of the field. It must understand when it desires in one instant and then prolongs its own desire instant after instant, sinfully. It feels and understands and desires. What a horrible thing! Who made it to be like that, a bestial part of the body able to understand bestially and desire bestially? Was that then he or an inhuman thing moved by a lower soul than his soul? His soul sickened at the thought of a torpid snaky life feeding itself out of the tender marrow of his life and fattening upon the slime of lust. O why was that so? O why? (*Portrait*, 139–40)

The heightened emotions involved in his meditation on mortal sin are framed by the external narration – the "He was in mortal sin" and the "Was that then he or an inhuman thing" – with its tell-tale third person pronouns. But by the scene's mid-portion, the obtrusive "he" disappears, lending the passage the illusion of penetration into Stephen's mind. It is Stephen who knows that mortal sin "could happen in an instant"; he also knows it is "a horrible thing." This complex blending of direct narrative voice with a plunge into Stephen's mind is delicately balanced and very effective.

Second, Joyce wears away the barrier that exists between art as subject and art as object. The novel revolves around Stephen, the aspiring artist, and his attempts to come to terms with art. At the same time, *Portrait* embodies the principles being discussed by Stephen with the other characters in the book, so that Joyce's novel is in fact the one we expect Stephen to write someday. Art is thus double-layered here, with Joyce becoming like his creation and Stephen becoming like his creator. Indeed, it is usual for critics to dwell on the biographical significance of this conflation of novelist and character. Here Joyce was working out his fundamental concern that art be as close an approximation of "real" (inner) life as it could be; he was using his own inner life as a model because that was the only one he had.

Stephen describes the process necessary to turn life into art. While discussing Aquinas with Cranly, he uses the opportunity to lay out his aesthetic theory. Although the lengthy speech will not be quoted in full here, some brief excerpts are important. First, Stephen describes how we know a thing:

In order to see that basket, said Stephen, your mind first of all separates the basket from the rest of the visible universe which is not the basket. The first phase of apprehension is a bounding line drawn about the object to be apprehended. An esthetic image is presented to us either in space or in time. What is audible is presented in time, what is visible is presented in space. But, temporal or spatial, the esthetic image is first luminously apprehended as self-bounded and selfcontained upon the immeasurable background of space or time which it is not. You apprehend it as *one* thing. You see it as one whole. You apprehend its wholeness, That is *integritas*. (*Portrait*, 212)

Then he talks about "the instant wherein that supreme quality of beauty, the clear radiance of the esthetic image, is apprehended luminously by the mind which has been arrested by its wholeness and fascinated by its harmony [this] is the luminous silent stasis of esthetic pleasure" (*Portrait*, 213). He concludes that he has been talking about

beauty in a wider sense of the word, in the sense which the word has in the literary tradition ... When we speak of beauty in [this] sense of the term our judgement is influenced in the first place by the art itself and by the form of that art. The image, it is clear, must be set between the mind or senses of the artist himself and the mind or senses of others. If you bear this in memory you will see that art necessarily divides itself into three forms progressing from one to the next. These forms are: the lyrical form, the form wherein the artist presents his image in immediate relation to himself; the epical form, the form wherein he presents his image in mediate relation to himself and others; the dramatic form, the form wherein he presents the image in immediate relation to others. (*Portrait*, 213–4)

The Bergsonian echoes are resounding: the "thingness" of an object is discovered by intuitive interaction with the object itself, and the recreation of the object results in an aesthetic awareness of its beauty. Stephen's outline of artistic beauty encapsulates the process involved in Bergson's aesthetic – each of these stages is involved in Bergson's aesthetic experience – while Stephen implies that mature artists need to go through each stage in order to produce truly beautiful art. In other words, dramatic art is the culmination of the artists' apprenticeship, because this is where they can give their art over to their audience so that the viewer may join them in its essence. Joyce's work reflects the progression that Stephen outlines here, leading one to assume that Stephen's statement about art expresses Joyce's views. Although Aquinas, Shelley, and others are also factors, Bergson should not be overlooked as a source for Joyce's aesthetic ideas. At this stage, however, Joyce, just like his characters, does not use his intuitive abilities to enter into and then recreate the worlds of objects and persons around himself. This results in the single focus on Stephen. It also results in the novel's unity being developed mainly from a collection of disparate epiphanies.

The novel dispenses with a formal time scheme in favour of putting together important moments in Stephen's life. Few external events intrude on his world, although there are glimpses of Stephen's traditional childhood and youth that reinforce the inner portrait presented without assuming centre stage. However, this external world becomes unimportant compared to the flow of his inner life, his *durée*. The moments that constitute the novel's actions are epiphanies; the most vivid moments are those in which a significant growth in Stephen's personality occurs because he is able to understand the importance of the epiphany he is experiencing and is capable of putting the new knowledge to work in his process of self-delineation. Stephen's most important epiphanies are moments of catharsis; they include his confession at the end of chapter 3, his reawakening to life prompted by the bird-girl scene of chapter 4, and his departure from Dublin at the novel's end. The bird-girl episode is particularly vivid:

A girl stood before him in midstream, alone and still, gazing out to sea. She seemed like one whom magic had changed into the likeness of a strange and beautiful sea bird. Her long slender bare legs were delicate as a crane's and pure save where as emerald trail of seaweed had fashioned itself as a sign upon the flesh. Her thighs, fuller and softhued as ivory, were bared almost to the hip where the white fringes of her drawers were like featherings of soft white down. Her slateblue skirts were kilted boldly about her waist and dovetailed behind her. Her bosom was as a bird's soft and slight, slight and soft as the breast of some darkplumaged dove. But her long fair hair was girlish: and girlish, and touched with the wonder of mortal beauty, her face.

She was alone and still, gazing out to sea; and when she felt his presence and the worship of his eyes her eyes turned to him in quiet sufferance of his gaze, without shame or wantonness. Long, long she suffered his gaze and then quietly withdrew her eyes from his and bent them towards the stream, gently stirring the water with her foot hither and thither. The first faint noise of gently moving water broke the silence, low and faint and whispering, faint as the bells of sleep; hither and thither, hither and thither: and a faint flame trembled on her cheek. (*Portrait*, 171)

How much time elapses in this moment is uncertain; the external world ceases to exist for Stephen and all that matters is the moment in which he savours the girl's blend of innocence and sensuality. It is only some time later, after he leaves the girl and wanders aimlessly away, that he becomes aware of the external world again: "He halted suddenly and heard his heart in the silence. How far had he walked? What was the hour?" (*Portrait*, 172). The encounter is a pivotal moment. The girl symbolizes life – both immediate life because of her youth, sensuality, and vibrance; and life in an abstract sense because she is immersed in water, the universal symbol of life, and, as woman, she is the bearer of life. By metaphorically embracing her and absorbing her life as his, Stephen embraces life.

As if to underscore the Bergsonian nature of these moments, Joyce surrounds them and even permeates them with Bergsonian images. Bergson's works are filled with references to the "stream of life" and the flow of existence. The dominant metaphors in his rhetoric are streams, rivers, oceans – images that convey simultaneously the continuity and novelty of life. Although Joyce certainly has many models for this imagery, Bergson's writings are one likely source. Joyce uses these images extensively: Stephen's confession occurs in a church reached by a long walk through the twisting, narrow streets of Dublin; the bird-girl stands thigh deep in the ocean, the water lapping around her raised skirts; and Stephen decides to leave Dublin after a series of walks through the city. The teeming streets of Dublin's poorer quarters are symbolic representations of the stream of life: their depiction of various types of life and their winding, often haphazard directions, provide a perfect image for Stephen's uncertainty. Many descriptions indicate how Joyce uses the streets to make life tangible. For example: "Consciousness of place came ebbing back to him slowly over a vast tract of time unlit, unfelt, unlived. The squalid scene composed itself around him; the common accents, the burning gasjets in the shops, odours of fish and spirits and wet sawdust, moving men and women. An old women was about to cross the street, an oilcan in her hand. He bent down and asked her was there a chapel near" (*Portrait*, 141). The vivid squalor mirrors Stephen's spiritual state. The river and the ocean are powerful symbols, too, of incessant change in the midst of permanence. The bird-girl standing in the ocean welcomes Stephen back into the secular world by reviving his sensual instincts and by also symbolizing the interpenetration of the present moment (the actual instant of Stephen watching the girl) and the whole of time (the ocean symbolic of past and future time.) As all of the action in the novel centres around Stephen's growth, so all the epiphanies must reflect his immediate concerns and his growth process.

Loosely linking episodes in Stephen's life through shared imagery provides a bare narrative structure that gives the novel a sense of unity and coherence. But the main source of unity arises not from imagery, but from the continuity of Stephen's character. Stephen's nature is revealed from the reader's privileged position inside his inner world. Using epiphanies to reveal that inner world, and limiting the novel's focus to this world alone, allows Joyce to break down the barrier between subject and object in the novel. He also makes great strides in developing a mode of representation that expresses his own view of the world. However, *A Portrait* did not completely satisfy Joyce, who wanted to demonstrate even more fully and clearly that representation, in whatever form it assumes, is a matter of intuitively understanding the things one wishes to represent and then finding a way of conveying this understanding. Nor did it fully illustrate Joyce's belief that no single form of representation can incorporate the totality of the object under scrutiny. Many means of representing the same intuitive experience, says Joyce, should be combined to capture and display adequately the "thing" he identifies as the essence of art and which he said was the goal to which artists, like his own Stephen Daedelus, should aspire. The more readers experience this thing, says Joyce, the more they will appreciate and understand its elements. As Bergson would argue, this process of discovery leads to a better understanding of a thing's "uniqueness" and "inexpressible qualities."

## ULYSSES

One important element in *Ulysses* – that complex modern novel that is a consciously fashioned and meticulously wrought manipulation of every aspect of fiction – is Joyce's experimentation with time. *Ulysses* recounts one day in the life of Dubliners: Leopold and Molly Bloom and Stephen Dedalus; this is the novel's overt time, its *l'étendu*. The actual novel engenders a sense of universal time by ranging through many different eras and places, times belonging specifically to the characters themselves – it is the totality of their experiences – and universal and historical times belonging to them by virtue of the fact that they are alive on this day in history and are able to share in a cultural heritage. This time is the characters' *durée*. The past, present, and future of each of the characters exist in the one day.

The tension between clock time and inner time provides the framework for the novel: the clock time gives overt structure to Stephen's and Bloom's wanderings; inner time provides the novel's substance, its psychological portraits. The representation of *durée* gradually attains prominence and reaches its most forceful expression in the novel's final episode, the Molly Bloom soliloquy in "Penelope." Here Molly's mind ranges over various moments in her life. Echoes of all her choices in life are heard in the resounding "Yes" with which the episode ends, making the one moment her entire lifetime.

These Bergsonian time elements are emphasized by Joyce's images of streams, rivers, and oceans, which convey the incessant passage of individual life within the permanence of the natural world. The streets of Dublin, as well, provide a wonderful image of the impermanence of human life in contrast to the permanence of physical surroundings. The "Lotus-Eaters," for example, starts with a descriptive account of Bloom's wanderings: "By lorries along sir John Rogerson's Quay Mr Bloom walked soberly, past Windmill lane, Leask's the linseed crusher's, the postal telegraph office. Could have given that address too. And past the sailor's home. He turned from the morning noises of the quayside and walked through Lime street. By Brady's cottages a boy for the skins lolled, his bucket of offal linked, smoking a chewed fagbutt" (*Ulysses*, 72). In this chapter, as well as in the rest of the novel, his route can easily be retraced, allowing the reader to move along the same streets as Bloom. Bloom's physical surroundings thus function as a permanent backdrop to the flux of time that encompasses the lives of Dubliners who come before and after Bloom.

The structure of the novel inevitably results in the widespread use of epiphanies. Stephen's walk on the beach, Bloom's journey through

Dublin's streets, their time in the brothel in the "Circe" episode, their talk in the cafe in "Eumaeus," and the memory-filled penultimate episode "Ithaca" (in which, even as he undresses, Bloom's mind attempts to reconcile past and present events in order to come to an understanding of the importance of the meeting with Stephen) – all are achieved partly through the use of memory-based epiphanies. The most important epiphany in the novel, and the purest example of what Joyce means by the term, belongs to Molly Bloom. Her soliloquy acts as a coda to the day's action, and as such is definitely in the present moment. Inasmuch as it is also a general reflection on her life, it recaptures the past. Bloom has just related an edited version of his activities for the day and, after making an ineffectual attempt at sexual intercourse, he settles down to sleep. His unusual request, to have breakfast brought to him in bed the next day, sparks off Molly's extended reflection on her life. She recalls their courtship on Gibraltar, their marriage, their life together, and her lovers; in fact, her mind ranges over her entire life. Each memory-image provokes another, which holds centre stage until it is replaced by another which it again has provoked. For example, the monologue starts with Molly musing about Bloom's odd request and then flows on to other memories:

Yes because he never did a thing like that before as ask to get his breakfast in bed with a couple of eggs since the *City Arms* hotel when he used to be pretending to be laid up with a sick voice doing his highness to make himself interesting to that old faggot Mrs Riordan that he thought he had a great leg of and she never left us a farthing all for masses for herself and her soul greatest miser ever was actually afraid to lay out 4d for her methylated spirit telling me all her ailments she had too much old chat in her about politics and earthquakes and the end of the world let us have a bit of fun first God help the world if all women were her sort down on bathingsuits and lownecks of course nobody wanted her to wear I suppose she was pious because no man would look at her twice I hope Ill never be like her a wonder she didnt want us to cover our faces but she was a well educated women certainly. (*Ulysses*, 659)

The immediate past, her day, and Bloom's tale of his also find a place in her thoughts, thereby uniting the major moments of the day with those of the past. Her soliloquy performs a future role as well, suggesting to the readers what is likely to happen next in the lives of the three central characters. Stephen will leave Dublin again, Bloom will attempt to reform his life, and Molly will attempt to revive her career as a singer. Her resounding "Yes" may be interpreted as an affirmation of life because it follows the memory of a time when she started a new life, when Bloom proposed to her "and then he asked would I yes to say yes my mountain flower" (*Ulysses*, 704). Thus a recollection affects present and future life. The mixture of distant past, immediate past, present, and future depends upon memory for its coherence and unity. This soliloquy not only renders Molly's consciousness; it also demonstrates just how central involuntary memory is to the whole process of life.

Joyce employs a great variety of techniques to place the reader in the consciousness of the characters. By doing so, he hopes to give the fullest possible insight into each character. He also underscores the fact that different representations of the same characters or events may reveal different aspects of them. By presenting the inner worlds of Bloom, Molly, and Stephen as chaotic and constantly in flux, Joyce makes readers see them as similar to themselves; he anticipates, too, that readers will recognize the nature of their lives in the fictional ones. Joyce also forces the readers to see the world through the characters' eyes, by placing the readers within their *durée*. His shifting from character to character and from outside world to inner one, in a manner reminiscent of Bergson's intuition, allows the readers to know all the characters and to see their world in many different lights. Moreover, by presenting the characters from this wide variety of viewpoints, Joyce challenges the subject-object barrier. The readers do not simply follow Bloom as he wanders around Dublin on this day; they join him on his trip and in his experiences. Indeed, they become the readers' experiences because the readers not only need to recreate them to understand them, but also to relate the different versions of the events in order to reconstruct them.

One of the best examples of this is found in "Sirens," in which the actual association of every event in the interchange between Miss Douce and Miss Kennedy, although related to the seemingly random noises that initiate the section, is left to the reader. For example, the first sentence in the section is "Bronze by gold heard the hoofirons, steelyringing in Imperthnthnthnthnthn" (*Ulysses*, 254). Later this is fleshed out: "Bronze by gold, Miss Douce's head by Miss Kennedy's head, over the crossblind of the Ormond bar heard the viceregal hoofs go by, ringing steel" (*Ulysses*, 256). The first sentence does not make sense until related to the second. But relating one to the other gives a fuller sense of the fragmented experience that presents sensory impressions and the pattern imposed on them to render them intelligible. The absence of a central narrative voice further pushes the readers into the consciousnesses of the characters and various narrators, for only by entering into them may the readers make sense of the novel. In the end, readers create the consciousnesses of the novel because they control the characters through their acceptance or rejection of the various versions of the events. For example, although Gerry fantasizes about Bloom in the "Nausicaa" episode, it is also clear that she is correct about his interest in her, for the reader later discovers that the man she believes is attracted to her is in fact masturbating while she is watching him. This episode gives an insight into both the characters and the loneliness that assaults them equally, although for different reasons and in different ways. The variations of the consciousness and the process of piecing them and their stories together are thus central elements in the novel's structure.

The process by which each event of *Ulysses* is reconstructed and then related to other events demonstrates Joyce's central aesthetic principle. To find the "thingness" of an object, he says, one must understand it; and to understand it one needs to relate the various parts of the object to each other, before determining their relative significance and their significance to the object itself. It is not surprising that Joyce patterned this novel after one of the central myths of Western society, for he wanted to demonstrate that the storytelling process of novels is also central to the way in which we construct our reality. Human existence, he feels, is based on the ability to make order out of the chaos of experience, while life is a montage of random events and moments organized by humans in order to express the inexpressible. Novels, too, are like life: they mirror the process of living in their construction of a "reality" from events and characters created, developed, and related by the author in different ways. *Ulysses* shows that any series of events may be given a coherent shape in retrospect because, in seeking order, we relate events or things to each other, encoding them in an organized fashion. Myth is then like life, not simply in the mimetic sense of art mimicking life, but in a more profound sense; indeed, Joyce's free play with narrative conventions reveals that while living is chaotic, representing living is less chaotic, because we inevitably fit our experiences into preexisting patterns. *Ulysses* is patterned, as is perhaps all life, implies Joyce, on a variation of Homer's ancient myth in which the aged warrior returns to his faithful wife and loyal son. The journey to home and renewed awareness of self is long and arduous; Bloom, like Odysseus, undergoes many adventures, still incomplete by the end of the story. Joyce adapts the myth to contemporary conditions and to his less idealistic view of the world: Bloom, his Odysseus, is far from the Homeric ideal and his Penelope, Molly, is equally distanced from the virtuous woman who spins her tapestry and waits for her husband's return. Joyce's characteristic twentieth-century irony works throughout the novel to subvert its mythic structure. Nevertheless, his placing of this portrait of modern society in a form that inevitably brings into play the nature of myth, and specifically the Ulysses myth, invites readers to see Joyce's novel as a contribution to the ongoing life of this ancient story as well as the process of creation. Adaptation renews old stories or myths, extending their life and their cultural significance. Joyce's adaptation of the Ulysses myth links his age with all previous ages and ensures a continuity of time as well as consciousness. In so doing, Joyce creates in this long novel one extended, time-filled moment that captures the essence of human consciousness. All humankind, all time, become players in *Ulysses*, with the novel itself fulfilling Bergson's vision of reality, with its representation of individual moments in a life and its representative of *durée* that holds within it all life and all experiences.

Joyce's masterpiece is indeed the "time-book" which Wyndham Lewis calls it, but it is a far different book than Lewis thought it was. The time which Lewis believed that Joyce, and Bergson, advocated was relativistic – one in which only the present moment counted and one in which the moral and ethical values were noticeable by their absence. But this is a falsification of Bergson's theory and Joyce's writings. Joyce's novel is permeated by the ethics and morality not only of Homer's age but of all ages, inasmuch as his vision of a relative time means that the values, ethics, morals, religions, and social structures of these times are relative too. All these things, and, from all ages, are in the background of Bloom's society; all of them are implicitly compared to their counterparts in Bloom's world. Because Joyce preferred to have his readers draw their own comparisons, this aspect of *Ulysses* is less prominent than it might be; thus readers like Lewis may miss it entirely. *Ulysses* reflects Joyce's command of the aesthetic he wanted to create when he gave his definition of aesthetics in *Stephen Hero*: readers only see a novel as a thing when they appreciate its aspects and their intricate interrelationships. Also, the novel illustrates the representational methods Joyce developed to convey his sense of reality, the variety of forms employed indicating the underlying sense that there is no one form of reality and that all forms contribute to an organized vision of the chaos of life. Although Joyce's debts to Bergson are evident in this novel, they are subtle as well; not only has he assimilated the aspects of Bergson's thought that help him to make sense of the world and of his art, he has been able to use previous works to refine those aspects. Joyce borrowed much from Bergson – not just his notion of the relativity of all times. To overlook that debt is to deny a rich source of additional insights into Joyce's works and their underlying aesthetic and cultural significance.

### CHAPTER SEVEN

# Dorothy Richardson: The Subjective Experience of Time

Although Dorothy Richardson has attracted more attention in the last ten years, particularly from feminist critics as they question and re-draw literary boundaries,[1] Robert Humphrey's description of Richardson's position in modern literature is in many senses still accurate: "Unlike most originators of artistic genres, the twentieth-century pioneer in stream-of-consciousness remains the least well known of the important stream-of-consciousness writers" (Humphrey, 9). Another of Richardson's biographers makes this same point, when he says that she "changed the course of the modern novel, only to become one of the great unread" (Rosenberg, 1).

One of the major reasons cited for her low profile is the nature of her work. *Pilgrimage* is often seen as an unwieldy and formless novel, little more than a loosely "fictionalized" account of Richardson's life. W.Y. Tindall's comments on the lengthy novel illustrate this common critical position: "Held together only by the continuity of person, such as it is, *Pilgrimage* falls into separate fragments. Plot and action have virtually disappeared, character has lost its elegance of shape, and personality has been all but replaced by a series of reactions; for the interest is no longer centered upon what occurs without, but upon what flows within" (Tyndall, 195). Virginia Woolf's assessment of Richardson illustrates a second, often voiced criticism. When Woolf first began to think about writing her "unwritten novel" in a new style, she remarked "I suppose the danger is the damned egotistical self; which ruins Joyce & [Dorothy] Richardson to my mind: is one pliant & rich enough to provide a wall for the book from oneself without its becoming, as in Joyce & Richardson, narrowing & restricting?" (*Diary* 2, 14). Yet this sort of commentary fails to see, or chooses to ignore, the real contribution that Richardson made to experiments with the novel. Long before Woolf wrote *Jacob's Room* and a few months before Joyce published *Portrait*, Richardson published *Pointed Roofs*, the first volume of the very experimental and innovative *Pilgrimage*. Like Woolf and Joyce, Richardson was fundamentally concerned with the issues of representation and the subject-object split; like them, her work seeks to resolve these problems while at the same time developing a new way of reflecting her vision of art and the world from which she drew her inspiration.

Richardson shares common ground with Woolf and Joyce in her appropriation of Bergsonian ideas. Although Thomas F. Staley, one of her biographers, states in a letter to a graduate student (Shiv Kumar) that Richardson denied ever having read any of Bergson's works (Staley, 35),[2] this does not mean that she was unaware of his philosophy. Richardson was very interested in philosophy; part of her time in the British Museum Reading Room was spent investigating past and present philosophical works. She also attended many series of philosophical lectures, including those given by McTaggart. It seems likely that in the course of her studies she would have come across Bergsonian ideas, even if they were not presented as such. The real indication of Richardson's share in the Bergsonian heritage is found in those issues central to her own writing. Richardson practises stream-of-consciousness and is interested in breaking down conventional narrative structures and replacing them with what she sees as the flow of her character's life. This involves devising a new fictional form that might accommodate the radically different time of the inner world, new methods of characterization, and a new narrative structure that would lend the various incidents of the inner world shape and unity. The way that Richardson goes about addressing these issues links her to Woolf and Joyce, but it also permits her to develop her own brand of stream-of-consciousness.

In her review of the fourth volume of *Pilgrimage*, Woolf wrote: "The reader is not provided with a story; he is invited to embed himself in Miriam Henderson's consciousness" (*Times Lit. Sup.*, 1). She correctly hits upon a central element of Richardson's work here. Richardson was less concerned with the external world than she was with the inner one, and this results in the sacrifice of a neat, chronological plot line to the rather more chaotic story of the growth of consciousness. To tell this story adequately, Richardson had to draw the reader into the world of her central character Miriam Henderson. This meant abandoning the world of *l'étendu* and entering the world of *durée*. Her method is well described by A.A. Mendilow, who says that she enters into time "in depth, vertically, by sinking a deep and narrow shaft into the present moment of feeling and sensation, the moment contains within itself the whole of the past" (Mendilow, 84). Writing in this manner, Richardson abandons many of the eighteenth- and nineteenth-century novelists' techniques. She does not structure the novel around significant events in Miriam Henderson's external life, for society is less important than Miriam's inner life. All sorts of events from Miriam's daily life are presented, but they are all meant to serve as a springboard into the inner life. Miriam's growth is not portrayed in logical or progressive terms – she simply evolves in an apparently haphazard manner. A chronology of sorts does hold the disparate adventures together, but this chronology is simply the skeleton of Miriam's world and does little to define her actual nature. While the Miriam who is part of the external world leaves home, finds employment first as a teacher then as a dental assistant, and then becomes a writer, the "real" Miriam is undergoing such growth and change internally that the actions in the social world pale in comparison to those of her inner world. When Woolf praised Richardson for embedding the reader in Miriam's consciousness, she was also praising Richardson's handling of the novel's two narrative times. In effect, Richardson places the reader within *durée*, while at the same time using the more conventional external time to form the novel's framework. The thirteen volumes of *Pilgrimage* include the events of ten years in Miriam's life; these events, by creating a showcase for Miriam's inner world, provide unity in the novel. As a result *Pilgrimage* combines the two worlds in a plausible and powerful portrait of Richardson's vision of "reality." Exactly how Richardson combines the two times and generates from this her different approach to the novel's nature may be grasped by examining the novel itself for clues to her treatment of time, self, and narrative structure.

TIME

When Miriam finally assumes the role of writer, near the novel's end, she contemplates what it is she wishes to write about and how she intends to do it; her reflections throw a great deal of light on how her creator, Richardson, approaches the task of writing. Miriam writes in *March Moonlight*: "While I write, everything vanishes but what I contemplate. The whole of what is called 'the past' is with one, seen anew, vividly. No, Schiller, the past does not stand 'being still.' It moves, growing with one's growth. Contemplation is adventure into discovery, reality. What is called 'creation' imaginative transformation, fantasy, invention, is only based on reality" (vol. 4, 657). Contained in this statement are the two overriding impulses in Richardson's creative method. The past is transferred to the present, bringing the present vividly to life, while the act of contemplation, a solitary process, brings the individuals in touch with their inner world and, through awareness of this world, puts them in touch with reality.

The first point is strikingly similar to Bergsonian *durée*. Gillian Hanscombe discusses Richardson's perception of time in her introduction to the Virago edition of *Pilgrimage*. She says that the major structures of time and subjective states, are for Richardson, "simply categories of space and time which our culture has developed in order to define for the individual his place in nature and society. The subjective experience of time becomes the framework within which reality exists and the corresponding task of fiction becomes the conscious bringing into being relationships of meaningful moments" (vol. 1, 9). Richardson fashions a series of meaningful moments that she relates to each other in order to represent Miriam's consciousness. The innovation she brings about is twofold: she creates the sensation of each moment being the present one, while creating a style that almost dispenses with conventional form. Punctuation, sentence structure, and paragraphs cease to be important and apparently haphazard shifts in narration and tense occur frequently. Gertrude Stein calls this type of time sequence the "prolonged" or "continuous present" (Stein, 17). Apparently, the unusual physical form of the novel – its long rambling sentences, for example – was developed to convey just this sense of continuity, of each moment lingering into the next. At any one point in *Pilgrimage* – Miriam's months as a teacher in Germany (*Pointed Roofs*), her career as a dental secretary (*Tunnel*), her time in Switzerland (*Oberland*), or her life with the Quakers (*Dimple Hill*) – the reader can enter into one of her present moments. The reader need not be aware of her past or her future in order to come to know Miriam, for she is revealed in each moment. Yet all moments do impinge on all others; there is no single moment that stands divorced from the others.

A good example of this is found in Miriam's continuing relationship with her employer Mr Hancock. It weaves in and out of her life; sometimes, as when he takes her to the Royal Society lectures, it is at the forefront and, sometimes, as when she leaves the dental practice, it fades into the background. Her feelings of excitement and awe are evident when she is at the Royal Academy:

To sit hearing the very best in the intellectual life of London, the very best science there was; the inner circle suddenly open ... the curious quiet happy laughter that went through with the idea of the breaking up of air and water and rays of light; the strange *love* that came suddenly to them all in the object-lesson classes at Banbury Park. That was to begin again ... but now not only books, not the strange heavenly difficult success of showing the children the things that had been found out; but the latest newest things that from the men themselves – there would be an audience, and a happy man with a lit face talking about things he had just found out. Even if one did not understand there would be that. (vol. 2, 100–1)

The gradual diminution of Hancock's influence is visible from *Deadlock* on. Yet because the relationship helps to define Miriam's personality, it is never really absent from the reader's attention. Most of the events and relationships in Miriam's story assume a similar form – no matter how apparently insignificant they may be. Thus she becomes an assemblage of all the events, moments, and relationships presented in the novel and not just an assemblage of the important external events. That this type of world is similar to Bergson's *durée* is clear; in fact, of all the British novelists dealing with the nature of this inner world at this time, none came closer than Richardson to putting into practice what Bergson's theory presents as the "real" world.

Hanscombe's second point, that "the subjective experience of time becomes the framework within which reality exists," goes hand-in-hand with the notion that contemplation of one's self may bring about awareness and knowledge of a new reality. Bergsonian time is essentially subjective: through his *durée* each individual creates his own reality. Richardson's original purpose in writing *Pilgrimage* was to "produce a feminine equivalent of the current masculine realism" (vol. 1, 9). In doing this, she not only chose to write about what she knew best, the feminine consciousness, but also chose to do it in a manner she saw as characteristically feminine. The de-emphasizing of the external time-frame in the novel is a deliberate attempt to rid herself of a dominant, controlling masculine view of the world. The subjective world of the novel, with its frequent disregard of external events, is Richardson's way of creating a distinctly feminine reality. Richardson plunges her reader into the depths of Miriam's *durée*, achieving a very successful portrait by presenting the reader with the internal facts of Miriam's existence. I will examine three examples of this technique from different stages of the novel, thereby showing the continuity of Miriam's character and also the accessibility of her nature at any single moment in her life.

In *Pointed Roofs*, Miriam's fears about her new position in Germany reveal the indecisive, immature girl facing a challenge she is not sure she can meet. This passage brings her to life:

It was a fool's errand … To undertake to go to the German school and teach … to be going there … with nothing to give. The moment would come when there would be a class sitting round a table waiting for her to speak. She imagined one of the rooms at the old school, full of scornful girls … How was English taught? How did you begin? English grammar … in German? Her heart beat in her throat. She had never thought of that … the rules of English Grammar? Parsing and analysis … Anglo-Saxon prefixes and suffixes … gerundial infinitive … It was too late to look anything up. Perhaps there would be a class to-morrow … The German lessons at school had been dreadfully good … Fräulein's grave face … her perfect knowledge of every rule … her clear explanations in English … her examples … All these things were there, in English grammar … And she had undertaken to teach them and could not even speak German. (vol. 1, 29)

Most of us have faced the prospect of a new challenge for which we feel unprepared or inadequate and thus can identify with Miriam's anxiety. We can enter into her experience.

In *Deadlock*, Miriam again enters a new phase, where she begins to appreciate the force that writing exercises over her. Although again her character is fully revealed, as are the changes that have occurred in it – her self-confidence is particularly notable – her position as an outsider, existing in her own world, joins her to her previous self. This passage shows a maturing Miriam:

She drew forth her first page of general suggestions, written so long ago that they already seemed to belong to some younger self, and copied them in ink. The sound of the pen shattered the silence like sudden speech. She listened entranced. The little strange sound was the living voice of the brooding presence. She copied the phrases in a shape that set them like a poem in the middle of the page, with even spaces between a wide uniform margin; not quite in the middle; the lower margin was wider than the upper; the poem wanted another line. She turned to the manuscript listening intently to the voice of Mr Lahitte pouring forth his sentences, and with a joyous rush penetrated the secret of its style. It was *artificial*. There was the last line of the poem summing up all the rest. Avoid, she wrote, searching; some word was coming; it was in her mind, muffled, almost clear; avoid – it flashed through and away, just missed. She recalled sentences that had filled her with hopeless fury, examining them curiously, without anger. Avoid ornate alias. So *that* was it! Just those few minutes glancing through the pages, standing by the table while the patient talked about her jolly, noisy, healthy, thoroughly *wicked* little kid, and now remembering every point he had made … extraordinary. But this was life! These strange unconsciously noted things, living on in one, coming together at the right moment, part of a *reality*. (vol. 3, 133)

Apart from the Bergsonian sense of life that Miriam arrives at by the end, this passage shows clearly the growing confidence she has in her intuitions about the world. It also shows Miriam beginning her journey as a writer – the journey at the heart of the novel.

The third passage comes from the end of the novel, in *March Moonlight*. Here we see a mature Miriam contemplating a significant past moment – when Densley proposed. She finally understands herself and her actions. She says:

Just as I must dimly have recognized, in that decisive moment with Densley, my unsuitability to manage the background of a Harley Street practice. Yet that surprising moment brought revelation. Down from behind me as I sat idly at home and at ease in his consulting-room – scene of our endless discussions – came his arms surrounding me while they held before my eyes that picture of the Grand Canal. Then his deepest tone, a little shaken: "Isn't that where people go for their honeymoon?" For what may have been a whole minute I was alone in the universe, all my garnered experience swept away as I moved forward in a mist of light. No temple this, but bringing later to my mind the meaning, for him, of one of his quiet generalizations: in marriage, women enter a temple where no man can follow. Certain it is that in the long moment I was aware only of myself as traveler. Sorry I was, disappointed, when I returned to my surroundings, big book vanished and his arms withdrawn, to find that my silent unresponsiveness had driven him to stand, an offended stranger, elbow on the mantel piece in the neighbourhood of one of those dreadful framed photographs of soul's awakening young women displaying long hair draped carefully waistwards down the fronts of their shoulders. Even then I could have recalled him. Was it because I knew myself not only beloved but, henceforth, free from the inconveniences of living, as Hypo had remarked long ago, only just above the poverty line, that I had stepped out alone, in blissful silence? Or because I suddenly realized that speech and emotional display in face of a lifelong contract were out of place. Sacred that moment had been, undisturbed by my knowledge of our incompatibilities. For I knew that in one way or another all men and women are incompatible, their first eager enthusiasms comparable to those of revivalist meetings and inevitably as transient. Only in silence, in complete self-possession, possession of the inwardness of being, can lovers fully meet. An enthusiastic vocal engagement is a farewell. Marriage usually a separation, lifelong? (vol. 4, 645–6).

Although the anxieties of youth are gone, replaced by confidence won by experience, her maturity is only possible because of those past experiences. Miriam is who she is now because of who she was in the past and because she understands the reasons for choices she made. At the time she was not aware of the full reasons for her decision not to marry Densley, but in retrospect she sees them, for they have emerged from the depths of her consciousness to assume a prominent place in her current self. This is how Richardson maintains continuity in Miriam's character; later versions of Miriam are always linked to previous ones through shared experiences that are transformed by the newer manifestation of Miriam's self. The process of self-definition is emphasized in the novel, but at each moment in Miriam's life we see her whole. There is never a perfectly developed self, just a constantly evolving one; thus each depiction of Miriam is as important as any other. Novelty and continuity are thereby achieved in Richardson's portrait of Miriam.

## SELF

By presenting Miriam's life as a collection of internal moments, progressing in no particular order toward no determined goal, Richardson makes her real. The complaint that *Pilgrimage* is monotonous or shapeless stems from Richardson's refusal to deviate from her purpose: to represent the feminine equivalent of masculine realism. *Pilgrimage* is a rare novel since it actually recreates one form of "reality" in fiction; nevertheless, because the average readers demand more than a sheer reproduction of life in fiction (they require entertainment or some profound revelation of truth, for example), *Pilgrimage* has ceased to be a widely read novel. Yet it, more than any other novel produced in Britain during this period, achieves what most experimental writers were trying to accomplish. Woolf said: "Life is not a series of gig lamps symmetrically arranged; life is a luminous halo, a semi-transparent envelope surrounding us from the beginning of consciousness to the end. Is it not the task of the novelist to convey this varying, this unknown and uncircumscribed spirit, whatever aberration or complexity it may display, with as little mixture of the alien and external as possible?" ("Modern Fiction," 150). But she never really achieved this goal even in her most experimental novel, *The Waves*. Richardson, on the other hand, accomplished this goal by persevering in her presentation of Miriam's character. Not every moment in a life is exceptional, but all contribute to growth; although some moments in a life are more important then others and Richardson recognizes this by emphasizing them, she nonetheless includes less important moments side by side with important ones. In her portrait of Miriam, Richardson displays the "semi-transparent envelope" surrounding humans; by including all the moments, "whatever the aberration or complexity" (or lack thereof), she adheres fully to Woolf's definition of the novelist. But to realize her intention of creating this "feminine equivalent" of the "masculine realism," Richardson had to grapple with more than presenting Miriam's *durée* as the central focus of her novel. She had to develop a viable manner of characterization, as well as a workable narrative structure that would unify the various actions and characters in the novel.

The first passage from *March Moonlight*, quoted earlier in this chapter, does more than outline Richardson's approach to time. In her description of the place that the past holds in the present, Richardson aligns herself with Bergson. Miriam's past is part of her present because she carries it with her, yet her present also impinges on the past, reshaping those moments in light of present experience. Instead of the anticipated chronological account of Miriam's life, as is the pattern of other *Bildungsroman*, the reader is given a privileged position within Miriam's consciousness from which to observe the disparate moments of her existence. Through these moments, and Miriam's reactions to them, the reader comes to know her. The creation of these moments illustrates Bergson's involuntary memory at work. A good way to examine Richardson's technique, then, is to select certain moments that illustrate both what she is attempting to do in *Pilgrimage*, and the way she progressively polishes her use of this form of memory.

The first passage comes from *The Tunnel*. Miriam has returned from a visit to the Wilsons, where she was given a glimpse of an alternative life. She settles into work at the dental practice on Wimpole Street with renewed vigour, enjoying the routine and feeling safe from the challenge that she experienced at the Wilsons. She believes that she has left her old life – both her family and her life as a teacher – behind her forever. This nice, comfortable niche is shattered by the appearance of an old friend whom she had once found attractive, Mr Grove. Her past world collides with the present: "At the door of the waiting-room she hesitated. Mr. Grove was on the other side of the door, waiting for her to come in. She opened the door with a flourish, and advanced with stiffly outstretched hand. Before she said 'Teeth?' she saw the pained anxiousness of his face and the flush that had risen under his dark skin" (vol. 3, 133). Miriam's new found contentedness and her plans for the future are assaulted by the past. Awareness of Grove's anxiety conjures up the image of a Miriam of past times, a Miriam whose existence had been consigned to the deepest stores of memory. Miriam is led to conclude: "He's seen one in the new life changed ... and I'm not really changed" (vol. 3, 135). She recognizes, at this early stage, that her past is always part of her present and that her present also colours her images of her past.

Richardson is just beginning to exploit the properties of involuntary memory in this passage. The sudden appearance of an old friend provokes memory of past days, a natural response. This event, occurring at such an important point – the world of literature is being dangled before her as a possible way of life – underscores the centrality of the memory process. Her life may have been filled with potential that was unimagined when she lived at home, but she has not changed fundamentally since that time. Voluntary recollections may be edited in a manner that suits Miriam, but involuntary memory often recalls things or events that she has little inclination to remember.

The second passage comes from *Interim*. Miriam, in North London for Christmas with the Brooms, is going up to her room to replace a gift. In this remarkable scene, the physical surroundings so affect her that a mixture of memories and feelings spill out. It is worthwhile to quote this passage at length:

Left alone with silence all along the street, Christine inaudible in the kitchen, dead silence in the house, Miriam gathered up her blouse and ran upstairs. As she passed through the changing lights of the passage, up the little dark staircase past the turn that led to the little lavatory and the little bathroom and was bright in the light of a small uncurtained lattice, on up the four stairs that brought her to the landing where the opposing bedroom doors flooded their light along the strip of green carpet between the polished balustrade and the high polished glass-doored bookcase; scenes from the future, moving in boundless backgrounds, came streaming unsummoned to her mind, making her surroundings suddenly unfamiliar ... the past would come again ... Inside her room – tidied until nothing was visible but the permanent shining gleaming furniture and ornaments; only the large box of matches on the corner of the mantel piece betraying the movement of separate days, telling her of nights of arrival, the lighting of the gas, the sudden light in the frosted globe preluding freedom and rest, bringing the beginning of rest with the gleam of the fresh quiet room – she found the nearer past, her years of London work set in the air, framed and contemplable like the pictures on the wall, and beside them the early golden years in snatches, chosen pictures from here and there, communicated, and stored in the loyal memories of the Brooms. Leaping among these lives came today ... The blouse belonged to the year that was waiting far off, invisible beyond the high wall of Christmas. (vol. 2, 312)

The passage starts with Miriam's awareness of silence followed by her notice of physical objects and their sensations; these lead her into a contemplation of other things. The familiar staircase carpeting, room, and furnishings become unfamiliar in the presence of musings about the future which enter her mind "unsummoned." The box of matches, an insignificant everyday object, brings her back to the present and then plunges her into a more distant past world. Here the Bergsonian undertones are obvious. Richardson's passage demonstrates the working of involuntary memory: recollections about past events are brought to Miriam's mind without conscious effort, needing only the stimulus of a familiar object. The process also involves a redefinition of the past by the present moment, the early years at home that she found frustrating are "golden", the harsh reality of the physical and spiritual poverty of her London life becomes less severe, becomes in fact "contemplable" rather than the contemptible existence which she faces daily. The passage provides not only an example of Bergson's involuntary memory in action, but also a convincing portrait of Miriam's consciousness. We believe that we enter Miriam's experience because we see how each phase of her recollection comes about, and also because the process is one with which we are undoubtedly familiar from our own recollective moments. At the passage's end, however, Miriam flings off both future and past in order to rejoin the present: "She dropped [the blouse] on the bed and ran downstairs to the little drawing room" (vol. 2, 312).

The third passage comes from *Dawn's Left Hand*. Miriam has returned from her rest-cure in Switzerland and is dining with Hypo and Alma prior to attending an evening at Covent Garden. A spirited discussion of the way people speak is broken off by the appearance of the main course, lark pie. This provokes a series of memories that prompts Miriam to withdraw from the general conversation in order to dwell on her thoughts. The crucial impact of this impromptu resurgence of the past is on her sense of belonging. She thinks: "The *What am I doing here*? that had sounded from time to time during their past association came back on this evening created by that past and yet fitting so perfectly into the present that had seemed to exclude them, and indeed was admitting them only as participators, more favourably circumstanced than herself, in the Oberland life" (vol. 4, 166). As Miriam's mind ranges over her life, including her time in Germany and at Wimpole Street, she attempts to place the various stages alongside her present life in order to understand the direction that she should take. In each of these places Miriam had looked for "the individual deep sense of being" (vol. 4, 167); in each she had searched in vain. Here a random object, the lark pie, plunges her into memories that give her a renewed awareness of what it is she seeks, re-affirming the belief that she can find this sense of belonging somewhere: "In the midst of Hypo's talk, she smiled towards the visible radiance that was drawing her forward and felt that within some as yet unknown life her being had set in that moment a small deep root" (vol. 4, 168). Miriam's moment of awareness is made possible through her recollection – a recollection in a Bergsonian form. Knowing her past has told her what she is lacking, a sense of belonging, and understanding this she may be able to shape her present and future in a way that will allow her to find what she desires.

## NARRATIVE STRUCTURE

Richardson delves deeper into Miriam's consciousness as *Pilgrimage* progresses, thus needing to make full use of all the narrative techniques at her command. In fact, she manipulates the narration so frequently that the reader is often in Miriam's mind in one passage and outside it in the next. One constant technique, however, is the use of memory-images that bring together Miriam's past and present lives. Since there is no consistent or detailed biographical account of Miriam's life, these memory-induced moments give valuable insights into her character. Thus, whereas Bergson was among the first to view memory in a way that explained the centrality of involuntary recollections to the whole memory process, Richardson was one of the first writers to use this type of memory extensively. The result is a novel structured around these memory-enhanced special moments. Like Woolf's moments of being and Joyce's epiphanies, Richardson's recollective moments supersede conventional narrative structure, becoming the backbone for her lengthy novel. By relating them to each other, Richardson and the reader, whom she involves in the reconstructive process required by her implied affective aesthetic, bring order and pattern to Miriam's ever-changing inner world.

Richardson's major innovation lies in her approach to character. She attempts to break down the barrier between subject and object (character and its representation) by altering the way in which character is represented. Miriam's many layers of self are revealed throughout the novel, as is her surface, or social, self that collects all the layers together and changes as they alter their internal alignments. Bergson's statement "If that which is being unmade endures, it can only be because it is inseparably bound to what is making itself" (*CE*, 362) illuminates her method of depicting Miriam's growth. Each stage of Miriam's life, from Hanover to the day years later when she begins to write her story, is built upon the previous stage and each one is retained within the new Miriam. The older, more experienced Miriam in *Dimple Hill* or *March Moonlight*, for instance, retains in herself the desire for freedom and self-possession that motivated the young Miriam's actions in *Pointed Roofs*. The desire is transformed by experience, but it still exists. By the end of *Pilgrimage* Miriam becomes a collection of different Miriams all housed together in one person; by following her inner life closely over the many volumes, the reader knows many of Miriam's different attributes and thus the entity Richardson calls Miriam Henderson.

The internal world is revealed in Miriam's thoughts as she expresses them, though Richardson's narrative technique often makes it difficult to know when Miriam is thinking and speaking directly and when a narrator is relaying her thoughts. Early in the novel Richardson uses a conventional omniscient narrator who has free access to Miriam's mind. The line between this indirect presentation of Miriam's thoughts and a new direct presentation becomes so blurred as the novel progresses that at one moment the reader is directly immersed in her mind, only to be brought up sharply a moment later by the narrator's intrusion. In *Dimple Hill*, when Miriam attends a meeting of the Quakers, we see an example of this type of narration:

What prevents the spreading, throughout Christendom, of a practice born of belief in the presence of God; necessarily following on that belief?
   Be still and *know*. Still in mind as well as in body. Not meditating, for meditation implies thought. Tranquil, intense concentration that reveals first its own difficulty, the many obstacles, and one's own weakness, and leads presently to contemplation, recognition.
   Bidding her mind to be still, she felt herself once more at work, in company, upon an all-important enterprise. (vol. 4, 498)

Until the final sentence with its tell-tale "her" and "she," readers could almost believe that they were inside Miriam, that her consciousness was being directly relayed from mind to written page. The obtrusive pronouns shatter this illusion, making it obvious again that someone is controlling the presentation of Miriam's consciousness. Nonetheless, the frequency of similar passages creates the illusion of a direct rendering of Miriam's inner world.

While Richardson succeeds in developing a new novel form, her real achievement is far more fundamental, with consequences beyond that of reshaping the traditional novel. Her first, major contribution is in the area of subject matter. She makes the events of Miriam's maturation as an individual and a writer the novel's central focus. Although previous novelists had done this with male figures, Richardson's variation of the *Bildungsroman* form is significant for two reasons. First, it centres on a female figure, thereby encouraging others, such as Virginia Woolf, to do the same. Second, and more important here, the characterization of Miriam demonstrates the overriding importance of the character's inner world, and that a focusing

on the way in which the inner world works can yield a story of interest and import. This approach concurs with Bergson's insistence that
"real" life occurs inside the individual and not in the external world.
Miriam is not a remarkable person, nor is her life filled with particularly interesting events. Yet she is a type of twentieth-century Every
Woman in that her struggles represent the struggles of many in her
era. She wins our interest because we assume a place within her consciousness and share in her struggles directly. Richardson's second,
major achievement lies in the way she represents Miriam's world. By
presenting the story of Miriam from inside the character's world,
Richardson blurs the line that separates fiction and "reality." In effect
she says that feminine reality is inside the self while masculine realism is external to the self. This understanding of reality led her to a
new style of writing, a style that attempted to mimic the inner world.
It also led to a profound, if implied, aesthetic, which may be Richardson's central artistic legacy.

Susanne Langer wrote, in *Feeling and Form*:

The contrast between the chaotic advance of the actual present and the sur-
veyable form of remembered life has been remarked by several artist-philoso-
phers, notably Marcel Proust, who maintained that what we call "reality" is a
product of memory rather than the object of direct encounter; the present is
"real" only by being the stuff of later memories. It was a peculiarity of
Proust's genius to work always with a poetic core that was a spontaneous and
perfect formulation of something in actual memory. This intense, emotionally
charged recollection, completely articulate in every detail, yet as sudden and
immediate as a present experience, not only was the catalyst that activated his
imagination, but also constituted his ideal of poetic illusion, to be achieved by
the most conscious and subtle kind of story-telling. (Langer, 266)

Richardson, whose writing has a much closer affinity to Proust's than
does the writing of either Woolf or Joyce and whose novels are so
clearly imprinted with his influence, achieves this "conscious and
subtle kind of storytelling." Because a line cannot be drawn between
the "fictional" parts of the novel and the "fictionalized" accounts of
her own life, the reader becomes aware of the artificiality of such
distinctions. Indeed, if all of what is customarily called "real" life is
simply a reconstruction of the chaotic events of experience, then reality is a "fictionalized" account of these events. When creating reality,
we organize our various disparate moments into a coherent pattern;
when a novelist does the same thing, the events are said to be imaginative and not "real." By creating fiction that mirrors the same process used to generate our reality, Richardson subtly points out the

similarity of the two processes and, in so doing, she punctures the notion that the "real" world is different from her "fictional" one. Like Proust, Richardson works with her own life and memories as the "poetic core" from which she fashions her story of Miriam's life. The intensity of the emotions and experiences that fill *Pilgrimage* attest to her ability to transform the events of her own experience into the events of Miriam's life. The line between art and life is thus drawn so fine that it becomes almost invisible. Bergson said that "what the artist tries to regain, in placing himself back within the object by a kind of sympathy, by breaking down, by an effort of intuition, the barrier that space put up between him and his model" (*CE*, 186), is a sense of the very "inwardness" of life. Richardson, by presenting Miriam's inner world and inviting the reader to share in her process of self-discovery, creates a Bergsonian novel. It is difficult to understand why, until recently, Richardson's novel has been so neglected by critics. But perhaps they had no real sense of what she was trying to accomplish. Realism for her is the inner world, and like Proust she handles this world with consummate skill. But again perhaps her female realism differed too greatly from the world inhabited by her mostly male critics and so she remains "the genius they forgot."

### CHAPTER EIGHT

# Joseph Conrad: Bergsonian Ideas of Memory and Comedy

Although Joseph Conrad has been linked with Bergson's philosophy on a number of occasions,[1] the degree to which his works reflect and embody central Bergsonian ideas remains understudied and under-appreciated. Unlike those novelists already examined in this study, Conrad's central debt to Bergson is not linked to his ideas about time. Furthermore, despite the psychological presentation of many of his characters, Conrad does not borrow Bergson's ideas about the self, for he stops short of direct representations of self and never really eliminates the barrier between subject and object that Bergsonian ideas about representation of the self would require. Two areas in Conrad's writing however, do seem to be heavily indebted to Bergson's philosophy. First, Conrad's distinctive impressionistic style of writing in his stories and novels depends in part on Bergson's ideas about memory for some of its form and unity.[2] Second, Conrad infuses comedy into his moral tales using Bergson's theories put forth in *Laughter*.

## MEMORY

But how is Conrad's approach to writing so remarkably Bergsonian in its use of memory? Conrad does not merely alternate flashbacks with current experience in his fiction, as is common in the novel; rather he uses a sophisticated blending of memories with current experiences to develop a pattern that eventually reveals a central truth. Frederick Karl remarks that Conrad "was attempting to grapple with Bergson's warning, close to his own sense of things, that the logical mind created continuity where none really existed; that this logical mind shaped mechanistic theories of existence because it had no other way of dealing with life" (Karl, 743n). Though Karl says this in reference to

*Chance*, it is applicable to many of Conrad's best works, the narrative style illustrating how much the mind does fashion life and how the recollection of past events combines with present experiences to reveal the essential nature of existence. For Conrad, though, it is not simply a case of blending the two. Like Bergson, Conrad's present experiences reshape past memories so that past moments are not merely pictures of what happened, but are tinged with the narrator's current experiences. Thus past moments are affected by present ones, but since they also clarify present experience, they affect the present moment. Thus, rather than allowing memory to fall into mechanical use – as the keeper and retriever of past experiences – Conrad's memory is the bridge in a dynamic interaction of past and present.

The narrator in *Heart of Darkness* describes Conrad's method when he says about Marlow that "to him the meaning of an episode was not inside like a kernel but outside, enveloping the tale which brought it out only as a glow brings out a haze" (*Youth*, 48). It is the external action of a story, the way both past and present events form patterns, that reveals the meaning behind Conrad's tale. In *Heart of Darkness* itself, it is not the story Marlow tells (the kernel) which is most important, but the total effect of his experience (the glow) as he sees it now, after it is over, that is the truth. This is also Bergson's vision of reality: "If there be memory, that is, the survival of past images," he says, "these images must constantly mingle with our perception of the present, and may even take its place" (*M&M*, 70). Conrad's version of this aesthetic principle allows him to blur the line between fiction and reality, resulting in fiction that is at the forefront of the school of realism despite its impressionistic style. This form of Bergsonian memory, a central element in Conrad's narrative structure, is found in both the stories and the novels.

Conrad usually starts his tales with static scenes: Marlow on the deck of the *Nellie* at twilight in *Heart of Darkness*; the physical descriptions of Jim given to Marlow by a mutual acquaintance in *Lord Jim*; or the description of Mr. Powell dining in the same room as the narrator and Marlow in *Chance*. The scene is used as the point from which the movement back in time, the actual time of the story, occurs. This method is not new; in fact, the oldest Anglo-Saxon sagas often start this way. What is new is that some chance comment or sensation – such as seeing Mr. Powell, or Marlow's comment "And this also … has been one of the dark places on the earth" (*Youth*, 48) – sparks off a tale that offers penetrating insights into human behaviour. As well, the method combines past and present moments to provide a double layer of reality: the tale told by the narrator, and the circumstances in which the tale is being told.

In *Heart of Darkness*, for example, the story's world at first appears to be the African jungle where Marlow meets Kurtz. In fact, the story takes place on the deck of the *Nellie*, since the retelling of Marlow's tale is only possible after its formative events have occurred. Although his memory of the events, prompted by the darkness of London, is the basis for the tale, his separateness from these very memories allows a logical, coherent story to emerge. The memories are augmented with later experiences, thus allowing Marlow to make sense of his past experiences in a way previously impossible. The struggle between memory and present time is visible at least twice in the course of Marlow's narrative, indicating both how difficult it is to combine the two and yet how inextricably bound together they are. The first time occurs when Marlow breaks off from his story to address his audience directly: "No, it is impossible; it is impossible to give the life-sensation of any given epoch of one's existence" (*Youth*, 82). He then returns to his attempt to do just that with his narration of Kurtz's life. The second is nearer the tale's end, when a question from a listener interrupts Marlow's flow, forcing him to emerge from his almost trancelike state to a level of consciousness in which he appears confused about the very story he is relating: "Girl! What? Did I mention a girl? ..." (*Youth*, 115). Here, Marlow's almost complete mental submersion in the past is counterpointed by his physical existence in the present; the moment is Bergsonian in the sense that past images are constantly mingling with present ones, creating at each moment a new reality.

*Lord Jim* illustrates this Bergsonian form even more clearly. Both Jim's story and Marlow's story about Jim are presented through their various experiences. Although the experiences are seen in light of past ones – Jim's actions at the end are prompted by memory of his failure to save the *Patna* – the past helps to change the present course of action and leads Jim to a completely different experience. Marlow's life receives a similar treatment: although the memories of past events affect his present life – his assessment of Jim's character – those present experiences also prompt him to assess his own past activities. Thus the multiple levels of narration – the novel is told by Marlow, but also contains an independent narrator who tells both Jim's and Marlow's stories – mingle past and present, thereby creating a Bergsonian time-filled moment.

*Under Western Eyes* also manipulates memory. Razumov is consumed by memories; in fact, they direct his present life. Yet Razumov is not a revolutionary; he adopts the role of revolutionary because everyone thinks he is one. Razumov is merely a weak man who will not stand up for himself; through association with Haldin, who was the real revolutionary, and because of the climate of suspicion surrounding the students, he finds himself labeled a revolutionary. When he is co-opted by the secret police, Razumov must pass himself off as a genuine revolutionary; he fails, ultimately, because he does not have the past experiences and memories of a real revolutionary. Incapable of balancing his present life with his past, he cannot maintain his covert role. Under the strain of events, he crumbles. In Bergsonian terms, his "privileged image" (social or surface self) is false because the "aggregate of images" (inner selves) which constitute it are false; thus Razumov is unstable because this "privileged image" is false. Nevertheless, Razumov's spontaneous images, the result of the working of his involuntary memory, inform the reader of Razumov's real self. It is when he is no longer physically capable of holding this repressed self back that he collapses mentally. Although the novel obviously has heavy Freudian undertones (repression of memory as the cause of psychological illness), its central action revolves around the way in which memory may be manipulated, thereby pervading present perceptions until it becomes difficult to distinguish truth from fiction.

Bergson was among the first to maintain that memory helps to define existence and that false memories prevent an assimilation of past experience by the present self, thus rendering the self's existence impossible. Conrad's psychological portraits of Razumov and others illustrate his acceptance of the idea that past events play a powerful role, not only in the perception of present events but also in an individual's subsequent ability to cope with each new moment of life. Razumov, like so many other Conradian characters, fails as a person because he lacks the stability necessary for the union of inner world and outer self. While memory is the bridge that unites these two worlds, falsification of memory, or denial of experiences, results in a schism between the two. Since so much of Conrad's fiction focuses on the nature of self, as well as the gulf between the selves we present to the world and the ones that remain harboured within our own consciousnesses, this use of Bergsonian memory is significant. An even more compelling case for Bergson's influence on Conrad, however, may be found in Conrad's use of Bergsonian comic theory.

### COMEDY

Although many observers of the modern scene claim that Bergson's only real excursion into the realm of art is found in *Laughter,* it does not appear to have had much impact on the writers generally recognized as having affinities to Bergson. Of the four novelists in this study, it is interesting to note that only Conrad uses comedy in a Bergsonian way. Conrad's greatest debt to Bergson lies in the ideas of comedy developed in *Laughter*. However the various critics who have examined Conrad's work for comedy have placed him in different traditions, even remaining skeptical about the presence of any comedy in his works;[3] clearly, there is little consensus as to the nature of Conradian comedy. In James F. English's recent study, "Scientist, Moralist, Humorist: A Bergsonian Reading of *The Secret Agent*," the author aims "not to settle the controversy" that has surrounded *The Secret Agent* since its publication, "but to provide a description of the novel's humor that might help account for the multiple and conflicting responses it has elicited" (English, 139). In so doing, he raises three issues, the significance of which goes far beyond that raised by a brief "Bergsonian reading" of one novel.

The first issue is the almost insoluble problem of whether Bergson had a direct influence on Conrad's approach to comedy. Though English, in agreement with others, concludes that "neither writer is likely to have been influenced directly by the other" (English, 141), I believe that a careful reading of *Chance* suggests not only the presence of such a link, but that Bergson's comic theory served as a model for Conrad's comedy. The second issue revolves around English's contention that the "basic tenets of Bergson's essay [*Laughter*] provide a reasonable, if somewhat too superficial and familiar commentary on *The Secret Agent*" (English, 143). Although it is true that both the mechanism and grotesque nature of the characters in this novel have been frequently noted as examples of the novel's "black comedy," I feel that English dismisses them too quickly. This type of comedy, though both pervasive and familiar in *The Secret Agent*, is no less pervasive, though less familiar, in Conrad's other late works. In fact, Bergson's basic contention "that the comic represents *'something mechanical encrusted on the living'* " [author's italics] (*Laughter*, 141) actually serves to illuminate the many other Conrad characters who are comical in a Bergsonian sense, thereby illustrating how pervasive Bergsonian comedy is in Conrad's work. The third issue raised by English is perhaps the most important. He says that "in his intimate concern with tensions between traditional humanism and radically scientific detachment, Bergson provides a key to both the humor of Conrad's novel and the startlingly divergent responses of its readers" (English, 141). English focuses his study on one manifestation of this tension – *The Secret Agent*'s narrative tone; however, I would argue that the scope here can be expanded to include both Conrad's social didacticism and his works other than *The Secret Agent*.

Even though I will focus specifically here on Conrad's two political novels – *The Secret Agent* and *Under Western Eyes* – the appropriateness of all of Conrad's work being given a "Bergsonian comic reading" will emerge. English is correct when he says that the essence of Bergson's comic theory may be expressed as "something mechanical encrusted on the living," that is, that living beings become comical when mechanical or habitual behaviour replaces the free flow of life. However, specific components of Bergson's theory were used for specific effects by Conrad.

Henri Bergson wrote in 1900:

> The comic is that side of a person which reveals his likeness to a thing, that aspect of human events which, through its peculiar inelasticity, conveys the impression of pure mechanism, of automatism, of movement without life. Consequently it expresses an individual or collective imperfection which calls for an immediate corrective. This corrective is laughter, a social gesture that singles out and represses a special kind of absent-mindedness in men and events. (*Laughter*, 87–8)

Two main elements of Bergson's theory of comedy are outlined here: the notion of inelasticity, or mechanism, as its chief cause; and the idea that detached laughter is a social corrective for those whose lives are rigid and mechanical. The third element of Bergson's theory is that "the comic does not exist outside the pale of what is strictly *human*" (*Laughter*, 3). Bergson advocates, then, a form of comedy of the ridiculous. At the same time, he speculates on the motivation of laughter, which he says stems from society's insistence on a "constant striving after reciprocal adaptation." So while society's laughter prompts its recipients to alter their behaviour, the very impulse to laugh also prompts society to reassess its own behaviour.

Bergson's view of life as an overflowing, vibrant stream affects his view of comedy. When we behave in a mechanical or automatic fashion, we consciously or unconsciously arrest the flow of life and therefore need correction. In other words, the transgressor's actions are comic, and laughter is the corrective. Bergson is not concerned with rebuking the wicked with this type of laughter; rather, his central concern is to ridicule the foolish. His laughter is essentially devoid of moral content; it is more concerned with unsociability than with morality. Bergson says: "We may therefore admit, as a general rule, that it is the faults of others that make us laugh, provided that we add that they make us laugh by reason of their unsociability rather than of their *immorality*" (*Laughter*, 139). He also states: "In laughter we always find an unavowed intention to humiliate, and consequently to correct our neighbor, if not in his will, at least in his deed" (*Laughter*, 136). Bergson's emphasis on the social function of comedy and his assertion that it has no moral function make his theory original. He argues that unsociability contains no moral overtones – man decides what behaviour is acceptable, not some absolute authority or some abstract moral code – and the decision as to what is sociable depends on both the circumstances and the observers. Bergson's insistence that comedy is a detached form of social criticism – "Comedy can only begin at the point where our neighbor's personality ceases to affect us. It begins, in fact, with what might be called *a growing callousness to social life*" [author's italics] (*Laughter*, 134) – makes him a forerunner of later twentieth-century theoreticians of comedy. The absurdist dramatists such as Unesco, for instance, see comedy as essentially amoral.

It is not farfetched to suppose that Conrad knew of Bergson's work on comedy. As Karl suggests, though "Conrad did not respond directly to Henri Bergson's work ... he would surely have had some sense of its impact" (*Three Lives*, 743n). Conrad himself supplies a more compelling piece of evidence in his novel *Chance*. The narrator and Marlow are discussing Flora de Barral when Marlow suddenly laughs and is accused of discovering something funny in the conversation. His reply, and the discussion that ensues, gives a remarkably clear statement of Conrad's idea of comedy. Its tantalizing allusion to various comic theories includes a thinly veiled reference to Bergson's theory. The passage deserves to be quoted at length:

"Comic!" he exclaimed. "No! What makes you say? ... Oh, I laughed – did I! But don't you know that people laugh at absurdities that are far from being comic? Didn't you read the latest books about laughter written by philosophers, psychologists? There is a lot of them ..."

"I dare say there has been a lot of nonsense written about laughter – and tears, too, for that matter," I said impatiently.

"They say," pursued the unabashed Marlow, "that we laugh from a sense of superiority. Therefore, observe, simplicity, honesty, warmth of feeling, delicacy of heart and of conduct, self-confidence, magnanimity, are laughed at, because the presence of these traits in a man's character put him into difficult, cruel or absurd situations, and makes us, the majority who are fairly free as a rule from these peculiarities, feel pleasantly superior." (*Chance*, 283–4)

Later in the novel, in the description of de Barral's court appearance, there is another important description of comedy:

"And it might have been the tenacity, the unintelligent tenacity, of the man who has persisted in throwing millions of other people's thrift into the Lone Valley Railway, the Labrador Docks, the Spotted Leopard Copper Mine, and the other grotesque speculations exposed during the famous de Barral trial, amongst murmurs of astonishment mingled with bursts of laughter. For it is in the Courts of Law that Comedy finds its last refuge in our deadly serious world." (*Chance*, 377)

The first passage is significant for two reasons. First, it reveals Conrad's awareness of the variety of comic theories, particularly of contemporary ones – "Didn't you read the latest books?" Although the satiric tone of the comment suits Marlow, it conveys Conrad's knowledge of the works by "philosophers, psychologists" – an obvious allusion to Bergson's *Laughter* and Freud's *Jokes and their Relation to the Unconscious* (1905). Second, we see underlying Marlow's theory, the idea that laughter is provoked by people who operate outside society's normal bounds. This behaviour prompts laughter from those who wish to see such reprobates conform to conventional standards. The similarity to Bergson's contention that laughter has a socially corrective function is clear.

The second passage is even closer to Bergson's notions of comedy. The realization of de Barral's very tenacity in sticking to his foolish course of investments in the face of all their failures draws laughter from those in the courtroom. The laughter is prompted by de Barral's rigidity, as well as by his unsociability in depriving his investors of their money. The laughter functions as both a social corrective and as a comment on his rigid, mechanical persistence in his business ventures. The second sentence, in which Conrad states that the Court of Law is the last home of comedy, is a wonderfully Bergsonian observation. English common law is based on a series of traditions and precedents: everything from the dress of the participants in a trial, to the manner in which evidence is submitted, scrutinized, and judged conforms to rigid conventions. Conrad's ironic statement here is aimed at this rigidity and the mechanical dispensing of justice, thereby illustrating Bergson's contention that comedy arises when there is "an automatic regulation of society" (*Laughter*, 47). Some of Conrad's other works also make use of Bergsonian comedy; while they do not discuss it as overtly as *Chance* does, it nonetheless becomes an integral part of these works. Two excellent examples of Conrad's Bergsonian comedy are *The Secret Agent* and *Under Western Eyes*.

Both novels are departures from Conrad's usual metier – stories of the sea and of sailors. This alone should alert the reader to possible differences in Conrad's usual form. The most important departures arise in how Conrad treats the novels' characters and in the ideas, or themes, discussed. These elements may not seem to be such radical departures from Conrad's usual works; if they are examined in terms of Bergsonian comedy, however, it is evident that Conrad is concerned with many of the same things.

## Comic Characters

Bergson said that "the comic is that side of a person which reveals his likeness to a thing" and that automatic behaviour in man is comical because it deprives him of his freedom and renders him less than human. The characters in both novels exemplify this reduction of man to thing or automaton.

The major characters in *The Secret Agent* are static; they are remarkable for their lack of spontaneity and their plodding adherence to the recurring rhythms of their lives. Each character, to a greater or lesser extent, lives an automatic life. Verloc, as the most automatic, is the most comical. At the novel's outset, where he is presented as being "thoroughly domesticated" and where the reader is told "Neither his spiritual, nor his mental, nor his physical needs were of the kind to take him much abroad" (*Agent*, 5), the reader sees Verloc's complacent acceptance of life. If Verloc's profession were different, his behaviour would not necessarily be comical; however, complacency and love of creature comforts are not normally associated with anarchy. Yet it is here that Conrad initiates the comic portrayal of Verloc, later extending it in the depiction of Verloc's responses to the series of crises that befall him.

In the first interview, in response to Mr Vladimir's intimidation, Verloc assumes the passive, plodding persona that has served him well in his career as an anarchist. The narrator's comments, however, are unfavourable, thus casting doubt on Verloc's fitness for this role. In fact, the narrator compares Verloc with a fly: "The useless fussing of that tiny energetic organism affected unpleasantly this big man threatened in his indolence" (*Agent*, 27). Vladimir's command that an outrage be perpetrated creates a dilemma for Verloc. Even his highly anxious state manifests itself in a subdued, almost frozen, mechanical fashion, for Verloc is as incapable of disobeying Vladimir as he is of successfully committing the act. The narrator, comparing Verloc to the other anarchists at this point, remarks:

And Mr. Verloc, temperamentally identical with his associates, drew fine distinctions in his mind on the strength of insignificant differences. He drew them with a certain complacency, because the instinct of conventional respectability was strong within him, being only overcome by his dislike of all kinds of recognized labour – a temperamental defect which he shared with a large proportion of the revolutionary reformers of a given social state. For obviously one does not revolt against the price which must be paid for the same coin of accepted morality, self restraint, and toil. (*Agent*, 53)

"Conventional respectability" and a "dislike of all kinds of recognized labour" are not the traits of someone committed to social upheaval. Thus it is this gap between his profession and his complacent shrugging off of both its moral and physical realities that creates comedy, that causes the reader to laugh at Verloc's mechanical, lifeless imitation of a secret agent. Conrad completes his comic portrayal of Verloc, appropriately, at Verloc's moment of greatest danger. As he is about to be killed by Winnie, Verloc ceases to be human. He becomes first a "veiled sound [that] filled the small room with its moderate volume" (*Agent*, 261); he is then reduced to sound waves that are "propagated in accordance with correct mathematical formulas" (*Agent*, 261); and finally, when Winnie kills him, he becomes a "mortal envelope" that "expire[s] without stirring a limb" (*Agent*, 263). His gradual reduction to a thing, coupled with his passive acceptance of his fate at the moment of extreme jeopardy, only enhances the comic properties of his character, adding to the novel's general comic tone. The other characters are dealt with in a similar manner.

Before considering Winnie and Stevie, who appear to have some capacity for free action, let us examine some of the other major characters. On the side of the anarchists are a motley collection of conspirators – Ossipon, Yundt, Michaelis, and the Professor – who, although superficially diverse, are fundamentally similar. The narrator's comments on revolutionaries is aimed at them all:

The majority of revolutionists are the enemies of discipline and fatigue mostly. There are natures, too, to whose sense of justice the price exacted looms up monstrously enormous, odious, oppressive, worrying, humiliating, extortionate, intolerable. Those are the fanatics. The remaining portion of social rebels is accounted for by vanity, the mother of all noble and vile illusions, the companion of poets, reformers, charlatans, prophets, and incendiaries. (*Agent*, 53)

The Professor is clearly a fanatic, determined to create the perfect detonator. His apparent strength of character is undercut by the very rigidity that permits his resolute search for the detonator. He lives an automatic life, frightening in its inhumanity; in the powerful final description, he ceases altogether to be human. He becomes "a force" like his bombs, and then "a pest in a street full of men" (*Agent*, 311). The willful obliteration of his humanity is terrible yet comical, given his unsociable actions and the laughter that may negate some of the reader's fear and some of the Professor's strength. The other three anarchists are much more obviously comical. Ossipon, Yundt, and Michaelis are social rebels because of their vanity: Ossipon, a charlatan who preys on women attracted to the cause and to his physical charms; Michaelis, a poet whose martyrdom inspires the cause but who is incapable of sustained thought; and Yundt, a fiery reformer who "had never in his life raised personally as much as his little finger against the social edifice" (*Agent*, 48). The fact that all three persist in their behaviour despite their ineffectiveness renders them insignificant and mechanical. They are automatons; even Ossipon is automatic in his attempt to defraud Winnie and in the predictability of his subsequent remorse. Such lack of freedom underlines their comedy, which is still further enhanced by their resemblance to things. Michaelis, for example, is like a pliable mannequin, "with [an] elbow presenting no appearance of a joint, but more like a bend in a dummy's limb" (*Agent*, 42), while Yundt, scarecrowlike, has a "clawlike hand" (*Agent*, 51) and resembles a "swaggering spectre" (*Agent*, 52). Michaelis's obesity only adds to his physical deformity, making him mechanical in his movements, again adding to the comedy.[4] The anarchists' counterparts on the law-and-order side fare no better.

Sir Ethelred, Chief Inspector Heat, and the Assistant Commissioner resemble the anarchists in their rigidity. Sir Ethelred is the very model of a statesman whose sole concern is the preservation of the status quo. He is presented as imperturbable – "The great man manifested no surprise, no eagerness, no sentiment whatever. The attitude in which he rested his menaced eyes was profoundly meditative" (*Agent*, 217). His appearance is statuelike, so that he is not flesh-and-blood but a mind encased in stone. Indeed, he is a robot. This dehumanizing portrait renders Ethelred an object of laughter. Chief Inspector Heat is similarly dehumanized, but in his case the dehumanization results from a lack of mental agility. He is "a loyal servant" (*Agent*, 89) of the state, an "average man, whose ambition is to common events" (*Agent*, 90) and whose mind "was unaccessible to ideas of revolt" (*Agent*, 92). The inflexibility of Heat's mental outlook makes him a fine policeman, for as the narrator remarks, "[Heat] could understand the mind of a burglar, as a matter of fact, the mind and the instincts of a burglar are of the same kind as the mind and the instincts of a police officer" (*Agent*, 92). Yet this very inflexibility makes him comical, because he is clearly incapable of any premeditated action. Although the Assistant Commissioner appears to be more nearly human than either Ethelred or Heat, he is just as mechanical. All of his actions are calculated to preserve and enhance his position, an aim he shares with his counterpart Vladimir. Both men are engaged in an elaborate "game" – part diplomatic, part political, part legal – that ignores the fact that the counters in the game are human beings. Indeed, the Assistant Commissioner fails even to acknowledge that Verloc is human, calling him a "sprat." His comment to Ethelred's young assistant suitably illustrates his vision of the game: "But a sprat is also thrown away sometimes in order to catch a whale" (*Agent*, 216). Such callous disregard for human life reflects both Vladimir and the Assistant Commissioner's lack of humanity, thereby making them comical. Clearly, the characters on both sides of the novel's political spectrum – the anarchists and the guardians of society – are equally dehumanized and rigid, thereby contributing to the novel's comedy. Winnie and Stevie, however, who live outside the novel's political framework, also provide it with comedy.

Although both Winnie and Stevie appear to be capable of spontaneous actions – witness Winnie's murder of Verloc and Stevie's occasional outbursts – this is deceptive. Winnie's action is the logical culmination of her life's work for Stevie. Not to kill Verloc would be the exceptional action; to kill Verloc and then herself are inevitable by-products of Stevie's death. Although the narrator says that Winnie "had her freedom" and that "her contract with existence, as represented by [Verloc] was at an end" (*Agent*, 251), her actions display her inability to accept and exercise freedom. She does not shout for help when she first discovers the circumstances of Stevie's death, nor does she do anything during her subsequent liberation, because "she do[es] not exactly know what use to make of her freedom" (*Agent*, 254). When she finally does act, she is portrayed as a somnambulist, a creature unaware of her actions. At the murder she is even reduced to a thing, a "moving shadow of an arm with a clenched hand holding a carving knife" that "flickered up and down" (*Agent*, 262) in a curiously mechanical way. When the deed is done she is apparently free: "She had become a free woman with a perfection of freedom which left nothing to desire and absolutely nothing to do" (*Agent*, 263). But her freedom is illusory; she is unable to make any decisions and foolishly turns to Ossipon in a vain attempt to avoid her inevitable death. Freedom with no desire or ability to exercise it is not really freedom; it is simply another form of enslavement (surely the complete absence of action being the complementary opposite of rigid adherence to a set course of action). Winnie depends on Stevie for meaning in her life; in a perverse way her devotion to, and complete submersion in, him dehumanizes her, thereby negating her own existence. His death, rather than liberating her as it might, pushes her even further into a dehumanized state – that of murderer, deluded woman, and suicide victim.

Stevie, too, is in a perverse way mechanical. His mental deficiency robs him of rational thought, forcing him to live a largely emotionally-reactive existence. Although he shows glimmers of social awareness, as in his comments on the cabbie and his horse – " 'Poor! Poor!' ... 'Cabman poor, too'" (*Agent*, 170) – he has little understanding of why the man is poor or why society allows poverty. His devotion to Verloc dehumanizes Stevie because it is presented as doglike. As long as Stevie is good, Verloc tolerates his presence as he would that of an animal; and all Stevie wants is to be near Verloc. Conrad's irony comes through here, because Stevie attracts sympathy and our compassionate laughter. Even when he is blown apart and clearly dehumanized, our pity is tinged by laughter at his graphic demise. The description Winnie receives is cruel in its vividness, yet comical because it presents Stevie as a firework: "A park – smashed branches, torn leaves, gravel, bits of brotherly flesh and bone, all sprouting up in the manner of a firework" (*Agent*, 260). What should be most natural, a "simple" boy who is cruelly killed, is changed into a vivid show, thereby underscoring Conrad's bitter attack on the mechanical nature of both Stevie's existence and his destruction.

Conrad connects the comic characters of this novel to each other by this continual dehumanization, though the actual process of dehumanization assumes different forms. He achieves a similar type of comic portraiture in other works – Marlow, Kurtz, Jim, and de Barral are all comic because of their rigidity and lack of humanity – and uses these characters to illustrate society's shortcomings. He does this again very powerfully in *Under Western Eyes*.

*Under Western Eyes* resembles some of the best Russian literature of the late nineteenth and early twentieth centuries; that comparisons can be made with Dostoevsky's *Notes from the Underground*, for example, is readily evident. Like the Russian literature it echoes, Conrad's novel focuses specifically on a relatively limited number of characters, although the cast of participants is large. Because of the fairly restricted focus, few characters are developed beyond the stereotype: Haldin is the idealist who is also a terrorist; Natalie is the beautiful but naive young woman; Sophia Antonova is the devoted but frustrated spinster, and so on. Three fully realized figures do emerge from the novel: Razumov, Councilor Mikulin, and the narrator. It is not coincidental that the first two reprise and extend roles played by characters in Conrad's previous political novel, while the narrator is a variation of Conrad's other first person narrators, the most notable of which is Marlow. Razumov is like Verloc, a highly unusual secret agent, while Mikulin performs a role similar to those played by Vladimir and the Assistant Commissioner. Again, it should not be surprising to find that both Razumov and Mikulin are Bergsonian comic characters, for Conrad is employing the same comic mode here as he did in *The Secret Agent*. It is interesting that the narrator, too, is rendered in a comic fashion, for he is also functioning, in the usual Conradian manner, as a social critic. The combination of comedy and social criticism that is so crucial to Bergson's theory assumes a prominent role in this novel, exemplified perhaps by the novel's central character: Kirylo Sidorovitch Razumov.

Razumov is unquestionably the novel's central figure. Although his actions provide compelling drama, many readers are hard pressed to feel much sympathy for his progressive decline and virtual disintegration; indeed, most readers are inclined to laugh at his predicament. Yet it is a laughter prompted less by an uncharitable failure to recognize Razumov's legitimate suffering than by his failure to do something, anything, to alter the path of his own destruction. Razumov's passive acceptance of Haldin's intrusion into his life appears initially to be borne out of a sense of practicality, as the following passage illustrates: "He shuddered. Then the peace of bitter calmness came over him. It was best to keep this man out of the streets till he could be got rid of with some chance of escaping" (*Eyes*, 22). Little does Razumov realize that Haldin's mere presence condemns him as fully as if Razumov himself were a terrorist. Yet this self-rationalization is deceptive, because subsequent events soon establish that Razumov habitually chooses to accept what is done to him rather than consciously act to avoid or alter situations. For instance, when Mikulin first interviews him, Razumov does little to help his case; in fact, his strange behaviour fosters in Mikulin the idea that Razumov can be useful, thereby eventually contributing to Razumov's downfall. Razumov's claim that he has "a faculty of independent thinking – of detached thinking" that makes him "more free than any social democratic revolution could" (*Eyes*, 86) is undercut by Mikulin, who responds to Razumov's announcement of his departure by saying "Where to?" (*Eyes*, 87). Implied is a critique of Razumov's belief that intellectual detachment is equivalent to political or even physical freedom: Mikulin knows that without the capacity to apply the fruits of intellectual discoveries, there can be no freedom. Razumov's inability to apprehend that basic principle leaves him perpetually falling short of any action. The unsubstantiated belief in his own intellectual superiority and the well-documented demonstration of Razumov's crumbling mind are most powerfully revealed in the final diary entry: "Have I then the soul of a slave? No! I am independent – and therefore perdition is my lot" (*Eyes*, 303). The independence he so proudly proclaims is illusory, however, since he becomes dependent on Sophia Antonova after his break with the revolutionaries; yet he fails to see that his pretense of independence causes his perdition. Just as he rationalizes his lack of action as stemming from intellectual superiority, so he rationalizes his failure by claiming moral or spiritual superiority. As readers, we laugh at Razumov because we can see through his self-delusion; we find comical his rigid adherence to a course of action guaranteed to destroy him. This clear self-delusion reduces Razumov's status from that of tragic figure to that of comic character; it allies him with Verloc.

Mikulin combines the two roles of Vladimir and the Assistant Commissioner. He is both policeman and spy-master, and, like his counterparts in *The Secret Agent*, he is a comic figure because his profession robs him of his humanity. Conrad is particularly damning in his portrait of Mikulin. The physical descriptions are noteworthy for their emphasis on Mikulin's lack of warmth. His is a "mild gaze" that rests on Razumov "almost without expression" (*Eyes*, 76). In a brilliant description of the gaze, Conrad encapsulates Mikulin's nature: "In its passionless persistence there was something resembling sympathy" (*Eyes*, 76). That the gaze is "passionless" implies Mikulin's lack of human understanding; its resemblance to "sympathy," however, implies a deliberate attempt to manufacture, mechanically or by force of will, a human response. Again, Mikulin is "mysteriously self-possessed like an idol with dim, unreadable eyes" (*Eyes*, 84); even Mikulin's wiping of his face with his hand implies for Razumov "an alarming aloofness" (*Eyes*, 85). Physically, too, Mikulin is detached, cold, and incapable of human emotional responses; he is dehumanized. Yet he is even more dehumanized by his profession. For example, in order to protect the state he serves, he treats people like pawns in some sort of elaborate game. Razumov interests him because he appears to differ from the terrorists Mikulin normally encounters and because he may prove to be a particularly effective pawn. Mikulin is adept at manipulating others for abstract philosophical or political purposes, but this activity only increases the gulf between his feelings and his intellect. Comedy is a result of this discrepancy between spontaneous feelings (which are almost non-existent) and overpowering intellect. Thus Mikulin – incapable as he is of living a spontaneous, free human life – like Razumov, elicits our laughter.

Conrad's narrator also assumes a comic role. He is presented as an elderly man, who consistently undermines his own status by such proclamations as "I wish to disclaim the possession of those high gifts of imagination and expression which would have enabled my pen to create for the reader the personality of the man who called himself, after the Russian custom, Cyril son of Isidor – Kirylo Sidorovitch – Razumov" (*Eyes*, 7). A teacher of languages, the narrator finds himself party to the intrigues of the expatriate Russians in Zurich, and thus privy to Razumov's story and presence, largely because of his friendship with the young Natalie Haldin. His fussy manner and thinly disguised romantic attraction to Natalie would make him a slightly comic character even in a conventional sense, but Conrad's clever use of him as a spokesman for social reform makes him a comic character in a Bergsonian sense as well. Remembering that for Bergson laughter is meant to function as a social corrective illuminates Conrad's treatment of his narrator here. Just as readers must routinely question the motives and involvements of Conrad's other first-person narrators, so they must question this narrator. The narrator's rendition of Razumov's story carries with it the tone of disapproval: both the society which creates a Razumov in the first place and then casts him off, and Razumov himself come in for a certain amount of criticism. The criticism consists mainly of highlighting the rigidity or mechanism of a society that allows no deviation from its conventions. A good example of this is the ironic tone employed to describe Mr de P—: "It is said that his execrated personality had not enough imagination to be aware of the hate he inspired. It is hardly credible; but it is a fact that he took very few precautions for his safety. In the preamble of a certain famous State paper he had declared once that 'the thought of liberty has never existed in the Act of the Creator'" (*Eyes*, 11). The narrator's facility with words makes this a vivid and effective portrait; it is a portrait that is critical of the man's lack of imagination and his mechanical adherence to what he believes is right. It questions Mr de P—'s character, which is condemned with laughter, and the narrator's reliability, which is questioned because of the caustic language he employs.

The characterizations also establish the grounds for the novel's social criticism. We criticize Razumov, for the narrator's portrait of him presents him as a man incapable of living a free life. Thus the narrator uses laughter to censure both society and Razumov. But Conrad also laughs at the narrator. By presenting the narrator as an aging, fallible man who has obvious biases and who follows a life of convention that is as rigid as the lives of those he condemns, Conrad forces his reader to examine the narrator closely. The reader sees, as he does when he is forced to examine Marlow closely in *Heart of Darkness*, for example, that the narrator is caught up in the very world he criticizes. We laugh at his belief that he is not part of this world, but our laughter is uneasy; we are aware, because we participate in the novel through the agency of the narrator, that, in effect,

Conrad is saying that we too belong to a similar world. Just as Marlow's experience of Kurtz's life allows readers to experience it, the narrator's experience of Razumov's world makes this world accessible. This type of reader involvement in fiction is not new, but by having the reader laugh at both the characters and the narrator in an effort to reform their behaviour, and by closely involving the reader in the narrator's experience, Conrad is inviting us to laugh at ourselves and thus correct our own unsociable behaviour.

### Comic Gesture

The comic nature of the major characters in both *The Secret Agent* and *Under Western Eyes* clearly owes a debt to Bergson's ideas on comedy. Less obvious, but even more central to the ideas or themes of both novels, is a second facet of Bergson's comic theory – his comedy of gesture. Bergson, contending that comedy arises when there is "an automatic regulation of society," discusses gesture as one way of regulating society. He writes: "*Instead of concentrating our attention on actions, comedy directs it rather to gestures* [author's italics]. Gesture here means the attitudes, the movements, and even the language by which a mental state expresses itself outwardly without any aim or profit, from no other cause than a kind of inner itching" (*Laughter*, 143). On two different levels – the action of the novels and the implied social criticism in each one – gestural comedy is pervasive in these two Conradian tales.

Although both novels contain a number of dramatic events – in the first: the Greenwich outrage, Verloc's murder, and Winnie's suicide; in the second: Razumov's forced occupation as a secret agent, the 'heroic fugitive's' orations, and the final assault on Razumov – the actions never really affect the societies they are meant to change. In the broad social context, none of the actions really amounts to much. Verloc's actions are a good example of Bergsonian gesture. He is a secret agent employed by three different groups: the anarchists, a right-wing Continental regime, and the British police. Any action he performs for one group is negated by an action he commits for another. For example, Verloc's position as "One of the Vice-Presidents" of "The Future of the Proletariat," a group "not anarchist in principle, but open to all shades of revolutionary opinion" (*Agent*, 26), is undercut by his position as "the famous and trusty secret agent … whose warnings had the power to change the schemes and the dates of royal, imperial grand-ducal journeys, and sometimes cause them to be put off altogether" (*Agent*, 27). Ultimately Verloc's actions achieve little more than a justification for his continued employment as a secret agent. As long as he appears to be doing something, he can justify his existence; yet his existence has little concrete purpose and is only a physical manifestation of the game other characters are playing.

The whole thematic structure of *The Secret Agent* revolves around mistaking gestures for actions. The Professor best exemplifies this in his dogged determination to create "a perfect detonator" (*Agent*, 69). By itself a detonator is useless; it must be connected to a bomb to cause any action. Creating the perfect detonator is a grand gesture, which the Professor uses to assert his independence. Although he says "My superiority is evident" (*Agent*, 68), this is undercut by the futile way he chooses to express his superiority. What good is a detonator without a bomb? And what good is superiority without some real activity in which to demonstrate it? In a similar fashion, all the novel's actions are futile gestures. Winnie's murder of Verloc does not set her free, nor does it bring Stevie back to life; it is a gesture that soothes her despair momentarily, but that does nothing to alter her fate. The game played by Vladimir, Ethelred, and the Assistant Commissioner is equally without real action, because it involves an elaborate sequence of gesture and countergesture. Most people are directly affected by the mundane events of life, but Ethelred and the others dismiss these "details" in favour of much more important things such as the "Nationalization of the Fisheries" (*Agent*, 145). While these larger, more abstract things do eventually have some impact on people, the real living continues despite them. People will live, die, marry, work or starve regardless of whether the fishing industry is nationalized or a bomb destroys Greenwich Observatory. The artful manipulating indulged in by the masters of the game is no more than the use of humans as pawns in the players' efforts to soothe their "inner itching." The great comedic impact Conrad creates here is that the characters fail to distinguish between gestures and actions; they thus order their lives in an automatic fashion largely around futile, but dramatic, gestures. He employs a similar comedic approach in *Under Western Eyes*, with the character Razumov.

As his central action, Razumov is forced to assume the role of agent for the Russian secret police. His job is to infiltrate a circle of expatriate Russian revolutionaries in Zurich and report on their activities to Mikulin. On the surface, this seems like a role which is both socially meaningful and full of action. However, the leader of this circle of conspirators – Peter Ivanovitch, the "heroic fugitive" – is a member of the Russian secret police, operating "undercover." In essence, a spy – Razumov – is reporting on the activities inspired by another spy – the "heroic fugitive." Both men are controlled by

Councilor Mikulin, so that Razumov's and Peter Ivanovitch's actions are really gestures and countergestures dictated from afar. Once again, the comedic impact stems from the calculated and callous manipulation of humans, the object of which is to reinforce the position of the government. Clearly, none of the characters has an individual importance in Mikulin's political forum; all are expendable; the real life of the novel surrounds Razumov's struggle, Natalie's battles with her own emotions, and the lives of the other characters. When the gulf between the importance Mikulin assigns his game and the dismissal of the others' daily dramas is viewed as insignificant, the discrepancy between gesture and action becomes apparent. When Razumov can no longer distinguish between the two – his decision to tell the revolutionaries the truth about himself is not based on some sense of the use that can be made of the confession, but is prompted by an intolerable inner itching – he destroys himself, eliciting not compassion, but laughter. What should be a great tragedy, the demise of an innocent man, is a comedy because of the routine substitution of gesture for action.

Although both novels are clearly comedies because of widespread use of gesture, there is another element in Bergson's comic theory that establishes the novels' wider social impact. Bergson said that comedy arises from "an individual or collective imperfection which calls for an immediate corrective," and that laughter is "a social gesture that singles out and represses a special kind of absent-mindedness in man and events." In both novels there are individual and collective imperfections in need of correction. Razumov and Verloc, for example, represent the absent-mindedness that self-absorbed individuals display; laughter might well shock them out of their mechanical routines and back into so-called real life. The organization of society in each novel is equally absent-minded or imperfect, not only because each society fails to consider the importance of the individual but also because each society is static. Laughter – generated by Conrad's vivid depiction of the shortcomings of a world designed and run by men such as Mr de P—, Sir Ethelred, or Councilor Mikulin – is meant to correct the societies' imperfections. The worlds of the novels are not open to change; they are fictional and the events in them are fixed. But the novels' implied social criticism seems to ask us to examine our world for similar flaws and, if they exist, to repair them. Conrad emphasizes the importance of human beings and their right to free, spontaneous action by showing us the dire consequences of societies that deny such things. Consistent with the body of Conrad's work, the social didacticism of these novels, although achieved in a comic manner, is an integral element.

Although these two political novels are his only sustained comedies, Conrad's other works contain certain comic elements as well. The native woman in *Heart of Darkness*, for instance, is comical because her gesture of love for Kurtz is at once vividly alive and mechanical. As Marlow describes it, her gesture is almost a reflex action: "Suddenly she opened her bared arms and threw them up rigid above her head, as though in an uncontrollable desire to touch the sky" (*Youth*, 136). "Rigid" arms bind the "uncontrollable desire"; conventional taboos, which prevent her from keeping the dying white man in her society, circumscribe her love. As Bergson said, "Action is intentional or, at any rate, conscious; gesture slips out unawares, it is automatic" (*Laughter*, 143). Not only is the woman's action a conscious expression of her despair at Kurtz's departure, it is also a symbolic gesture that acknowledges the futility of her desire, thus rendering this magnificent woman an object of the white man's laughter. Other incidents of gesture and other comic characters are found throughout Conrad's work. Jim, in *Lord Jim*, provides some comedy; certainly his adherence to a moral code that is not applicable to the Malay way of life affords some humour. Again, de Barral's comedy has been noted; his rigid behaviour is a classic example of mechanical, and hence, comic, action.

Psychological, moral, and spiritual states were Conrad's chief concerns. His knowledge of contemporary psychology and philosophy enabled him to treat human beings and society at great depth in his fiction. Conrad's use of Bergson's comic theory is understandable and significant. Not only does it relieve Conrad's often somber tales and make his harsh social criticism more palatable, it also allows him to probe another side of human nature. Whether it constitutes an integral aspect, as in *The Secret Agent* and *Under Western Eyes*, or simply provides momentary relief, Conrad relies on Bergsonian comedy in many of his tales. Thus, in his treatment of comedy and in his use of memory as a structural device in his narratives, Conrad illustrates that he – like Eliot, Woolf, Joyce, and Richardson – participated in the appropriation of Bergsonian philosophy that occurred in the first years of this century.

# Conclusion

The preceding chapters have set out the case for Bergson's role in the evolution of British Modernism. The first part of the book, chapters 1 to 3, illustrates the philosopher's prominence in British intellectual and social life during the first decades of this century. The second part, chapters 4 to 8, provides close readings of major modernist writers whose works testify to their interaction with Bergson's theories. Let me conclude this study by taking a step back from the immediacy of the project in order to make two observations.

The first centres on the relevancy of Bergson to today's questions. I first discovered Bergson's work while taking an undergraduate course on early twentieth-century British literature. In Bergson I found a key that enabled me to decode many of the hitherto undecipherable texts with which I had been struggling. For a time, I saw every modernist text through Bergsonian-tinted glasses. I believed that he was, without question, the central source of the major concepts underlying European intellectual life in the first half of this century. Time, wider experience with other intellectual works, and a more sophisticated and subtle appreciation of the complex web of forces shaping modernist cultural production have tempered this early enthusiasm. Nonetheless, I believe that this initial phase was significant, both to my own intellectual growth and to the reassessment of Bergson's place in Modernism.

Since to a certain extent we are bound by our own time and place, it is impossible to recapture fully the ebb and flow of intellectual debate from any particular period. Nevertheless, my initial experiences with Bergson's ideas may well have been similar to those of the writers presented in this book. Most of them encountered Bergson's philosophy early in their intellectual development, as I did, and most were swept up by his ideas, as I was. Certainly, I was for a time converted to a Bergsonian view of the world, as was Eliot by his own admission. Moreover, like Hulme, Murry, and other modernist theorists, my approach to issues such as language, form, consciousness, and representation have been profoundly influenced by Bergsonian concepts. But like many of these writers, I, too, have gone beyond my Bergsonian phase and have begun to articulate ideas perhaps rooted in his philosophy, but which pursue other courses of investigation. As much as any significant influence may be called temporary, mine, like Eliot's, was.

I provide this narrative of my experiences to illustrate that the process I went through to some degree parallels that of modernist writers. I believe that this voyage alerted me to many of the complexities surrounding modernist writers' interactions with Bergson, thereby providing me with some common ground from which to study them. The late twentieth century is undergoing a period of instability and searching that parallels that which occurred at the end of the nineteenth century. While the forces provoking the questioning in our time are different from those of a hundred years ago, the search for meaning as well as for representational modes is remarkably similar. It is not surprising, then, that I, like writers early in this century, have found some measure of comfort in Bergsonian solutions to these issues. That the last fifteen years of renewed interest in Bergson has come about at just this juncture also seems reasonable, given the revisiting by so many writers of similar issues and challenges.

My second observation is prompted by my puzzlement over Bergson's relative obscurity at this point in the century. I never did understand how he could have been so thoroughly consigned to the intellectual margins. As I worked on this study, I have drawn certain conclusions about this obscurity – some of which are indicated in chapter 2. A much larger issue, however, is at work here – one that is at the heart of contemporary reassessments of Modernism.

As Janet Wolff and other cultural theorists have argued, any object is a product of the myriad of forces at play in a particular culture at a particular point. What determines the valorization of objects by later cultures is an equally complex mixture of factors. In the case of British modernist writing, later assessments of value have, to a large degree, been shaped by the influence of a limited number of figures – Eliot, Pound, Virginia Woolf, F.R. Leavis, and I.A. Richards initially. What fascinates me is the degree to which these individuals' ideas have remained, and still remain, entrenched in contemporary debates. Perhaps one explanation of this is that we are still too close to the period in which modernist art was produced. Only recently, for example, have we begun to subject Eliot's proclamations about Modernism to the same kind of scrutiny employed when examining the ideas of writers from other times. By problematizing the definitions of the period provided by those who participated in the construction of the art that gave rise to these definitions, we open a broad spectrum of concerns. For instance, a reexamination of Eliot's concept of poetic impersonality suggests that the gap between Eliot's practice and theory is significant. Indeed, Maud Ellmann's provocative account of this gap in both Pound's and Eliot's poetry exemplifies the ongoing difficulties with received modernist constructions of cultural practice. It seems to me that this reassessment of Modernism will result in markedly different accounts of the period. I believe that my rescuing of Bergson from the intellectual margins is part of this broader process of challenging the static view of Modernism, a view that dominated criticism for much of the middle years of this century.

# *Notes*

1 Throughout the study, I refer to Bergson's works by their English titles
  and use the authorized English translations for purposes of quotation.
2 Appended to Alun Jones's biography of T.E. Hulme is a short article on
  Bergson written by Hulme, entitled "A Personal Impression of Bergson."
  In it, Hulme discusses a conversation he had with Bergson at the Bologna
  Philosophical Congress of 1910, in which Bergson said, "When I do write
  a new book it will probably be on aesthetics and ethics." Alun Jones, *The
  Life and Opinions of T.E. Hulme*, 208.
3 Others before the modernists had also used similar subjects; for example,
  Baudelaire was quite influential in this respect in modern literature. I am
  not arguing that modernists came to these types of subjects first, but that
  the period as a whole was more inclined to select them.
4 This is a summary of Bergson's discussion in *Time and Free Will*, in a section on "The Aesthetic Feelings," 11–18. Dance is specifically mentioned
  on 12–13.
5 I mention French and American literature because recent full-length studies have demonstrated Bergson's significant role. See Pilkington's *Bergson
  and his Influence* or Grogin's *The Bergsonian Controversy in France* (on
  France) and Paul Douglass's *Bergson, Eliot, & American Literature* and Tom
  Quirk's *Bergson and American Culture* (on America). But Bergson's influence was not restricted to these countries. Because his work was translated
  into many different languages and was widely debated, one may conjec-
  ture that his influence was also widespread. Many interesting studies on
  Bergson and Russian, German, or Spanish literature remain to be written.
6 See Grogin, chapter 7 (especially 186–92), for a good account of the political intrigues involved in Bergson's election to the French Academy on
  12 February 1914.

7 Here there are many works that deal with Bergson's ideas in different ways. Studies devoted exclusively to Bergson and Anglo-American Modernism are, as yet, hard to come by, except for those of Paul Douglass and Quirk or the early pioneering work of Shiv Kumar. Studies that devote chapters or lengthy sections to Bergson's role are more common; these include works by Schwartz, Maude Ellmann, Levenson, and a host of others. Articles on Bergson have proliferated in the last twenty years as scholars begin to recognize Bergson's important position. P.A.Y. Gunter's excellent bibliography, recently revised, contains thousands of entries that show the range and manner of interest that Bergson has attracted in this century.

CHAPTER TWO

1 Russell's initial foray into the controversy prompted by Bergson's philosophy was an article in *The Monist* entitled "The Philosophy of Bergson." It ends with the damning comment that "those to whom activity without purpose seems a sufficient good will find in Bergson's books a pleasing picture of the universe. But those to whom actions, if it is to be of any value, must be inspired by some vision, by some imaginative foreshadowing of a world less painful, less unjust, less full of strife than the world of our every-day life, those, in a word, whose actions is built on contemplation, will find in this philosophy nothing of what they seek, and will not regret that there is no reason to think it true" (*The Monist*, 347). Russell later wrote a book on the subject that was very critical of Bergson's philosophy. However, Lindsay's book, *The Philosophy of Bergson*, contains a highly favourable account of Bergson's philosophy.
2 Evelyn Underhill, "Bergson and the Mystics" in *English Review*.
3 See James Johnstone, *The Philosophy of Biology*.
4 The range of articles is extensive. I refer the reader to P.A.Y. Gunter's admirable bibliography of Bergson for further reading.
5 This is the date for the American edition. In 1913 it appeared with an English printer as *Introduction to Metaphysics*, with an authorized translation by T.E Hulme (London: Macmillan).
6 Reviews of *Time and Free Will*: appeared in *Nation* 91, no. 2369 (24 November 1910): 499–500; *Athenaeum*, no. 4330 (13 October 1910): 482–4; and *Saturday Review* (London) 90, no. 2866 (1 October 1910): 430. Reviews of *Creative Evolution* appeared in *Lancet* 181 (10 February 1912): 1710–11; *Athenaeum* 1, no. 4355 (April 1911): 206; and *Saturday Review* (London) 91, no. 2901 (3 June 1911): 685–6.
7 See the *Times*, 29 May 1911: 5.
8 "University Intelliegence," *Times*, 20 October 1911: 8.
9 The series of four articles was entitled "Professor Bergson on the Soul." See the *Times*, 21 October: 4; 23 October: 4; 28 October: 11; 30 October: 10.

10  "Professor Bergson on the Soul," *Times*, 28 October: 11; 30 October: 10.

11  This lecture, somewhat expanded, was published as "Life and Consciousness" in *The Hibbert Journal* 10, Part 1 (October 1911): 815–36.

12  Julian Huxley, *Essays of a Biologist*, 34. Quoted in Gunter, *Bergson and the Evolution of Physics*, 15.

13  This is true, despite the challenge of Samuel Butler whose theories suggested that the mind could select the direction of evolution. Although there are similarities between Bergson and Butler, Bergson's stress that the creative impulse was not, ultimately, controlled by humans distinguishes the two approaches to evolution.

14  Frederick Burwick and Paul Douglass, eds., *The Crisis in Modernism* 1. This is an engrossing account of the vitalist tradition and Bergson's place in it. I am indebted to it for my thinking about Bergson and biology.

15  See *Bergson and the Evolution of Physics* for interesting studies of Bergson and physics. Čapek has also written extensively on the topic, most notably in *Bergson and Modern Physics*.

16  Carr wrote over two dozen articles on Bergson. They range from reviews of Bergson's work, to reviews of other writers' works on Bergson, to his own analysis of Bergson's major statements.

17  Bertrand Russell was an outspoken critic of Bergson. In eight different works, he varied his arguments around the basic theme that Bergson's work is anti-intellectual and favours the mystical rather than the scientific.

18  I am speaking here of Russell's early phase, when he was most interested in mathematical models and explanations for physical phenomena. It is appropriate to note that Whitehead was a disciple of Bergson early in his career. The irony of this collaboration with Russell should be noted.

19  Although Balfour as a young man had written two books on philosophical subjects and maintained interest in the debates whirling around in the philosophical community, I would argue that his interest in philosophy was that of an amateur, and not of a professional philosopher like Russell.

20  I distinguish between those people who adopted Bergsonian vocabulary without necessarily understanding the concepts behind the words (they used Bergsonisms) and those I call Bergsonians (my term), who studied and understood Bergson's philosophy. Whether or not they agreed with it is unimportant.

21  Balfour and Bergson both shared an interest in psychical phenomena and both became president of the Society for Psychical Research – Balfour in 1894 and Bergson in 1913.

22  It is artificial to talk of society figures as separate from those of the literary or political worlds, for the worlds were locked together. For example, while Balfour was very much a society figure, being well connected among the landed gentry, he was also an important politican and welcome at the

various literary salons of the day. Although the distinction I am trying to make is a fine one, it is important. I believe that Bergsonism was promulagated by those who met at social functions, who wanted to appear up to date with all the current trends or fads – and Bergson was one of the most notable trends. It is also worth noting that Bergson stopped lecturing at the Collège de France because of those very society figures whose presence had prompted such scornful reactions from Bergson's many critics.

### CHAPTER THREE

1 There is some disagreement over the group's name – it is also known also as the Poetry Society – as well as the date of its establishment – both 1908 and 1909 are mentioned. However, I have taken my information from Humphrey Carpenter's biography of Ezra Pound, where he discusses Hulme, the Poetry Club, Imagism, and Pound, pp. 112-ff.
2 Patricia Rae's article, "T.E. Hulme's French Sources: A Reconsideration," provides an interesting and thorough account of the influence of both Bergson and Ribot on Hulme. My sense of Bergson's impact on Hulme was determined before reading this article.
3 Hulme's influence on each of these has been well documented. For his influence on Pound, see Humphrey Carpenter's biography *A Serious Character*; for his relation with Eliot, see Piers Gray's *T.S. Eliot's Intellectual and Poetic Development 1909–1922*; for his role in the Imagist movement, see Graham Hough's *Image and Experience*.
4 Here I am indebted to Michael Levenson's excellent discussion of Hulme's career in *A Genealogy of Modernism*. However, although I agree that Bergson's influence is most prominent in the first phase of Hulme's career, I also believe it was a lasting influence; one can detect it in Hulme's concern for precision and accuracy in language, a concern that I believe he encountered in Bergson and subsequently adopted for his own use.
5 The first two points here are discussed by Levenson on pages 37–47, especially 46–7. The final point, about the clarity of language, is one that Levenson overlooks with respect to Bergson's influence on Hulme, deciding to concentrate instead on this aspect of Ford Maddox Ford's contribution to Imagism.
6 Carpenter's biography of Pound, *A Serious Character*, and Hugh Kenner's *The Pound Era* are excellent books on this subject.
7 See Maud Ellmann's book, *The Poetics of Impersonality*, in which she carefully dissects both Pound's theories and his poetry, arriving at just such a conclusion about the inevitability of their reflecting his personality.
8 Both Levenson and Carpenter provide good, detailed accounts of the motivations and circumstances surrounding Pound's sudden move away from the stances he held to 1913. Here I am also following the line of

thought that Levenson provides in *A Genealogy of Modernism*, though my later discussions will be founded on the idea that the early form of Modernism is not replaced by the later "high" Modernism, but rather remains as an important subversive element in the theories and works of later modernists such as Eliot.

9 Sue Ellen Campbell's article "Equal Opposites: Wyndham Lewis, Henri Bergson and Their Philosophies of Time and Space" provides an insightful account of Lewis's tangled relationship with Bergson. She argues that while "Lewis dismisses Bergson as insignificant, at the same time he assails him with invective at every opportunity" (353). I agree with her that Lewis's attack is often submerged or indirect – criticizing those he saw as Bergson surrogates (Proust, for example) – but believe that Bergson is an important influence on Lewis himself.

10 It is worth noting that in the 1930s Bergson's philosophy was openly embraced by some Fascists who saw in it ideas amenable to Fascist doctrine. Although Bergson was horrified by the associations drawn and denied the conclusions drawn by the Fascists, it is nonetheless a fact that they found his ideas appealing and useful.

11 Poole is one of many who discuss Woolf's position in the intellectual world of Bloomsbury. The memoirs, letters, autobiographies, and other accounts of the men themselves make clear that Virginia's position in their eyes was as an adept at the feet of her "Gods." It is ironic, however, that she seems to have understood the essence and spirit of Modernism better than they did. It is ironic, too, that it is Virginia Woolf whose works are read by later generations and who is cited as a leading modernist, while Strachey and Leonard Woolf are no longer the important figures they were in the early years of this century.

12 Forster, Strachey, and Leonard Woolf were seen by Bloomsbury at the time to be writers of note. From today's perspective, Forster remains a novelist of the first rank, although Strachey, and to a greater degree Leonard Woolf, have fallen from this top rung. This is not to say that both men were not and, indeed, are not important figures in the period. It is rather that Virginia Woolf is a more important representative of the sentiment of the age. Woolf incorporates the essence of Modernism in her work, while Strachey and Leonard Woolf have at least one foot still firmly fixed in the Victorian or Edwardian eras.

13 This label for Bergson had been widely employed, largely by those who did not agree with his philosophy. For example, it was used in derision by Lewis; see *Blast* no. 1, 132.

14 See, for example, Woolf's "A Sketch of the Past" in *Moments of Being*.

15 See "French Books" in *Blue Review*, vol. 1, no. 1 (May 1913), 56–62.

16 The statement of interest comes from the 1947 edition of Mattheissen's study of Eliot, which included his treatment of Eliot's masterful long

poem, *Four Quartets*. Whether Eliot's comments in his sermon were a response to Mattheissen's remarks on Eliot's relationship with Bergson, especially the remarks that Mattheissen abstracts out of context from Eliot's essay on Bergson, is difficult to establish so long after the fact. However, it is interesting that both men talk about Bergson and attempt to dismiss him from a place of prominence in Eliot's development as critic and poet. Such efforts to deny Bergson a prominent role in Eliot's work hint at the type of process Harold Bloom describes in *Anxiety of Influence*, when he talks about the concept of "misprison" and the necessity of the young artist to absorb, then discard and transcend, the work of his master or artistic role model. While no hard conclusions may be drawn from the evidence presented here, it seems likely that Eliot's denial of long-term influence, coupled with the ready acceptance of the Mattheissen's statement by the critical world, resulted in the the long passage of time it took to have Eliot's relationship with Bergson studied in detail and in depth.

17 Both my master's thesis, "T.S. Eliot and Henri Bergson: 1909–1920. A Study of Influence" (Oxford, 1983) and my doctoral dissertation "The Influence of Henri Bergson on Early Modern British Literature" (Oxford, 1988) deal with Eliot's relationship with Bergson. Douglass, as well as M.A.R. Habib in "Bergson Resartus' and T.S. Eliot's Manuscript," also examine this relationship. Both men focus on Eliot's unpublished essay on Bergson, Habib much more extensively than either Douglass or I do, and both extend their discussions to a broader look at Eliot's thought. I encountered both studies after my initial work was completed; although we all cover much of the same ground, I believe I bring additional insights to the ongoing debate.

18 As I said at the outset of the study, I will not be exploring influence by outlining the various phases writers go through when dealing with the ideas of predecessors or teachers, as Bloom suggests we do in *The Anxiety of Influence*.

19 Pound's comments about the the experience of an image, which are very much in evidence here, are a possible source for Eliot's "objective correlative." I think that both notions owe something to Bergson's ideas and that Eliot is as likely to be indebted to Bergson as he is to Pound.

20 Many critics have begun to make strong cases for Bergson's role in Eliot's work. Two of the best are made by Maud Ellmann in *The Poetics of Impersonality* and by Paul Douglass in *Bergson, Eliot & American Literature*.

CHAPTER FOUR

1 Throughout this chapter I rely on the dates of composition supplied by Lyndall Gordon's study, *Eliot's Early Years*.

2 Donald Childs's "T.S. Eliot's Rhapsody of Matter and Memory" is a recent examination of Bergson's influence in the construction of this poem. Childs argues persuasively that "Rhapsody" is the "culmination" of Bergson's influence on Eliot, not the end as suggested by other, earlier critics, including Grover Smith, Gertrude Patterson, Lyndall Gordon, and Piers Grey. (484–5) While Childs may be on the right track in demonstrating how thoroughly Bergsonian "Rhapsody" is, I do not think that it represents a culmination of the Bergsonian influence. I would contend that Bergson's influence is pervasive throughout Eliot's body of work.

3 "Prufock" critics include Hugh Kenner in *The Invisible Poet*, 3–11; A.D. Moody in *Thomas Stearns Eliot: Poet*, 30–8; and Grover Smith in *T.S. Eliot's Poetry and Plays*, 15–20.

4 The line from *The Waste Land* is 63. The lines from the *Inferno* are: "So long a train of people/That I should never have believed/That death had undone so many" (*Inferno III*, 55–7).

5 In the notes to the poem, Eliot identifies the scene as II, ii, 90.

6 It has often been said that Eliot appended the notes to the original version of the poem in order to fill out the volume. Critics have used this explanation to claim that the notes have no real value in interpreting the poem. The notes have nevertheless become an integral part of the text, no matter what the original intent, and for this reason they will be used in our analysis.

7 Donald Childs discusses Eliot's interaction with Bergsonian thought in *Four Quartets* in his article "Risking Enchantment: The Middle Way between Mysticism and Pragmatism." While it is an interesting examination it doesn't convince me enough to alter my reading of the poem.

8 Elizabeth Drew's *T.S. Eliot: The Design of his Poetry*, Leonard Unger's "T.S. Eliot's Rose Garden," and Edith F. Cornwell's *The Still Point* trace various patterns in Eliot's work.

9 On this point, see Unger's work in *T.S. Eliot: A Selected Critque*.

CHAPTER FIVE

1 Hafley comments: "Virginia Woolf evidently never read Bergson: Leonard Woolf assured me in a letter, in 1949, that 'Mrs Woolf did not read a word of Bergson,' and that in spite of the fact that her sister-in-law Mrs Karin Stephen wrote a book on Bergson (*The Misuse of Mind*, 1921), I very much doubt that she ever discussed Bergson with Mrs. Stephen." Hafley further says that "Mr Woolf also wrote that 'I do not think that she was influenced in the slightest degree by Bergson's ideas'; but with this it is hard to agree" (Hafley, n. 21, 174). I agree with Hafley here and have outlined Woolf's aesthetic and Bergson's role in its construction in chapter 3 of this text. In this chapter I am primarily interested in Bergsonian readings of Woolf's major works.

2 David Daiches, *Virginia Woolf*, 54. Although Daiches does not see Bergson as a central influence, he does hold that Bergson's work had some influence on her.

3 John Graham, "A Negative Note on Bergson and Virginia Woolf"; James Hafley, *The Glass Roof*.

4 Jean Guiguet, *Virginia Woolf and her Works*, 33.

5 To survey the body of Woolf criticism for its treatment of Bergson is beyond the scope of this chapter, particularly since so many critics refer to Bergson in a cursory way, usually mentioning that his time theories had some influence on Woolf, but not following this up with detailed discussion. However, to give a sense of the nature of the existing criticism, I want to mention three studies that are, in a way, representative of the critical approaches taken toward Woolf and Bergson: two standard critical works, Maria Dibattista's *Virginia Woolf's Major Novels* (1980) and Harvena Richter's *Virginia Woolf: The Voyage Inward* (1970); and a fine recent study John Batchelor's *Virginia Woolf: The Major Novels* (1991). Dibattista refers to Bergson twice in her book; both references have to do with Bergson's notions of the comic – once vis-à-vis *Orlando* and once vis-à-vis *Between the Acts*. I have chosen not to discuss Bergson's sense of the comic and Woolf because the correspondence is much more visible and important apropos other areas. Although Richter's discussion of Bergsonian time apropos Woolf's moments of being is interesting, she pursues the connection somewhat differently than I do. Batchelor, too, discusses Woolf vis-à-vis Bergson's theory of time, saying "All Bergson's ideas are of the kind that Woolf would have found sympathetic, especially his resistance to analysis and classification and his notion that interior time, *durée réelle*, distinguishes itself from exterior or clock time" (47–8). The resulting examination of the way his time theories work in Woolf's fiction however, is brief.

6 Hafley, *The Glass Roof*, 43–4.

7 I am aware of the difficulties surrounding the use of this term. It is, to say the least, an imprecise and somewhat unsatisfactory blanket label for the mode of writing that many modern writers employed – and most of them in significantly different ways. However, as a convenient form of shorthand, the term will suffice to describe the apparently random presentation of a character's inner thoughts, in a manner that approximates the perceived way in which the human consciousness operates.

8 It received favourable reviews in the *Times Literary Supplement*, reviews that Woolf attributes in her Diary to boosting the sales of the book (*Diary 1*, 280, entry for Tuesday, 10 June 1919). Desmond McCarthy in the *New Statesman* of 9 April 1921 and R. Ellis Roberts in the *Daily News* of 2 May 1921 gave favourable reviews as well. Woolf was particularly pleased that T.S. Eliot praised the stories. In her Diary for Tuesday, 7 June

1921, she records his comments: "He picked out the String Quartet, especially the end of it. 'Very good' he said, & meant it, I think. The Un-written Novel he thought not successful; Haunted House 'extremely interesting'" (*Diary 1*, 125).

9 Hafley talks about this story as exhibiting Bergson's sense of *élan vital*. This is an astute observation, but he seems to miss the sense of relative times that becomes central in the later novels. (See Hafley, 42–4).

10 Harvena Richter says that Woolf creates special memory-filled symbols – "abstracting and condensing memories into symbols which, like Japanese paper flowers, would expand in the reader's mind, evoking almost auto-matically an entire scene from the past." She continues: "This type of complex symbol is what Virginia Woolf uses throughout *The Waves* as a mode of memory release, not in the mind of the characters but *in the mind of the reader*. The reader herself responds to the visual-emotional stimuli offered, calling up a past scene from the novel and, as the images repeat and vary, building up a fund of emotion around the remembered event" (Richter, 166). I would add that this very Bergsonian mode of memory is one that Woolf worked with as early as "Monday or Tuesday;" certainly she experimented with it before writing *The Waves*.

11 See chapter 2 of this text on Bergson's sense of self.

12 This is quoted in John Graham, "Point of View in *The Waves*: Some Ser-vices of the Style" in *Virginia Woolf: A Collection of Criticism*, 108.

13 Hafley argues that *The Years* is "possibly the best, and certainly one of the most interesting, of Virginia Woolf's novels" (Hafley, 132). His is not the majority position of critics, who generally see the book as a retreat from the experiments of *The Waves*.

CHAPTER SIX

1 Richard Ellmann, *The Consciousness of Joyce*, 7.

2 Ellmann, *James Joyce*, 788.

3 He rightly points out Joyce's attack on Lewis's anti-semitism: "Professor Jones demonstrates his anti-semitic tendencies by dismissing the works of Bitchison (Bergson) and Winstain (Einstein) as having no merit" (Manga-niello, *Joyce's Politics*, 230).

4 Lewis says: "Bergson's doctrine of Time is the creative source of the time-philosophy. It is he more than any other single figure that is responsible for the main intellectual characteristics of the world we live in, and the implicit debt of almost all contemporary philosophy to him is immense" (*Time*, 166). But Lewis maintains that the influence of the time philosophy is anything but good, given its resulting falsification of experience. He charges it, too, with fostering a discontinuity between the individual and the world outside, a characteristic typical of writers whom he assigns to

the time-school of Bergson, Einstein, Proust and Stein. He says: "It is our contention here that *it is because of the subjective disunity due to the separation, or separate treatment, of the sense principally of sight and of touch, that the external disunity has been achieved*" [author's italics] (*Time*, 419).

5 W.Y Tindall, *James Joyce*, 93.

6 Meyerhoff's *Time and Literature* mentions Bergson in passing. Mendilow's *Time and the Novel* examines Bergson's role in somewhat greater detail. And Friedman's *Stream of Consciousness: A Study of Literary Method* deals more extensively with Bergson's role in modernist fiction.

7 Kumar's tentativeness is evident in the following remarks: "To suggest that the new form of fiction emerged under the direct influence of Bergson would be rather misleading. In fact, Bergson was himself, like those he was supposed to have influenced, a manifestation of the *Zeitgeist*. It should, therefore, be more appropriate to say that in his philosophy one finds a most effective articulation of that intuitive sense of the fluid reality of which sensitive minds were becoming aware in the early years of this century" (S. Kumar, 13). He continues: "It would be wrong to presume, like Wyndham Lewis, that without Bergson's influence *Ulysses* could not have been written. Unlike Proust, Joyce makes no reference to Bergson in his *Letters*, nor did he ever acknowledge any such affiliations with the French philosopher. An attempt to trace Bergson's influence in his work would, therefore, be rather farfetched" (S. Kumar, 106–7). However, I believe that Bergson was more than just an articulate spokesman of the *Zeitgeist*: although, he was a man of his age in his preoccupation with the nature of reality, his opinions and theories were distinctive expressions of these concerns with their own readily identifiable Bergsonian twist. It is this Bergsonian twist that was absorbed by his contemporaries and that helped to shape modernist literature.

8 Although other studies have looked at Joyce and Bergson since Church's study in 1963, with a few notable exceptions they have done so in only an incidental fashion. Robert Klawitter, in his "Henri Begson and James Joyce's Fictional World," presents an argument that differs significantly from Church's and from mine. He writes: "I wish to contradict not only Wyndham Lewis but also the analysts of Joyce's stream-of-consciousness technique, who see *Ulysses* and the *Wake* as representations of Bergson's *durée réelle*. Rather Joyce's fiction is a representation of unreality – what Bergson held to be unreal" (432). I disagree with this and, as this chapter shows, I believe that the temporal reality Joyce presents us with is "real." Moreover, I think Joyce develops this world by placing his characters (and readers) in Bergsonian *durée*.

Eliot Gosse Jr.'s *The Transformation Process in Joyce's Ulysses* begins by discussing the impact that *Creative Evolution* had on Joyce. He argues that it "provided [Joyce] with more general principles for shaping the great work [*Ulysses*] on which he embarked" (xi). However, Gosse's arguments are not altogether convincing, because he fails to provide sufficiently convincing readings of *Ulysses*.

More recently, Udaya Kumar, in *The Joycean Labyrinth*, is persuasive when discussing the "two kinds of complicaton to the temporal progress of [*Ulysses's*] narrative. The first functions by the use of an associational connection between elements in the monologue and the second by a spatial unification of elements deployed throughout the novel" (54). Kumar centres the discussion of the first complication around Lewis and Bergson, concluding that the presentation of consciousness in terms of discourses and repetition does have some similarities to Bergson's notion of *durée*. Kumar notes that the profound relation between *durée* and the stream of consciousness is based on the continuous process of differentiation that informs them, and concludes that it is through the use of various discourses and of repetition that this differentiation operates in Joyce's text (79–80). Though Kumar focuses almost exclusively on time, this last description could embrace Bergson's theory of memory as well.

9 Church suggests this concept in relation to *Stephen* and *A Portrait*, but I think it holds true here as well.

### CHAPTER SEVEN

1 A check of the Modern Language Association Bibliography reveals thirty-one citations for Richardson since 1981. Most of the articles, books, or dissertations cited take feminist stands towards her work. For example, in " 'But how describe a world seen without a self?' Feminism, Fiction and Modernism," Sandra Kemp wants "to consider the issue of gender-genre-modernism in terms of what I see as this characteristic attention to detail and to 'things' or objects in narrative" (100). She mentions Bergson in passing, saying: "If Bergson's theory of *durée* engendered what have now become the clichés of modernist temporality, the [Feminist Modernist Fiction] substitution of space for time could be seen as a reworking of Bergson in terms of Bachelard's spatial alternative" (105). Although her argument is interesting, I think she oversimplifies Bergson's theory and fails to see the very real way in which Bergson's temporal theories are woven into the modernist novel. Other works – such as Ellen Friedman's " 'Utterly other discourse': The Anticannon of Experimental Women Writers from Dorothy Richardson to Christine Brooke-Rose"; Diane Filby Gillespie's "Political Aesthetics: Viriginia Woolf and Dorothy Richardson" in *Virginia Woolf: A Feminist Slant*; and Gloria Fromm's "What are Men to Dorothy Richardson" – all approach Richardson and *Pilgrimage* from expressly feminist standpoints and do not examine Richardson's Bergsonian heritage. In fact, many of the dissertations appear to explore Richardson's

place in the *Bildungsroman* tradition and her place in modernist literature.
2 Gloria Fromm makes the same point in her biography of Richardson, *Dorothy Richardson*.

CHAPTER EIGHT

1 Much of the criticism has focused on Conrad's Bergsonian comedy; see, for example, Wolfgang B. Fleischmann's discussion of comedy and *Chance* in his article, "Conrad's *Chance* and Bergson's *Laughter*." While other critics do not attempt to make a case for Bergson's full-fledged influence on Conrad, they do point out approaches to life and literature shared by the two. Paul Kirschner, for example, says that Conrad has "affinities with pragmatic thinkers such as Bergson, Vaihinger, F.C.S. Schiller ..." (*Conrad: The Psychologist as Artist*, 275). Others make more general references to Bergson as a force in the period, whose ideas expressed the era's general opinions. Frederick Karl, for instance, wrote, "Conrad was, in his way, grappling with what Bergson called the vital or intuitional part of man's mind" (*A Reader's Guide to Joseph Conrad*, 34).
2 Here I want to emphasize that many other figures contribute to Conrad's impressionistic writing style, notably Flaubert. What I am interested in establishing is the role Bergsonian memory plays in Conrad's style.
3 Little work has been done on assessing the nature of comedy in Conrad's body of work. Instead, most critics focus on the nature of comedy in individual works. Early reviews of *The Secret Agent*, for example, hotly debated the novel's comedy. Although some reviewers such as the one in *Truth* (20 October 1907) in *Conrad: The Critical Heritage* (ed. Norman Sherry, 817) focus on the novel's comedy in a positive light, others focus on it in a negative light – see the unsigned review in *Country Life* (21 September 1907) in *The Secret Agent: A Casebook* (ed. Ian Watt, 28–9). Wolfgang B. Fleischmann discusses comedy and *Chance* in his article "Conrad's *Chance* and Bergson's *Laughter*."
4 Most critics of *The Secret Agent* note the obesity of the principal characters. English draws a parallel between Bergsonian comedy and the characters' deformity due to obesity in his article. (See English, 143).

# Selected Bibliography

Abrams, M.H. 1953. *The Mirror and the Lamp*. New York: Oxford University Press.

Ackroyd, Peter. 1984. *T.S. Eliot*. London: Hamish Hamilton.

Balfour, Arthur. 1911. "*Creative Evolution* and Philosophical Doubt." *The Hibbert Journal* 10, part 1 (October): 1–23.

Batchelor, John. 1991. *Virginia Woolf: The Major Novels*. Cambridge: Cambridge University Press.

Beja, Morris. 1953. *Epiphany in the Modern Novel*. New York: Harcourt Brace.

Bell, Clive. 1914. *Art*. London: Chatto & Windus.

Bergson, Henri. 1928. *Creative Evolution*. Translated by Arthur Mitchell. London: MacMillan.

– 1913. *An Introduction to Metaphysics*. Translated by T.E. Hulme. London: MacMillan.

– 1911. *Laughter: An Essay on the Meaning of the Comic*. Translated by Cloudesley Brereton and Fred Rothwell. London: MacMillan.

– 1911. "Life and Consciousness." *The Hibbert Journal* 10, part 1 (October): 815–36.

– 1911. *Matter and Memory*. Translated by Nancy Margaret Paul and W. Scott Palmer. London: George Allen & Unwin.

– 1878. "Solution d'un problem mathématique." *Nouvelles annales mathématique* 17, no. 2: 268–76.

– 1910. *Time and Free Will: An Essay on the Immediate Data of Consciousness*. Translated by F.L. Pogson. New York: Harper & Row, 1910.

Blast. *The Review of the Great English Vortex*. 1914. no. 1 (June).

Bloom, Harold. 1973. *The Anxiety of Influence*. New York: Oxford University Press.

Burwick, Frederick, and Douglass, Paul, eds. 1992. *The Crisis of Modernism*. Cambridge: University of Cambridge Press.

Campbell, Sue Ellen. 1983. "Equal Opposites: Wyndham Lewis, Henri Bergson and Their Philosophies of Space and Time." *Twentieth Century Literature*

29, no. 3 (Fall): 351–69.

Carpenter, Humphrey. 1988. *A Serious Character: The Life of Ezra Pound*. London: Faber & Faber.

Carr, H. Wildon. 1970. *Henri Bergson: The Philosophy of Change*. New York: Kennikat Press.

Childs, Donald. 1993. "Risking Enchantment: The Middle Way between Mysticism and Pragmatism in *Four Quartets*." In *Words in Time: New Essays on Eliot's "Four Quartets,"* edited by Edward Lobb. Ann Arbor: University of Michigan Press, 107–30.

– 1991. "T.S. Eliot's Rhapsody of Matter and Memory." *American Literature* 63, no. 3 (September): 474–88.

Church, Margaret. 1949. *Time and Reality: Studies in Contemporary Fiction*. Chapel Hill: University of North Carolina Press.

Clements, Patricia. 1985. *Baudelaire and the English Tradition*. Princeton: Princeton University Press.

Conrad, Joseph. 1928. *Chance*. London: J.M. Dent & Sons.

– 1967. *The Secret Agent*. London: J.M. Dent & Sons.

– 1911. *Under Western Eyes*. London: Methuen.

– 1967. *Youth, Heart of Darkness, The End of the Tether*. London: J.M. Dent & Sons.

Cornwell, Edith F. 1962. *The "Still Point."* New Brunswick, N.J.: Rutgers University Press.

Daiches, David. 1942. *Virginia Woolf*. Norfolk, Conn.: New Directions.

De Broglie, Louis. 1969. "The Concepts of Contemporary Physics and Bergson's Ideas of Time and Motion." In *Bergson and the Evolution of Physics*, edited by P.A.Y. Gunter. Knoxville, Tenn.: University of Tennessee Press, 45–61.

Delattre, Florris. 1932. "La *Durée* bergsonienne dans le roman de Virginia Woolf." *Revue Anglo-Américaine* 9, no. 2: 97–108.

DiBattista, Maria. 1980. *Virginia Woolf's Major Novels*. New Haven: Yale University Press.

Douglass, Paul. 1986. *Bergson, Eliot, & American Literature*. Lexington, Kentucky: University Press of Kentucky.

Drew, Elizabeth. 1950. *T.S. Eliot: The Design of his Poetry*. London: Eyre & Spottiswoode.

Eliot, T.S. 1969. *The Complete Poems and Plays of T.S. Eliot*. London: Faber & Faber.

– 1951. "Hamlet." In *Selected Essays*, 3d ed. London: Faber & Faber.

– 1964. *Knowledge and Experience in the Philosophy of F.H. Bradley*. London: Faber & Faber.

– 1951. "The Metaphysical Poets." In *Selected Essays*, 3d ed. London: Faber & Faber.

– 1951. "The Music of Poetry." In *On Poetry and Poets*. London: Faber & Faber.

- 1948. *A Sermon Preached at Magdalene College Cambridge*. Cambridge: Cambridge University Press.
- 1950. "Tradition and the Individual Talent." In *The Sacred Wood*, 7th ed. London: Metheun.

Ellman, Maud. 1987. *The Poetics of Impersonality*. Cambridge, Mass.: Harvard University Press.

Ellmann, Richard. 1977. *The Consciousness of Joyce*. London: Faber & Faber.
- 1959. *James Joyce*. London: Oxford University Press.

English, James F. 1987. "Scientist, Moralist, Humorist: A Bergsonian Reading of *The Secret Agent*." *Conradiana* 19, no. 2: 139–56.

Fleischman, Wolfgang B. 1961. "Conrad's *Chance* and Bergson's *Laughter*." *Renascence* 4 (Winter): 66–71.

Friedman, Ellen. 1988. "'Utterly other discourse': The Anticanon of Experimental Women Writers from Dorothy Richardson to Christine Brooke-Rose." *Modern Fiction Studies* 34, no. 3 (Autumn): 353–70.

Fromm, Gloria. 1977. *Dorothy Richardson*. Urbana: University of Illinois Press.
- 1982. "What are Men to Dorothy Richardson?" *Women in Literature*, no. 2: 168–88.

Gillespie, Diane Filby. 1983. "Political Aesthetics: Virginia Woolf and Dorothy Richardson." In *Virginia Woolf: A Feminist Slant*, edited by Jane Marcus. Lincoln: University of Nebraska Press.

Gordon, Lyndall. 1977. *Eliot's Early Years*. London: Oxford University Press.

Gosse, Eliot, Jr. 1980. *The Transformation Process in Joyce's Ulysses*. Toronto: University of Toronto Press.

Graham, John. 1956. "A Negative note on Bergson and Virginia Woolf." *Essays in Criticism* 6, no. 1 (January): 70–4.
- 1975. "Point of View in *The Waves*: Some Services of the Style." In *Virginia Woolf: a Collection of Criticism*, edited by Thomas S.W. Lewis. New York: McGraw-Hill.

Gray, Piers. 1982. *T.S. Eliot's Intellectual and Poetic Development 1909–1920*. Brighton, Sussex: The Harvester Press.

Grogin, R.C. 1987. *The Bergsonian Controversy in France*. Calgary: University of Calgary Press.

Guiguet, Jean. 1965. *Virginia Woolf and her Works*. Translated by Jean Stewart. New York: Harcourt, Brace & World.

Gunter, P.A.Y. 1969. *Bergson and the Evolution of Physics*. Knoxville, Tenn.: University of Tennessee Press.
- 1974, *Henri Bergson: A Bibliography*. Bowling Green, Ohio: Philosophy Documentation Centre.

Habib, M.A.R. 1993. "'Bergson Resartus' and T.S. Eliot's Manuscript." *Journal of the History of Ideas* 54, 2 (April): 255–76.

Hafley, James. 1963. *Virginia Woolf: The Glass Roof*. New York: Russell & Russell.

Hanna, Thomas. 1962. *The Bergsonian Heritage*. New York: Columbia University Press.

Hanscombe, Gillian. 1979. "Introduction." In *Pilgrimage*. Vol. 1. London: Virago Press.

Holtby, Winifird. 1969. *Virginia Woolf*. Folcroft, Pa.: Folcroft Press.

Hough, Graham. 1960. *Image and Experience*. London: Gerald Duckworth.

Hulme, T.E. 1955. *Further Speculations*. Edited by Sam Hynes. Minneapolis: University of Minnesota Press.

– 1911. "Mr. Balfour, Bergson and Politics." *New Age*, n.s., 10 (9 November): 38–40.

– 1936. *Speculations*. Edited by Herbert Read. 2d ed. London: Routledge & Kegan Paul.

Humphrey, Robert. 1958. *Stream of Consciousness in the Modern Novel*. Berkeley: University of California Press.

Huxley, Julian. 1926. *Essays of a Biologist*. London: Chatto & Windus.

Hynes, Samuel. 1968. *The Edwardian Turn of Mind*. Princeton: Princeton University Press.

Johnstone, James. 1914. *The Philosophy of Biology*. Cambridge: Cambridge University Press.

Joyce, James. 1976. *Dubliners*. London: Penguin.

– 1974. *Exiles*. London: Jonathan Cape.

– 1976. *Finnegans Wake*. London: Penguin.

– 1977. *A Portrait of the Artist as a Young Man*. London: Penguin.

– 1980. *Stephen Hero*. London: Granada.

– 1980. *Ulysses*. London: Penguin.

Karl, Frederick. 1979. *Joseph Conrad: The Three Lives*. London: Faber & Faber.

– 1960. *A Reader's Guide to Joseph Conrad*. New York: The Noonday Press.

Kemp, Sandra. 1990. " 'But how describe a world without a self?' Feminism, Fiction and Modernism." *Critical Quarterly* 32, no. 1 (Spring): 99–118.

Kenner, Hugh. 1965. *The Invisible Poet: T.S. Eliot*. London: Methuen.

– 1972. *The Pound Era*. London: Faber & Faber.

Kermode, Frank. 1972. *Modern Essays*. London: Collins.

Kirschner, Paul. 1968. *Conrad: The Psychologist as Artist*. Edinburgh: Oliver & Boyd.

Klawitter, Robert. 1966. "Henri Bergson and James Joyce's Fictional World." *Comparative Literature Studies* 3, no. 4: 429–37.

Kolakowski, Leszek. 1985. *Bergson*. Past Master Series. Oxford: Oxford University Press.

Kumar, Shiv. 1962. *Bergson and the Stream-of-Consciousness Novel*. London: Blackie & Son.

Kumar, Udaya. 1991. *The Joycean Labyrinth: Repetition, Time and Tradition in Ulysses*. Oxford: Clarendon Press.

Langer, Suzanne. 1953. *Feeling and Form*. London: Routledge & Kegan Paul.

Leavis, F.R. 1932. *New Beginnings in English Poetry*. London: Chatto & Windus.

Le Brun, Philip. 1967. "T.S. Eliot and Henri Bergson." *Review of English Studies*. New Series 17, no. 70: 149–61, 274–86.

Lehan, Richard. 1992. "Bergson and the Discourse of the Moderns." In *Crisis of Modernism*, edited by Frederick Burwick, and Paul Douglass. Cambridge: Cambridge University Press: 306–29.

Levenson, Michael. 1984. *A Genealogy of Modernism*. Cambridge: Cambridge University Press.

Lewis, Wyndham. 1934. *Men Without Art*. London: Cassel.

– 1957. *Time and Western Man*. Boston: Beacon Hill Press.

Lindsay, A.D. 1911. *The Philosophy of Bergson*. London: Dent & Sons.

Manganiello, Dominic. 1980. *Joyce's Politics*. London: Routledge & Kegan Paul.

Matthessien, F.O. 1959. *The Achievement of T.S. Eliot*. 3d ed. New York: Oxford University Press.

Meisel, Perry. 1987. *The Myth of the Modern*. New Haven: Yale University Press.

Mendilow, A.A. 1952. *Time and the Novel*. London: Peter Nevill.

Meyers, Jeffrey. 1980. *The Enemy*. London: Routledge & Kegan Paul.

Moody, A.D. 1979. *Thomas Stearns Eliot: Poet*. Cambridge: Cambridge University Press.

Murry, John Middleton. 1920. *Aspects of Literature*. London: W. Collins & Sons.

– 1924. *Discoveries*. London: W. Collins & Sons.

– 1920. *The Evolution of the Intellect*. London: Richard Cobden-Sanderson.

– 1913. "French Books." *Blue Review* 1, no. 2 (May): 56–62.

– 1960. *The Problems of Style*. London: Oxford University Press.

Pilkington, A.E. 1976. *Bergson and his Influence: A Reassessment*. Cambridge: Cambridge University Press.

Poole, Roger. 1978. *The Unknown Virginia Woolf*. Cambridge: Cambridge University Press.

Pound, Ezra. 1954. "A Retrospective." In *Literary Essays of Ezra Pound*, edited by T.S. Eliot. London: Faber & Faber.

– 1914. "Preface." In *Des Imagistes*. New York: Albert & Charles Boni.

"Professor Bergson on the Soul." 1911. *Times* (London), 21 October: 4.

"Professor Bergson on the Soul." 1911. *Times* (London), 23 October: 4.

"Professor Bergson on the Soul." 1911. *Times* (London), 28 October: 11.

"Professor Bergson on the Soul." 1911. *Times* (London), 30 October: 10.

Quinones, Ricardo. 1985. *Mapping Literary Modernism*. Princeton: Princeton University Press.

Quirk, Tom. 1990. *Bergson and American Culture*. Chapel Hill: University of North Carolina Press.

Rae, Patricia. 1989. "T.E. Hulme's French Sources: A Reconsideration." *Comparative Literature* 41, no. 1 (Winter): 69–99.

"Review of *Creative Evolution*." 1911. *Athenaeum* 1, no. 4335 (April): 200.

"Review of *Creative Evolution*." 1912. *Lancet* 181 (10 February): 1710–11.

"Review of *Creative Evolution*." 1911. *Saturday Review* (London) 91, no. 2901 (3 June): 685–6.

"Review of *Time and Free Will*." 1910. *Athenaeum*, no. 4330 (13 October): 482–4.

"Review of *Time and Free Will*." 1910. *Nation* 91, no. 2369 (24 November): 499–500.

"Review of *Time and Free Will*." 1910. *Saturday Review* (London) 90, no. 2866 (1 October): 430.

Richardson, Dorothy. 1979. *Pilgrimage*. Vols. 1–4. London: Virago Press.

Richter, Harvena. 1970. *Virginia Woolf: The Voyage Inward*. Princeton: Princeton University Press.

Rosenberg, John. 1973. *Dorothy Richardson: The Genius They Forgot*. London: Duckworth.

Russell, Bertrand. 1912. "The Philosophy of Bergson." *Monist* 23, no. 3 (July): 321–47.

Scharfstein, Ben-Ami. 1943. *Roots of Bergson's Philosophy.* New York: Columbia University Press.

Schwartz, Sanford. 1985. *The Matrix of Modernism: Pound Eliot and Early Twentieth Century Thought*. Princeton: Princeton University Press.

Sherry, Norman, ed. 1958. *Conrad: The Critical Heritage*. Cambridge, Mass.: Harvard University Press.

Smith, Grover. 1974. *T.S. Eliot's Poetry and Plays: A Study of Meaning and Sources*. 2d ed. London: University of Chicago Press.

Spalding, Frances. 1980. *Roger Fry – Art and Life*. Berkeley: University of California Press.

Staley, Thomas. 1976. *Dorothy Richardson*. Boston: Twayne.

Stein, Gertrude. 1926. *Composition as Explanation*. London: Hogarth Press.

Szathmary, Arthur. 1937. *The Aesthetic Theory of Henri Bergson*. Cambridge, Mass.: Harvard University Press.

Tindall, W.Y. 1956. *Forces in Modern British Literature 1885–1956*. New York: Vintage Books.

Underhill, Evelyn. 1912. "Bergson and the Mystics." *English Review* 10, no. 2 (February): 511–22.

"University Intelligence: M. Bergson's Lectures." 1911. *Times* (London), 20 October: 8.

Watt, Ian, ed. 1973. *The Secret Agent: A Casebook*. London: MacMillan.

Wolff, Janet. 1980. *The Social Production of Art*. London: Oxford University of Press.

Wolsky, Maria de Issekutz, and Wolsky, Alexander A. 1992. "Bergson's Vitalism and Modern Biology." In *Crisis in Modernism*, edited by Frederick Burwick, and Paul Douglass. Cambridge: Cambridge University Press, 153–70.

Woolf, Virginia. 1989. *The Complete Shorter Fiction of Virginia Woolf*. Edited by Susan Dick. London: The Hogarth Press.

- 1978. *The Diary of Virginia Woolf*. Vol. 2. Edited by Anne Olivier Bell, assisted by Andrew McNeillie. London: Harcourt Brace Jovanovich.
- 1980. *The Diary of Virginia Woolf*. Vol. 3. Edited by Anne Olivier Bell, assisted by Andrew McNeillie. London: Harcourt Brace Jovanovich.
- 1980. *The Diary of Virginia Woolf*. Vol. 4. Edited by Anne Olivier Bell, assisted by Andrew McNeillie. London: Harcourt Brace Jovanovich.
- 1976. *Jacob's Room*. London: Triad/Panther.
- 1984. "Modern Fiction." In *The Common Reader I*. London: The Hogarth Press, 146–54.
- 1966. "Mr Bennett and Mrs Brown." *Collected Essays*. Vol. 1. London: Harcourt, Brace & World, 319–37.
- 1976. *Mrs Dalloway*. London: Granada.
- 1981. "A Sketch of the Past." In *Moments of Being*. London: Granada, 71–159.
- 1919. *Times Literary Supplement*, 13 February.
- 1977. *To the Lighthouse*. London: Granada.
- 1977. *The Waves*. London: Granada.

Wordsworth, William. 1974. "Preface to *Lyrical Ballads*." In *The Prose Works of William Wordsworth*. Vol. 1. Edited by W.J.B. Owen, and Jane Smyers. Oxford: Clarendon Press.

# Index